RESEARCH METHODS
in
PSYCHOLOGY

Second Edition

RESEARCH
METHODS
in
PSYCHOLOGY

A Handbook

Second Edition

Wendy A. Schweigert
Bradley University

WAVELAND
PRESS, INC.
Long Grove, Illinois

For information about this book, contact:
Waveland Press, Inc.
4180 IL Route 83, Suite 101
Long Grove, IL 60047-9580
(847) 634-0081
info@waveland.com
www.waveland.com

This book is dedicated to
Emma Jean Schweigert Sullivan

Contents

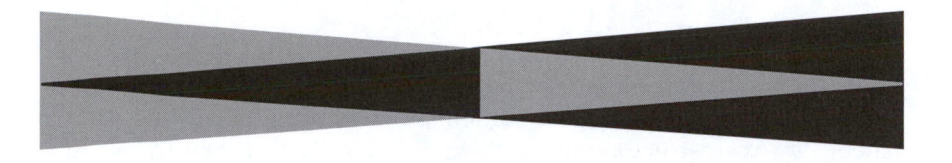

Preface

Often instructors will object to a text not because of the accuracy of its content or the thoroughness of its presentation, but because it doesn't present the material in a manner that fits their course. The primary goal of this book is to augment a course, rather than to dictate its organization; to that end, material is presented in a concise format that can be used flexibly by the instructor.

This handbook provides a brief but thorough introduction to the most commonly used research methods in psychology. It includes much of the same information presented in longer texts, but in a more succinct format. After reading each chapter, a student will be able to identify significant advantages and disadvantages of each approach and will be able to carry out a project using each method.

The book has been written for students with no previous research background and at a level easily understandable by college sophomores. Key terms are printed in boldface at their first appearance and defined within the text at that point; these terms also appear in a glossary at the end of the book. Beyond the introductory chapters on the scientific method, ethics, hypothesis testing, and statistics, each chapter focuses on a particular type of research approach, such as experimentation and the between-groups design (chapter 5), surveys and interviews (chapter 9), or quasi-experimental designs (chapter 10). Each chapter can stand as an independent unit; accordingly, the chapters can be presented in varying order. At the end of the text are three appendixes. The first explains how to use a number of statistical techniques. The second appendix contains numerous statistical tables and a random-numbers table. The third appendix describes research reports in psychology, with sections on literature searches and writing reports in APA style (using the fifth edition of the APA manual).

This handbook might be useful in a variety of courses. It can be the primary text in a research methods course, but I also picture it as a supplementary text for research-oriented content courses—for instance, in cognitive or social psychology—especially if these courses contain a laboratory component. It might also be used in combination with a statistics text in a course that introduces students to methods and statistics simultaneously. An instructor can combine this text with examples of published research to provide students with a broader perspective and knowledge base when considering research in psychology. It can be combined with other small handbooks, such as those on writing research papers, critical thinking, or multiculturalism in psychology. However this book is used, I hope it inspires in students the same excitement about research that I have felt since my first psychology course.

Acknowledgements

Thank you to all the users of the first edition of this book who have contacted me or Waveland Press with their comments and ideas. The second edition has been edited specifically with those thoughts in mind.

I would like to thank those who reviewed the first edition of this book for their valuable insight and suggestions: Debora Baldwin, University of Tennessee–Knoxville; Cynthia L. Crown, Xavier University; Jonathan Finkelstein, University of Maryland–Baltimore County; Ira Fischler, University of Florida; Robert Grissom, San Francisco State University; Merrill Hiscock, University of Houston; David E. Hogan, Northern Kentucky University; Janice H. Kennedy, Georgia Southern University; James Phillips, Oklahoma State University; Paul Schulman, SUNY Institute of Technology at Utica/Rome; and Bernard Whitley, Ball State University.

Special thanks go to my editors, Don Rosso and Diane Evans, and all the other behind-the-scenes people at Waveland Press. Their belief in this book saved it from an early demise.

Finally, I thank my husband, Jim Sullivan, and my children, Harry and Emma, for their continuous support and encouragement.

Wendy A. Schweigert

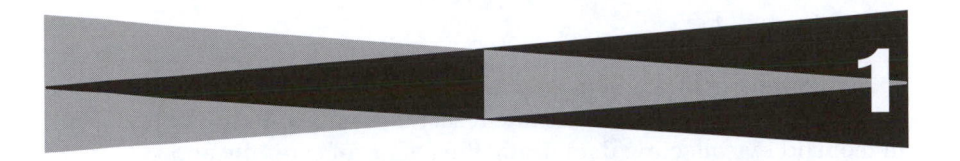

Introduction to the Scientific Method

I was in my introductory psychology class when I was bitten by the research bug. I suddenly realized the power of research, that by simply planning ahead and making observations carefully and objectively I could *know* something—something, in fact, that no one else had ever known before. And the process of learning this information involves no more than some problem-solving skills, creativity, and curiosity.

I have been addicted to research ever since—both to conducting my own and to teaching others how to conduct theirs. One of my greatest thrills as a teacher is to watch students discover for themselves that scientific research is not the dull, dry, uninteresting process they somehow thought it was but, instead, is downright fun.

Most students have conducted research by scouring the library for information relevant to a topic. Scientific research, however, is considerably different. Although it does require library work, the bulk of the information learned from scientific research is gained in the laboratory or in the field by collecting data. **Data**, the results of carefully and systematically recorded observations, are then organized and summarized so that the researcher can answer the question behind the study.

Scientific research is conducted using the **scientific method**, which is a general set of procedures used to gain information in the sciences. It is the process of making *systematic* observations in an *objective* manner. This approach is adopted so that the results of the research will be meaningful, unambiguous, and uncontaminated by the biases of either the participants or the researcher.

Psychology is the scientific study of behavior, and research psychologists use the scientific method to learn more about the behavior of animals and humans. The research psychologist's job is to identify and explore phenomena by collecting and analyzing data. For example, a research psychologist might investigate how young children learn to identify colors; another research psychologist might study the factors that predict whether a marriage will last or end in divorce.

In order to obtain sound and informative results, a research psychologist must have a solid knowledge of research methods. Perhaps less obvious, the knowledgeable clinical psychologist also must understand research methods. Only with an understanding of how research is done correctly can a clinician adequately comprehend and critique the articles published in professional journals. Research criticism involves identifying not only the flaws of a particular study, but also its contributions. With an understanding of research methods, for example, a clinician can determine whether the results of a study describing a new therapeutic technique reflect the benefits of the therapy or the poor research skills of the investigator.

Knowledge of research methods is not only important for professional psychologists but can also be of great value to any educated consumer. Research experiments can help the consumer determine if one product is better than another and if the advertised claims for a product are warranted. An understanding of research methods may also prove very useful to individuals who face important decisions—for example, to a shop owner who wonders if staying open on Sunday would be profitable or to a businessperson who needs to determine if an advertising campaign has been effective.

Although knowledge about scientific research is of practical value, the motivations of most researchers are less pragmatic. The research process at its best is wholly systematic and objective, but the drive to do research is very subjective. Scientific research is a very fulfilling means of satisfying our curiosity. The ability to contribute, bit by bit, to human knowledge is enticing. It is exciting to design a way of answering an intriguing question—a question that may not have even been asked before. Although the experimenter may feel momentarily discouraged when a research project does not provide the expected results, that feeling is soon replaced by more curiosity, more questioning, more research, and more answers.

Psychological questions are not always easy for the researcher to study. Psychologists collect data not only on overt physical movements, but also on more subtle physiological and psychological responses. Some psychologists might study reading, listening, comprehending, or the ability to store or recall information. Others might need to investigate emotions such as happiness, depression, boredom, anger, or fear. Not all objects of psychological research can be measured directly, and developing a way to make indirect measurements often proves challenging for a researcher.

A researcher who wishes to study hunger, for example, must decide how to measure hunger. Should the participants be asked to rate their hunger? What if the participants are small children or animals? If the participants can answer, does one person's report that he or she is very hungry mean the same as another person's report? Perhaps hunger could be measured in terms of blood-sugar levels, or by the number of calories ingested during the last 24 hours. There is more than one right way to make measurements; a researcher must choose among many alternatives, or even develop a new measure when necessary.

Making observations can be tricky; the process of studying a behavior can sometimes change the behavior itself. For example, a supervisor enters a classroom to observe the interactions between the students and their teacher. The students immediately put on their best behavior. The supervisor's own presence has affected the very behaviors that he or she was trying to observe.

Often behaviors are affected by subtle, unrecognized factors. A person's mood, for example, may be affected by the time of day, the color of the room, the weather, or even a tight pair of shoes. Obviously, a researcher cannot control everything that might affect the behaviors being studied. Part of the challenge of psychological research is to design projects so that the researcher can identify and study certain factors that cause or affect the behavior, while taking special precautions to prevent other factors from also having an effect.

The special challenges of psychological research, as well as the techniques that can be used to avoid the problems these challenges may cause, will be made clear in this book. This information will allow you to evaluate the research of others thoroughly and critically and will provide you with the skills to conduct quality research of your own.

WAYS OF KNOWING

The scientific method is the method of inquiry used by scientists to acquire knowledge. Scientists feel reasonably confident about the results of research obtained by the scientific method. What is known in the sciences today has been learned using this method. To better understand what this means, let's consider other ways of acquiring knowledge.

You know many things. Volumes could be filled with your specific knowledge of your hometown, family, friends, religion, and course work. But relatively little of what you know was learned through the use of the scientific method. When a person says that he or she knows something, that information may have been learned in a number of ways. No single way of acquiring knowledge is necessarily better than another, but some questions are better answered—or can only be answered—by a specific approach.

Intuition and Superstition

My grandmother firmly believed—she would say that she knew—that the number 13 was unlucky. She held a **superstition**, a belief or practice based on faith in chance, magic, or irrational feelings (Merriam-Webster, 2003). Superstitions are based on personal, **subjective** feelings, as opposed to **objective**, verifiable experience. Many otherwise rational people believe in superstitions. They often realize that their beliefs are irrational but continue to wear lucky shirts, to knock on wood, or to steer clear of black cats.

Intuition is knowledge that we acquire without conscious reasoning (Merriam-Webster, 2003). Like superstition, intuition is a wholly subjective experience; it is based totally on personal feelings. Intuition, however, has a better reputation than superstition, perhaps because knowledge gained without reason is not always contrary to reason. While few decisions should be based on superstitions, an argument can be made that intuition provides the best answers to some questions. Which summer job should you take? Which person should you date? Perhaps you've been advised at some point to "go with your gut feeling"—in other words, to use your intuition.

Authority

A more universally accepted approach to knowing is based on authority. In this method, information is learned from the reports of a trustworthy and credible source. People tend to believe information that has been reported to them by someone in a position of authority. Students listen to lectures, read textbooks, and rarely question the material presented to them by college professors because they are assumed to be authorities on their topics. Generally, television news anchors are not swamped with calls questioning the veracity of their news stories because viewers believe that they have valid sources. This is not to say that people blindly accept all they are told. Educated consumers do not believe everything that they see on TV or read on the cover of grocery store tabloids. How likely we are to believe some information depends on the source's reputation.

In September 2004, CBS news reported that they had documents that showed that President George W. Bush had not completed his National

Guard service. When it became public that the documents' authenticity could not be substantiated the reputation of CBS news was sullied. As a result, Dan Rather, the head anchor, retired earlier than he'd originally planned (Zurawik, 2005), and CBS fired four other reporters in an effort to convince the public that it had rectified the situation and could be trusted as an authority (UPI, 2005).

The method of authority is a more rational approach to knowing than belief in superstition or dependence on intuition, but it is not without its flaws. A person's perception of an authority figure is often tainted by personal feelings; I may tend to believe what one person tells me simply because I like that person. Also, in most cases, the learner has very little knowledge about how the information was acquired by the authority. Did the authority learn it from another authority? Was it learned originally through direct observation, or was it someone else's intuition? Urban myths—such as the tale of the person who dried a pet dog in a microwave—are spread and believed because people do not question the source: a friend of a friend of mine.

Rational-Inductive Argument

Perhaps one of the most highly respected methods of acquiring knowledge is through **rational-inductive argument**. This is the primary method of knowledge acquisition in nonscientific academic disciplines, such as history, philosophy, and literature. Based on the text of an author's works and the historical context in which they were written, a scholar draws some conclusions about that author's motivations, beliefs, and attitudes. Similarly, we may become familiar with what others have said about a topic and then form our own rational arguments to defend a different idea or thesis. Of course, this approach to acquiring knowledge is not limited to academicians. And not all use of the rational-inductive argument is based on extensive research on an area. We all use this approach every day when trying to explain why we voted for a certain politician, why we didn't like a movie, or why our friends should go to the restaurant we prefer.

A rational-inductive argument may be well-conceived and based on verifiable facts. In fact, rational-inductive arguments can be objective. The process of arguing, however, is susceptible to subjectivity and bias. A white supremacist who refuses to acknowledge the valuable contributions of other races is using rational-inductive argument in a biased manner. If I argue that a certain movie isn't worth seeing because I don't happen to like the starring actor, I am basing my argument on subjectivity, on my own personal feelings.

The contributions of rational-inductive argument to the world's body of knowledge, however, should not be undervalued. Although this approach is susceptible to subjectivity, users of rational-inductive argument often provide us with important, useful, and meaningful commentaries and theories. It is impossible to imagine our intellectual development without rational-inductive argument.

The Scientific Method

The scientific method is the method of inquiry used to acquire knowledge in the sciences. It is the collecting of observations in a systematic and objective manner. These observations are collected to test predictions called hypotheses. Typically, a **hypothesis** is a prediction about what causes a certain phenomenon to occur. For instance, a researcher might have a hypothesis that the stress of final exams might make students more susceptible to illness; another researcher might hypothesize that sleep deprivation will cause a person to perform poorly on a word puzzle. When the data are consistent with a hypothesis, the hypothesis is supported. If the researcher collects data that demonstrate that sleep-deprived people have more difficulty with word puzzles than those who are not sleep-deprived, the hypothesis is supported. Scientists, including psychologists, have high standards about what counts as supporting a hypothesis. Scientists like to be 95% confident in their results; in the section on statistics we will get a sense of how that is done.

Despite high standards and a focus on obtaining unbiased results, research in science is not totally objective. The choice of what topic to research and, to some extent, how the results of research are interpreted are vulnerable to subjectivity. Science differs from other ways of knowing, though, in that a system is created so that data are collected objectively and the hypotheses are tested objectively.

Each way of knowing is best suited to answering particular types of questions, thus the scientific method is not always the most appropriate way to gain knowledge. For instance, it is not likely to tell you whom you should marry or why you should eat at a certain restaurant. However, it could be used to answer questions about which factors affect a person's choice of a spouse or whether there is a relationship between entree prices and rated quality among restaurants. The scientific method is most useful for answering what are often called empirical questions—questions that can be answered by making observations or conducting experiments. In psychology, these questions often address, directly or indirectly, the underlying causes of events, behaviors, and other phenomena.

Concept Question 1.1

Identify the different ways of knowing (superstition and intuition, authority, rational-inductive argument, or the scientific method) used in each of the following scenarios.

a. A child believes that Santa Claus is real because Mom and Dad say he is.

b. Dr. Jones argues that the causes of the First World War were nationalistic feelings within the different European countries; he backs his arguments with evidence about the economic, social, and international conditions of the time.

c. The Tasty Company knows that its cola tastes better than competing brands because people who did not know which cola they were drinking chose Tasty Cola more often than the other brands.

d. I know the brakes are wearing out on my car because my mechanic looked at them and then told me so.

e. The electrician checked each of the circuit breakers independently before concluding that the problem was a short in the third breaker.

f. The athlete knew he would have a good game because he wore his lucky socks.

g. I think that people should go see my favorite movie because the plot is enthralling, the acting is well done, the photography is excellent, and the script is fantastic.

h. I knew that my house was going to be broken into because I've been very paranoid about the neighborhood ever since I came back from vacation.

The essential task in conducting scientific research is to collect the data in a manner such that there is only one explanation for the obtained results. The researcher attempts to design a study without **confounds**. Confounds are flaws in the design of a study that allow for competing explanations of the results. For example, imagine a study in which participants are randomly assigned to one of two groups. One group is simply told to study a list of 20 words for 5 minutes; a second group of participants is given instructions for a special mnemonic, a memory technique that may help them remember the words. If the only difference between the groups is the mnemonic instructions, any difference in performance between the groups is probably caused by those instructions. But what if the room is noisy for the first group and quiet for the second? Then differences in performance could be either a result of the mnemonic instructions or a result of the noise level in the room, or even a combination of the two. Now the results of the experiment are ambiguous—there is more than one possible explanation.

Concept Questions 1.2

1. An acquaintance mentions that the arthritis in her hands has been bothering her, but she has been rubbing herbal creams into her knuckles and this has helped. What explanations other than the effi-

cacy of the herbal creams might also account for the improvement she feels?

2. In a taste test between Tasty Cola and Quencher Cola, tasters are always presented with Quencher Cola first, followed by a salted cracker, and then presented with Tasty Cola. Although the tasters do not know which cola is which, they report that Tasty Cola tastes better than Quencher. Are there alternative explanations for the results? If so, how many can you identify? What improvements in the design of the study would you suggest?

When conducting research by the scientific method, a researcher is typically interested in knowing how one thing, such as mnemonic instructions, affects something else, such as memory performance. Let's return to the study where one group receives no instructions and the other group receives mnemonic instructions. The researcher will try to hold everything constant between the two groups of participants. The groups will be tested on the same day, in the same room, by the same experimenter. The two groups will have the same amount of time to study the same list of 20 words, and they will be given the same amount of time to recall the 20 words. The only difference between these two groups will be that one group will receive the mnemonic instructions and the other will not. What the researcher changes or *manipulates* in an experiment is called the **independent variable**. The different ways in which the independent variable is varied are referred to as the different **levels** (or **conditions**) **of the independent variable.** In this case, the two levels of the independent variable, mnemonic instructions, are whether the participant receives the mnemonic instructions or not. The group of participants given the treatment being tested is often referred to as the **experimental group**. The group that does not receive the treatment being tested (when there is such a group—in this case the group that does not receive the mnemonic instructions) is called the **control group**. The control group is treated in exactly the same manner as the experimental group, except for the manipulation of the independent variable. The control group is used to demonstrate that any difference between the performance of the control group and the performance of the experimental group was a result of the independent variable and not some other aspect of the experiment.

The effect of the mnemonic instructions in this experiment would be seen by measuring how well the experimental group remembers the 20 words and how well the control group remembers them. What the experimenter measures in both the experimental and control groups is called the **dependent variable**, because the experimenter wants to see if the participants' performance on this variable is *dependent* on the condition of the independent variable they have been assigned. In other words, the researcher wants to see if the independent variable causes a change in the dependent variable. In the present example, the researcher wants to know if the use of the mnemonic (the independent variable) does or does not affect the number of words recalled (the dependent variable).

In some types of research, it is not possible to manipulate the independent variable. For example, a researcher who is interested in the effects of gender on mathematical performance cannot manipulate gender. Gender is a **subject variable** (also called an **attribute variable**), a characteristic of the participants that can be measured. (Until recently, research participants were referred to as subjects and, correspondingly, a variable that reflects a characteristic of the participants, or subjects, was called a subject variable.) The levels of a subject variable can only be selected; they cannot be manipulated. A researcher can choose to study how mathematical performance is related to gender, but cannot decide which participants will be male and which will be female.

The distinction between subject variables and independent variables is important when drawing conclusions from the results of research. A researcher has little or no control over the many factors associated with a subject variable and, consequently, cannot determine conclusively that a subject variable caused a result to occur. On the other hand, if an independent variable is manipulated, and the results warrant such a conclusion, the researcher can claim that the independent variable had a *causal* effect on the dependent variable, because the researcher was able to control all the related factors that might have affected the results. So, having found that individuals of different gender differ in their mathematical performance, a researcher could conclude only that there is a *relationship* between the two variables (gender and mathematical performance). The evidence does not suggest, however, that gender causes a difference in mathematical performance any more than it suggests that mathematical performance causes a difference in gender. There is no way of ruling out numerous alternative explanations—for example, that members of one gender receive more background or more encouragement in mathematics. This distinction between causal evidence and evidence of relationships will be discussed more thoroughly in other chapters. For now, the more important distinction is between independent variables (including subject variables) and dependent variables.

As a general rule, researchers using the scientific method attempt to identify the effect of independent variables on dependent variables. In fact, if a study can be retitled so that it fits the form "the effect of _____ on _____ ," it will always be the case that we are looking at the effect of an independent variable on a dependent variable. So if a study can be called *The Effect of Mnemonic Instructions on Memory*, then we can see that "mnemonic instructions" is the independent variable and "memory" is the dependent variable.

A researcher is able to make systematic and objective observations by controlling for all possible confounds when designing and carrying out a research project. However, the fact that a researcher is able to identify an effect of an independent variable on a dependent variable does not, by itself, mean that the effect actually exists. The best support comes when different researchers using different participants and different types of research designs are able to replicate (or reproduce) the results. In that case, we conclude that the effect is strong enough to be found under a variety of circumstances. If an effect is sometimes replicated and sometimes not, then some other unknown and uncontrolled variables may be affecting the results. Studies that are unable to replicate an effect should not be considered failures. The information these studies provide is useful and important for guiding additional research, as researchers try to determine what factors might be causing the effect to appear on some occasions but not on others.

Concept Questions 1.3

1. In an experiment comparing the effect of study materials on test scores, participants in one group are instructed to take their own notes on a videotaped lecture and participants in the other group are instructed to look at an outline of the lecture while watching the video. Three days following the lecture, all of the participants take a short test on the material and their test scores are recorded.
   a. What is the dependent variable in this study?
   b. What is the independent variable in this study?
   c. How many levels of the independent variable are there in this study?
   d. Is the independent variable a subject variable?

2. Volunteers over the age of 21 participate in a study that is designed to study the effects of alcohol on visual acuity. The participants all have 20/20 vision. One-third of the participants drink 2 ounces of alcohol, one-third of the participants drink 1 ounce of alcohol, and one-third of the participants consume a drink with no alcohol. Then, each participant's visual acuity is measured.
   a. What is the dependent variable in this study?
   b. What is the independent variable in this study?
   c. How many levels of the independent variable are there in this study?
   d. Is the independent variable a subject variable?

3. To study the effect of gender on color preference, men and women were asked to choose their favorite shade of blue among seven possible choices. Their choices were then compared.

a. What is the dependent variable in this study?

b. What is the independent variable in this study?

c. How many levels of the independent variable are there in this study?

d. Is the independent variable a subject variable?

THE OBJECTIVES OF SCIENCE AND THE SCIENTIFIC METHOD

Research using the scientific method can provide information about how one variable affects another or about how two or more variables are related. This information can be used to reach a number of different goals: description, explanation, prediction, and control.

Description as a Research Objective

The results of scientific research can be used in the identification and **description** of phenomena. For example, I may be interested in studying how students learn in the classroom. By carefully observing classroom behavior, or by gathering information from surveys or interviews (or perhaps by some other research method), I might be able to identify different classroom styles. Perhaps, for instance, I find that some students are extensive note takers, while others take only cursory notes, and still others take no notes at all. Further research might address whether this distinction among styles is true in all types of courses or with all types of instructors. The goal of this research would be to describe the phenomenon of different classroom styles. Descriptive research plays an important role in science by identifying and describing phenomena so that later explanations of these phenomena may be proposed.

Explanation and Prediction as Research Objectives

Explanations in research attempt to offer reasons why a phenomenon occurs. For example, suppose researchers found that note takers scored higher on a test of lecture material than those who studied a lecture summary written by someone else. A researcher might propose that this phenomenon occurs because the process of note taking helps a student learn the material during the lecture, in contrast to listening without taking notes. From this explanation, specific **predictions** or hypotheses can be derived and tested.

Based on the explanation proposed above, one might predict that note takers would perform better on a test than listeners when neither group is allowed to study before the test. An experiment could then be designed to test this hypothesis. If the results of the experiment are consistent with the hypothesis, the explanation that the process of note taking is important in the learning of material is supported. Predictive ability adds value to an explanation; an explanation that can predict future results is of more worth to a researcher than an explanation that can only account for past research findings.

Control as a Research Objective

With an understanding of the causes of a phenomenon and the ability to predict results on the basis of that explanation can also come the ability to **control** the phenomenon. If we know that excessive stress can cause headaches and ulcers, we also know that we can reduce the chance of suffering from these ailments by reducing the amount of stress in our lifestyle. Not all research in psychology leads so directly from description to control, but control is one of the major goals of applied psychological research.

As in other fields, **applied research** in psychology is research with results that are immediately relevant in a practical setting. Research that attempts to identify new and effective therapy techniques is applied research, as is research testing the worth of different teaching methods or the most efficient layout for a keyboard. The results of such research can often be applied directly in order to control behavior; many practitioners find this aspect of applied research particularly satisfying.

Not all research results are immediately applicable to a specific problem, nor were they ever intended to be. The results of **basic research** may have no immediate practical use; explanation, rather than application, is typically the goal of basic research. The basic researcher's motivation often comes from an insatiable curiosity and a desire to gain knowledge for knowledge's sake. Basic and applied research are related, however. Results of previous basic research often lay the groundwork for applied research, and investigations into practical questions can also suggest theoretical research questions to the basic researcher.

A Word about Theories

A scientific **theory** is a set of related statements that explain and predict phenomena. The statements used in a theory can be laws, principles, or beliefs. **Laws** are very specific statements that are generally expressed in the form of a mathematical equation involving only a few variables. Laws have so much empirical support that their accuracy is beyond reasonable doubt. The law of gravity is an example of such a theoretical statement. My mental health would be questioned if I began to publicly doubt the validity of the law of gravity. While there are numerous laws within the natural sciences such as physics and chemistry, there are relatively few in psychology; most have been discovered in the area of psychophysics (the study of how physical stimuli are translated into psychological experiences). For example, Weber's law states that for any sensory modality, such as vision, the difference threshold (the smallest difference a person can detect 50% of the time) for a particular type of stimulus is constant; this law is written as $\Delta I / I = K$, where I is the magnitude of the stimulus, ΔI is the difference threshold, and K is a constant. This law is precisely stated and well supported by empirical research.

Principles are more tentative than laws. They are statements that predict a phenomenon with a certain level of probability. A description of positive reinforcement could be stated as a principle: Positive reinforcement increases the probability that a contingent behavior will occur again. The principle of positive reinforcement can be used to predict how likely it is that an event will occur, but not with total accuracy. Psychology is replete with principles.

Finally, psychological theories will sometimes incorporate **beliefs**. Beliefs (also called assumptions) are statements based on personal feelings and subjective knowledge about things that cannot be tested scientifically. Freud's theory of the id, ego, and superego contains a number of belief statements about the existence and function of these three entities. The theory is useful to psychoanalysts as a way to conceptualize the workings of the mind, but it is of less value to the scientific researcher because the belief statements cannot be tested. No one has been able to demonstrate the existence of the id, ego, or superego. Beliefs are avoided within scientific psychology theories because they are untestable. All theories, though, are based on some as-yet untestable assumptions. The goal is to keep the number of these assumptions to a minimum.

Theories often attempt to explain a set of related observations or phenomena; for example, the behavioral theory of learning attempts to explain the behavioral effects of positive reinforcement, negative reinforcement, punishment, and schedules of reinforcement. From this theory, as from any scientific theory, a researcher can derive specific testable hypotheses that serve as the bases for scientific investigations. A testable hypothesis is one that can be disproven if certain results occur. Thus, from behavioral learning theory in general, and the principle of positive reinforcement in particular, a researcher may predict that people who received positive comments about their progress would be more apt to stick with a weight-loss program than would people who received no feedback. This is a specific, testable hypothesis derived from a more complex theory. Support for the theory comes, of course, from support for the hypothesis. Should the hypothesis fail to be supported, the theory may require some modification; in the most extreme case, it may need to be discarded.

When there are two equally accurate explanations for a phenomenon, the explanation based on simpler assumptions is preferable. This preference for simplicity is called **parsimony**. For example, the theory of extrasensory perception (ESP) attempts to explain and predict occurrences such as the telepathic transmission of messages or the psychokinetic movement of objects. To accept ESP theory's explanation for these events requires us to abandon the assumptions of contemporary physical theory. For instance, psychokinesis suggests that physical objects can be influenced without transmitting or transferring any physical energy, an assumption that runs counter to present-day knowledge of physics. Until scientific research presents considerable solid, replicable evidence that supports ESP theory and refutes present-day theory, it is more parsimonious to explain apparent occurrences of psychokinesis or telepathy in terms of coincidence or magicians' tricks. It is simpler to use the assumptions of present-day theories to explain these events than it is to discard them in exchange for assumptions that are as yet unsupported (Kalat, 1990). In general, if two competing theories are equally good at explaining behavior, the theory with fewer assumptions or better-supported assumptions is deemed superior.

Another criterion with which to evaluate theories is **precision**. A good theory is precisely stated. This might mean that it consists of mathematical statements or a computer program. Or it might be stated in standard English, but with carefully defined terms. Regardless of the language in which it is stated, a precise theory is written to avoid ambiguity and misinterpretation.

Related to precision is a third criterion on which to judge theories—**testability**. A sound scientific theory is testable; that is, it must be possible, in principle, to prove the theory wrong (Popper, 1959). Consider an example. On the basis of learning theory, and in particular, the principle of positive reinforcement, a researcher predicts that, if two groups of people are asked to complete a meaningless task (such as circling every letter e on this page), the group that receives attention while completing the task will perform more rapidly and more accurately than the group that receives no attention. This is a testable hypothesis. We may conduct such a test and if the results do not occur as predicted, we can conclude that there is a flaw in either the hypothesis or the underlying theory. Now suppose that a researcher predicts, from Freudian personality theory, that fixation at the oral stage of psychosexual development will lead to some type of overuse or underuse of the mouth. In this case, oral fixation could predict overeating or anorexia, or it might predict loquaciousness or a refusal to speak. A theory that is capable of explaining all results is untestable and judged a poorer scientific theory than a testable one.

A fourth criterion for judging scientific theories is apparent **accuracy**. A parsimonious, precisely stated theory that yields testable hypotheses is of little value if all of its hypotheses are left unsupported. A good scientific theory should fit the known facts and predict new ones. This, however, leads to what might appear to be a paradox: A theory can never be proven true.

Results that are consistent with predictions derived from a given theory may be found over and over, but this does not prove that the theory is true; it simply supports the theory. The results may have been found because the theory is true, or perhaps because another theory that makes the same predictions is true. It could be that the theory is true thus far but is incomplete and cannot explain phenomena in yet unstudied areas. The research results may actually be an artifact (a by-product) of the research method, and would not be found if another method were employed. Or the results may simply have occurred by chance. Suppose I predict that when I let go of a pencil in the air, it will fall to the floor. But instead, the pencil floats. This evidence refutes the theory of gravity as it stands today. If the pencil hits the floor, in contrast, that does not prove the theory of gravity; it does, however, add additional support to it.

Just because a theory can never be proven does not mean that research is a waste of time. As support for a theory accumulates, confidence in the veracity of the theory increases. So, even though a theory may never be proven correct, it can accumulate enough support to be assumed correct. In science, the only way to accumulate this support is through research.

RESEARCH CRITICISM

The goal of this book is to serve as a guide as you learn to design and conduct psychological research. During the process of learning how to conduct well-designed research, you will also gain critical-thinking skills and the ability to critique other research. Do not believe that just because a study has been published, it must be good. Often, errors in design slip past the editors and reviewers of research journals, or what was not seen as a problem at first becomes a problem as new research is conducted. As you read research literature, you need to evaluate each study and determine if it provides useful information or if the researchers made errors that weaken their conclusions.

As you read a description of a research project, note whether the arguments made are logical. Are terms clearly defined? Was the manner in which the investigation was conducted clearly stated so that another person could repeat it? Were there any potential confounds in the design? Were the conclusions consistent with the results of the study? Do the researchers interpret the results and come to the same conclusions that you do? Are there any alternative explanations that the researchers may have missed?

You do not need to be the premier expert in a field to find flaws and weaknesses in other people's research. While I was researching possible dissertation topics I read a research project on idioms (or phrases such as "let the cat out of the bag" and "over the hill"). The materials used by the researchers included phrases that, while I may have heard of them, I certainly didn't encounter them on a daily basis (e.g., "upset the applecart"). It occurred to me that the results of the study may have been more an artifact of the rather unusual materials being used than an indicator of how idioms in general are processed. My observation of this potential problem led to my dissertation on idiom familiarity and to a research program that continues 20 years later. Sometimes it takes the fresh eye of a novice to see the most obvious problems.

SUMMARY

Research in psychology is conducted using the scientific method. In the scientific method, information is gained through systematic observations made in an objective manner.

There are other methods of inquiry that people use in various situations. No one method is better than another, but some methods are better than others in some situations or for some questions. Superstitions are a method of inquiry based on belief and subjective feelings. Intuition is based on subjectivity also, but many people argue that there are appropriate situations for using intuition. In the method of authority, knowledge is gained from the reports of a trustworthy source. The rational-inductive argument is the primary method of knowledge acquisition used in non-scientific academic disciplines. The person uses information gleaned from other sources and personal thoughts to construct a rational argument in defense of a specific point of view.

The scientific method differs from other approaches in its emphasis on systematic and objective observation. It attempts to avoid the effects of the possible biases of the research participants or the researchers themselves. Experimenters using the scientific method must take care to design a study without confounds. Confounds are flaws in the design of a study such that competing explanations of the results are possible.

Research projects based on the scientific method usually involve at least one independent variable and one dependent variable. The independent variable is manipulated by the experimenter. There may be several levels of one independent variable. When the independent variable cannot be manipulated but instead must be selected, as in the case of the sex, height, or weight of the participants, it is called a subject variable.

The dependent variable is the variable that is measured. The observation of changes in the dependent variable corresponding to different levels of the independent variable suggests that the independent variable caused the dependent variable to change. But note that, in the case where the independent variable is a subject variable, such an observation would simply suggest a relationship between the subject variable and the dependent variable.

Researchers conduct experiments for four major reasons: to describe phenomena, to predict phenomena, to explain phenomena, and to control phenomena. Applied research focuses on practical problems. Basic research focuses on theoretical problems and questions for which the results have no immediate application.

Theories guide much research in psychology. A sound scientific theory is parsimonious, precise, testable, and accurate.

Learning to evaluate research will help you gain important critical-thinking skills and also to become a better consumer of research in the day-to-day world. Perhaps it will also lead you to conduct research of your own.

IMPORTANT TERMS AND CONCEPTS

accuracy
applied research
authority
basic research
beliefs
confound
control
control group
data
dependent variable
description
experimental group
explanation
hypothesis
independent variable
intuition

laws
levels (or conditions) of
   the independent variable
objective
parsimony
precision
predictions
principles
rational-inductive argument
scientific method
subject (or attribute) variable
subjective
superstition
testability
theory

EXERCISES

1. A researcher is investigating the effect of mood on eating. Participants in a sample of undergraduate females (ages 18–22) are randomly assigned to one of two conditions, the depressed condition or the neutral condition. Participants assigned to the depressed condition are hypnotized and a depressed mood is induced. Participants in the neutral condition are hypnotized and a neutral mood is induced. Following the hypnosis, participants are offered a plate of cookies as they watch a travel film about Paris. The number of cookies eaten by each participant is recorded.

    a. Identify the experimental and control groups.

    b. What is the independent variable? How many levels of the independent variable are there?

    c. Is the independent variable manipulated or selected?

    d. What is the dependent variable?

2. During everyday speech we often use figurative phrases, such as "let the cat out of the bag" or "over the hill." Researchers are very inter-

ested in what phrases people use or are familiar with. One researcher selects a sample of 16–22-year-olds and another sample of 66–72-year-olds. The researcher interviews each participant for 5 minutes and records the number of figurative expressions each one employs. The researcher finds that the older participants use more figurative expressions than the younger participants.

   a. What is the dependent variable in this study?

   b. What is the independent variable? How many levels of the independent variable are there?

   c. Is the independent variable manipulated or selected?

   d. The researcher is tempted to conclude that, as individuals get older, they use more figurative language. Suggest another possible explanation for the results.

3. A television advertisement states that "scientific studies prove that this product works, and it will work for you too."

   a. If a viewer believes this advertisement, what method of knowing is being used?

   b. Explain why a scientific study cannot prove that a product will work for an entire population.

4. In this chapter, four ways of knowing were described—superstition and intuition, authority, rational-inductive argument, and the scientific method. The scientific method, which is the subject of this book, is not always the best way of acquiring knowledge. Provide examples of a situation in which (a) intuition, (b) authority, and (c) rational-inductive argument would be an adequate or superior way of gaining information, and explain why you believe so.

5. What is the difference between objectivity and subjectivity, and why is it so important that scientific research be conducted objectively?

6. A good scientific theory should be parsimonious, precise, and testable.

   a. Explain the concept of parsimony, and create an example (other than the one in the chapter) comparing two theories in terms of parsimony.

   b. Explain the value of precisely stated theories.

   c. Explain the concept of testability and its relationship to theories. What is the difference between testing a theory and proving one? Why do I rant and rave when a student claims to have proven a theory?

7. How do you think you might use information from this course and textbook in the future? Answer this question again after you have completed the book.

6

ANSWERS TO CONCEPT QUESTIONS AND ODD-NUMBERED EXERCISES

Note: There will often be more than one correct answer for each of these questions. Consult with your instructor about your own answers.

Concept Question 1.1
a. authority
b. rational-inductive argument
c. scientific method
d. authority
e. scientific method
f. superstition
g. rational-inductive argument
h. intuition

Concept Questions 1.2
1. Perhaps the act of massaging is what makes her hands feel better. Or perhaps she is experiencing a placebo effect; that is, her hands feel better because she thinks the cream is effective, although in reality it isn't.
2. Perhaps the second cola is always judged to taste better, regardless of which cola is first or second. Or perhaps Tasty Cola is judged to taste better because it follows a salted cracker, while the other cola does not. The study could be improved by alternating the order of the two colas and by preceding each cola with a cracker.

Concept Questions 1.3
1. a. test scores
   b. study materials
   c. two levels
   d. no
2. a. visual acuity
   b. alcohol consumption
   c. three levels
   d. no
3. a. color choice
   b. gender
   c. two levels
   d. yes

Exercises
1. a. Those in the induced-depression group make up the experimental group; those in the induced-neutral group make up the control group.
   b. Induced mood; two levels.
   c. The independent variable is manipulated.
   d. Number of cookies eaten.

3. a. Method of authority.

   b. The scientific method allows a researcher to be reasonably confident that a product will work for a group of people, but it cannot prove that it will work for everyone without actually testing it on everyone.

5. Subjectivity is reasoning based on personal beliefs and attitudes. Objectivity is reasoning that avoids the influence of personal beliefs and attitudes. It is important for scientific research to be conducted objectively, so that the personal beliefs and attitudes of the researcher (or participants) do not affect the results of the research.

7. There is no right or wrong answer to this question.

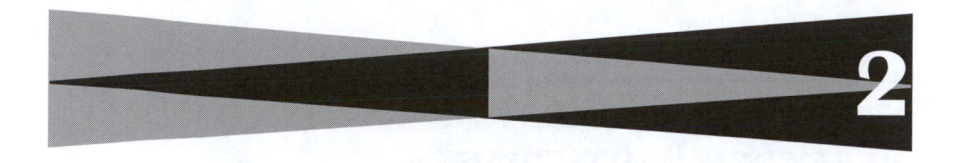

Ethics in Research

> For psychologists . . . one of their obligations is to use their research skills to extend knowledge for the sake of ultimate human betterment. Psychologists begin with the commitment that the distinctive contribution of scientists to human welfare is the development of knowledge and its intelligent application to appropriate problems. Their underlying ethical imperative, thus, is to conduct research as well as they know how. (APA, 1982, p. 15)

Psychologists conduct research not only because they enjoy the process, but also because psychology as a discipline is defined by, and dependent on, psychological research. However, conducting research requires awareness and consideration of a number of ethical concerns. Two major areas of ethical consideration are: the treatment of participants while conducting the research and the use of the research results.

ETHICAL TREATMENT OF
RESEARCH PARTICIPANTS

The participants of psychological research are usually either animals or humans. How the participants are treated during the course of a research project is in part mandated by law, in part regulated by guidelines developed by psychologists, and in part determined by the researcher's own conscience. Together, these factors lead to research that not only provides valuable information about behavior but also respects the dignity of the research participants.

Ethical Treatment of Human Participants

The ethical treatment of research participants is the primary responsibility of the researcher. It is the researcher who decides what research to do and what method to use. A researcher might decide not to investigate a certain topic or use a particular methodology because he or she is uncomfortable with the ethical ramifications. In other cases, a researcher may not easily perceive genuine ethical problems with a method he or she was planning to use. To help researchers see their projects from others' point of view, and in an attempt to ensure the safety and well-being of human participants in research, **institutional review boards (IRBs)** review proposals for research with human participants.

IRBs are committees of individuals with diverse backgrounds who review proposals for research with human participants. Members of an IRB at a college may include faculty members from different academic departments, as well as members of the community. The diverse backgrounds of the members help bring different perspectives to the review process. All research using human participants that is federally funded must be reviewed by an IRB, but changes in the law in 1981 and subsequent revisions exempted many other types of research from review. Such exemptions include research that involves common educational practices and research in which the participants remain **anonymous**, that is, no one, not even the researcher, knows the identity of the participants (Public Welfare, 2005). In an effort to guarantee the ethical treatment of human participants, however, most colleges and universities review all research proposals involving human participants that will be carried out at that institution, and many institutions do not allow exemptions from this review.

Typically, a researcher completes an application form for the IRB that asks specific questions about the procedures to be used in a research project, whether there are any known risks or benefits related to the procedure, and how the participants' confidentiality will be maintained. Often, a detailed research proposal is supplied with the application. An important part of the application to the IRB is the informed consent form.

The **informed consent form** is given to each participant prior to participation in the project. It describes the purpose of the study and what the participant will be asked to do. Any known risks or benefits related to the study are made clear to the participant. Even if the participant signs the informed consent form, that person is still free to stop participating at any point during the project; this is also clearly stated in the informed consent form. An example of an informed consent form is presented in figure 2.1.

If the participants are children, the consent form is read and signed by each child's parent or guardian. The children, however, should also be asked if they want to participate and should be free to say no or to end their participation at any time.

As a member of an IRB, I always put the most emphasis on the informed consent form when evaluating a proposal. It may be the only information the participants receive about what to expect and what risks and benefits may be involved. It is essential that it be accurate, understandable, and clearly written.

The goal of the informed consent form is not to convince the individual to sign it; rather, the goal is to provide enough information so that he or she can make an informed decision. The consent form simply documents that the person has consented to participate, and review of the form by the IRB ensures that he or she is given adequate information to make an informed decision. Although the consent form provides much information about the study, the researcher will typically describe the study to the participant orally and offer an opportunity for the participant to ask questions.

A researcher who has spent the time to plan and develop a research project may sometimes regard review by an IRB as an unnecessary hurdle before data collection can begin. However, the importance of an impartial review should not be underestimated. Ethical concerns are not always obvious; subtle and inconspicuous effects may easily be overlooked. I once used a procedure that involved rapidly presenting slides to the participant. During its development, I had tried the procedure on myself and a number of willing friends with no ill effects, but an impartial reviewer who experienced the procedure found it gave him a headache. Of course, the risk of headache or other discomfort was added to the informed consent form. If it had not been for that reviewer's comment and the inclusion of that risk in the information provided to participants, those who experienced headaches from the procedure may have believed that I was trying to hide a negative side effect. Ignoring ethical problems does not make them go away—they can also harm the reputation of the researcher and of psychology as a whole.

Concern for participants' welfare does not start at the IRB, nor does approval of the procedure by the IRB release the researcher from responsibility for any ethical violations the board may have missed. Ethical con-

Figure 2.1   A sample informed consent form

Bradley University
CONSENT FORM ON THE USE OF HUMAN SUBJECTS IN RESEARCH
Statement of Informed Consent

I, _____, am being asked to participate in a research project entitled _____. This project is being conducted under the supervision of _____ and was approved by Bradley University's Committee on the Use of Human Subjects in Research on _____.

From this project the investigators hope to learn _____.
(EXPLAIN, IN LAY LANGUAGE, WHAT THE PURPOSE OF THE STUDY IS.)

As a participant in this project I shall be asked to _____.
(IN THIS SPACE, EXPLAIN TO THE PARTICIPANT WHAT PROCEDURES WILL BE FOLLOWED. WHAT IS THE DURATION OF THE RESEARCH PROJECT? BE CONCISE, BUT FULLY INFORM THE PARTICIPANT. BE SURE TO AVOID LANGUAGE THAT IS TECHNICAL.)

The nature of this study has been explained to me by _____. I understand that the anticipated benefits of my participation are _____. I understand that the known risks of my participation in this study are _____. (FOR BENEFITS, YOU CAN INCLUDE BOTH DIRECT BENEFITS, SUCH AS EXTRA CREDIT POINTS, AND INDIRECT BENEFITS, SUCH AS THE BENEFIT TO SOCIETY DUE TO AN INCREASED UNDERSTANDING OF THIS AREA. FOR RISKS, INCLUDE POTENTIAL DISCOMFORTS. IF NO RISKS ARE APPARENT, STATE SO.)

The investigators will make every effort to safeguard the confidentiality of the information that I provide. Any information obtained from this study that can be identified with me will remain confidential and will not be given to anyone without my permission. (IF YOUR STUDY INVOLVES THE POSSIBILITY OF OBTAINING INFORMATION THAT YOU ARE OBLIGATED BY LAW OR ETHICS TO DISCLOSE, SUCH AS CHILD ABUSE OR A DANGER TO SELF OR OTHERS, INSERT A SENTENCE INDICATING THE SPECIFIC LIMITS OF CONFIDENTIALITY.)

If, at any time, I would like additional information about this project, I can contact _____ at _____. (GIVE THE NAME OF THE INVESTIGATOR AND GIVE AN ADDRESS AND PHONE NUMBER.)

I understand that I have the right to refuse to participate in this study. I also understand that, if I do agree to participate, I have the right to change my mind at any time and stop my participation. I understand that the grades or services I receive from Bradley University will not be negatively affected by my refusal to participate or by my withdrawal from this project. (IF THE PROJECT IS TAKING PLACE AT SOME OTHER ORGANIZATION, STATE HOW REFUSAL TO PARTICIPATE OR WITHDRAWAL WILL AFFECT THE SERVICES RECEIVED FROM THAT ORGANIZATION.) My signature below indicates that I have given my informed consent to participate in the above-described project. My signature also indicates that:

____   I have been given the opportunity to ask any and all questions about the described project and my participation and that all of my questions have been answered to my satisfaction.

____   I have been permitted to read this document and I have been given a signed copy of it.

____   I am at least 18-years-old.

____   I am legally able to provide consent.

____   To the best of my knowledge and belief I have no physical or mental illness or weakness that would be adversely affected by my participation in the described project.

_____   _____
Signature of participant   date

_____   _____
Signature of witness   date

Source: Reprinted with the permission of Bradley University.

siderations must be addressed throughout the development of the project. To aid researchers in identifying important ethical concerns, the **American Psychological Association (APA)**, a national organization of psychologists and people in related fields, has developed a set of fundamental principles. These **APA ethical principles in the conduct of research** are presented in box 2.1.

According to ethical research principles, a researcher is obligated to make a careful ethical evaluation of proposed methodology. If there is any question of an ethical violation, the researcher should seek ethical advice from others. Thus, even when an IRB review is not required, a researcher should not hesitate to ask other individuals for advice.

The primary ethical concern is whether the participants of the experiment would be at **risk** or at **minimal risk**. Risk can be defined as the potential for physical or psychological harm to a research participant. Although the APA does not define "minimal risk," the definition used by IRBs reviewing biomedical and behavioral research is as follows:

> *Minimal risk* means that the probability and magnitude of harm or discomfort anticipated in the research are not greater in and of themselves than those ordinarily encountered in daily life or during the performance of routine physical or psychological examinations or tests. (Public Welfare, 2005)

Thus, if the procedure involved in an experiment causes no more physical or psychological stress than a person would expect to encounter in everyday life, nor does it cause any greater risk of harm than a person usually faces, then a participant is at minimal risk. A person who spends an hour carrying out a very boring task in a psychological experiment may experience the discomfort of being bored, but this is not likely to be any more harmful or stressful to the individual than the boredom encountered in everyday life. Similarly, completing a paper-and-pencil psychological test—such as the Minnesota Multiphasic Personality Inventory (MMPI), which entails answering over 500 true/false questions—can be a long, somewhat stressful endeavor, however, since it is not unusual for students to be tested with long, somewhat stressful paper-and-pencil examinations, student participants completing the MMPI would probably be considered at minimal risk. In a study where the participants received painful but nonharmful shocks, the participants might very well be considered at risk, because the stress associated with the shocks might be deemed of greater magnitude than they would typically encounter.

It is the researcher's responsibility to assess whether the participants are at risk or at minimal risk. If the researcher believes the participants may be at risk, a decision must be made regarding whether the risk to the participants outweighs the possible benefits of the knowledge gained. When the risk is relatively small compared to the possible gains, most advisory boards allow the research to be conducted (with fully informed consent from the participants, of course). The greater the risk to the participants of a study, however, the greater is the researcher's obligation to consider alternative procedures that present a smaller risk.

Box 2.1

Excerpts from the American Psychological Association's *Ethical Principles of Psychologists and Code of Conduct*

8. Research and Publication

8.01 Institutional Approval

When institutional approval is required, psychologists provide accurate information about their research proposals and obtain approval prior to conducting the research. They conduct the research in accordance with the approved research protocol.

8.02 Informed Consent to Research

(a) When obtaining informed consent as required in Standard 3.10, Informed Consent, psychologists inform participants about (1) the purpose of the research, expected duration, and procedures; (2) their right to decline to participate and to withdraw from the research once participation has begun; (3) the foreseeable consequences of declining or withdrawing; (4) reasonably foreseeable factors that may be expected to influence their willingness to participate such as potential risks, discomfort, or adverse effects; (5) any prospective research benefits; (6) limits of confidentiality; (7) incentives for participation; and (8) whom to contact for questions about the research and research participants' rights. They provide opportunity for the prospective participants to ask questions and receive answers. (See also Standards 8.03, Informed Consent for Recording Voices and Images in Research; 8.05, Dispensing With Informed Consent for Research; and 8.07, Deception in Research.)

(b) Psychologists conducting intervention research involving the use of experimental treatments clarify to participants at the outset of the research (1) the experimental nature of the treatment; (2) the services that will or will not be available to the control group(s) if appropriate; (3) the means by which assignment to treatment and control groups will be made; (4) available treatment alternatives if an individual does not wish to participate in the research or wishes to withdraw once a study has begun; and (5) compensation for or monetary costs of participating including, if appropriate, whether reimbursement from the participant or a third-party payor will be sought. (See also Standard 8.02a, Informed Consent to Research.)

8.03 Informed Consent for Recording Voices and Images in Research

Psychologists obtain informed consent from research participants prior to recording their voices or images for data collection unless (1) the research consists solely of naturalistic observations in public places, and it is not anticipated that the recording will be used in a manner that could cause personal identification or harm, or (2) the research design includes deception, and consent for the use of the recording is obtained during debriefing. (See also Standard 8.07, Deception in Research.)

8.04 Client/Patient, Student, and Subordinate Research Participants

(a) When psychologists conduct research with clients/patients, students, or sub-ordinates as participants, psychologists take steps to protect the prospective participants from adverse consequences of declining or withdrawing from participation.

(b) When research participation is a course requirement or an opportunity for extra credit, the prospective participant is given the choice of equitable alternative activities.

8.05 Dispensing With Informed Consent for Research

Psychologists may dispense with informed consent only (1) where research would not reasonably be assumed to create distress or harm and involves (a) the study of normal educational practices, curricula, or classroom management methods conducted in educational settings; (b) only anonymous questionnaires, naturalistic observations, or archival research for which disclosure of responses would not place participants at risk of criminal or civil liability or damage their financial standing, employability, or reputation, and confidentiality is protected; or (c) the study of factors related to job or organization effectiveness conducted in organizational settings for which there is no risk to participants' employability, and confidentiality is protected or (2) where otherwise permitted by law or federal or institutional regulations.

8.06 Offering Inducements for Research Participation

(a) Psychologists make reasonable efforts to avoid offering excessive or inappropriate financial or other inducements for research participation when such inducements are likely to coerce participation.

(b) When offering professional services as an inducement for research participation, psychologists clarify the nature of the services, as well as the risks, obligations, and limitations. (See also Standard 6.05, Barter With Clients/Patients.)

8.07 Deception in Research

(a) Psychologists do not conduct a study involving deception unless they have determined that the use of deceptive techniques is justified by the study's significant prospective scientific, educational, or applied value and that effective nondeceptive alternative procedures are not feasible.

(b) Psychologists do not deceive prospective participants about research that is reasonably expected to cause physical pain or severe emotional distress.

(c) Psychologists explain any deception that is an integral feature of the design and conduct of an experiment to participants as early as is feasible, preferably at the conclusion of their participation, but no later than at the conclusion of the data collection, and permit participants to withdraw their data. (See also Standard 8.08, Debriefing.)

8.08 Debriefing

(a) Psychologists provide a prompt opportunity for participants to obtain appropriate information about the nature, results, and conclusions of the research, and they take reasonable steps to correct any misconceptions that participants may have of which the psychologists are aware.

(b) If scientific or humane values justify delaying or withholding this information, psychologists take reasonable measures to reduce the risk of harm.

(c) When psychologists become aware that research procedures have harmed a participant, they take reasonable steps to minimize the harm.

If an investigation involves some risk of negative effects, the risk must be made clear to the participant. If the risk is serious, the investigator is obligated to consider alternative procedures. If there are no alternative procedures, an important decision must be made. Should research on the topic be scrapped, or do the potential benefits of the knowledge from the research outweigh the risk to the participants? Research involving serious risk to the participants should only be undertaken if there are great potential benefits or when the risk to the participants would be even greater if the research were not conducted.

Regardless of whether an advisory board has given the go-ahead for a project, and regardless of whether the researcher is the person who actually collects the data for the project, the researcher is always responsible for ensuring that the project is conducted in an ethical manner. Often, students or technicians who work for a researcher will actually conduct the research. If a research assistant behaves unethically, both the assistant and the primary researcher are responsible for that behavior and for alleviating any negative side effects caused by it.

In addition to informing the participants of any risks (as well as any benefits) participation might involve, the researcher should also answer all of the participants' questions about the study. This may require some special efforts if the participants are children or people with mental or physical limitations that hinder communication, but it is an important step that ascertains that the participant fully understands what is expected and what to expect.

Special efforts to safeguard the participants are also required when full disclosure of the purpose of a study or the procedure prior to the investigation might impair the validity of the results. For example, in an investigation of reactions to emergency situations, the researcher cannot tell the participants that a staged emergency situation is about to occur and still be certain that the results reflect what the participants would do in real life. According to the APA, studies involving **deception** (lying or misleading participants) or concealment should only be conducted when no known alternative procedure is available and if the researcher does not deceive the participant about any factors that might affect their willingness to participate. Also, if studies involving deception or concealment are conducted, it is important to let participants know the true purpose of the study as soon as possible.

Even if a participant has signed the consent form, he or she still has the right to quit the study at any time. Of course, this can be very frustrating for an investigator. Moreover, if participants from one group quit the project more than do participants from another group, it can affect the interpretability of the results. However, as frustrated and disappointed as a researcher may be when a participant decides to withdraw from an investigation, no effort should be made to convince the person to stay. As a volunteer, it is the participant's right to terminate his or her participation, and that right must be respected.

Similarly, no undue effort should be made to convince a person to serve as a participant in an investigation. The participant must be in a situation allowing **free consent**. Free consent is consent given without coercion or pressure to comply. Clearly, whining and pleading by the researcher are unacceptable. However, it's also important to guard against situations in which a person feels coerced because the researcher is in a position of authority. For example, a student may feel pressure, imagined or not, to participate in an investigation conducted by his or her advisor. Or a patient may wonder if declining to participate in a study will affect the medical treatment provided. An employee may wonder if volunteering to serve as a participant might translate into a few more dollars in the next raise. A researcher who is in a position of influence or authority must make extra efforts to avoid any real or perceived coercion of potential participants.

Even in studies that do not involve deception, the actual purpose of the study may not be fully explained at the time the procedures are described. When the participants know the purpose of the study, they often try, in a spirit of helpfulness, to behave in the way they think the experimenter wants. Thus, while the procedure, risk, and benefits might be described in detail, the reason for conducting the research might not be explained thoroughly before the person participates. Standard 8.08 of the APA ethical guidelines states, however, that information about the purpose of the study should be provided as soon as possible after the data have been collected. This is called **debriefing** the participant. Often debriefing occurs immediately after an individual's data have been collected; at other times, debriefing may be provided at a later date, after the data are collected from all the participants. This may be necessary to prevent knowledge of the study's purpose from leaking to others before they participate.

Even when provided with the true purpose of an investigation, participants will often create their own additional misconceptions. As many psychology majors have noticed when talking to students of other disciplines, people often have the mistaken notion that psychologists can see into their souls. Participants asked to rate how often they have heard figurative phrases such as "let the cat out of the bag" may believe that how they rate a list of these phrases says something about their personalities. In debriefing, misconceptions about the purpose of a research project should be removed, so that the researcher—and psychology in general—will not suffer (or benefit) from them. When explaining the true purpose of the study during debriefing, the researcher should clarify any aspects of the study that were concealed or misrepresented. For example, if the study included a **confederate** (a research assistant who posed as a participant), this would be made clear during the debriefing. The researcher should also answer all the participants' questions about the study at this point.

Unless other arrangements have been made between the researcher and participant prior to data collection, all information collected during the course of the project is confidential, which means that the information collected will not be shared with anyone outside of the research project. **Confidentiality** is not a principle to be taken lightly. Off-hand comments to others about a silly thing a participant did during the study serve only to undermine the respectability of the researcher, the research, and psychology in general. In other cases, the information gained from a participant may be very sensitive and could cause the person great distress if it was learned by others outside of the experiment. Perhaps more importantly, if participants know that the information they give will be kept confidential, they can let down their guard and act naturally. This is essential in psychological research, where the value of the results depends on participants reflecting real behavior.

Ethical Dilemmas

Although these guidelines aid researchers in their decisions about how and when to conduct a research project, they are only guidelines, not laws. Researchers can stray from them with legal impunity. For example, a researcher who learns from a participant that he or she plans to commit a serious crime may feel morally entitled—and in some cases may be legally required—to breach confidentiality and report this information to the appropriate authorities. In fact, evidence supplied during the course of a research project can be subpoenaed by a court. Furthermore, these ethical guidelines were developed to be applicable to a broad array of research procedures and to reflect the ethical beliefs of a great number of psychologists. As such, they do not address ethical questions that some people find especially important. For example, when is it acceptable to observe behavior and when is observation a violation of privacy? Is it ever acceptable to use deception in research, or do such practices represent disrespect for human dignity?

Privacy. **Privacy** refers to an invisible physical or psychological buffer zone or boundary around a person (Sieber & Stanley, 1988). Not uncommonly, research is designed to access information within those boundaries; examples include studies on sexual behaviors, child-rearing practices, and personal relationships. In some cases, the researcher can ask permission to gain this information. When participants voluntarily complete a questionnaire on their buying habits or religious beliefs, they have agreed to share this private information. In other cases, researchers may observe people who are unaware that they are being watched. For example, in one investigation, men were observed by means of a periscope to study the effect of invasion of personal space on their rate of urination. In the condition in which the participant's personal space was invaded, a confederate in a public restroom would urinate in the urinal next to the participant. In the condition without invasion, the confederate was not present (Middlemist, Knowles, & Matter, 1976). Obviously, in this study there was no opportunity to gain informed consent from the participants. If you were a member of an IRB reviewing a proposal for this study, what would your decision be? Would you allow the study to be conducted as described, or would you suggest some modifications or perhaps simply deny permission for it to be undertaken? (For a critique of the ethical decisions behind this study, see Koocher, 1977; for the authors' response, see Middlemist, Knowles, & Matter, 1977.)

Deception.   In a now-famous study of obedience by Stanley Milgram (1963, 1977), participants were led to believe that they were inflicting dangerous levels of electrical shock to a second participant whenever the second participant failed to answer a question correctly. In reality, the shock machine was inoperable, and the second participant was a confederate who only pretended to be shocked. Approximately half of the participants continued to give shocks, as instructed by the experimenter, until the maximum shock level was reached. Milgram was criticized by colleagues, the press, and the general public for deceiving his participants and causing them to experience the stress associated with a distasteful truth about themselves. However, during immediate debriefings and during one-year follow-up interviews with his participants, Milgram reported that only about 1% of the people wished that they had not participated in the study and that most of the participants were very glad that they had.

The positive reaction of Milgram's participants to being deceived in psychological research appears not to be unusual. Pihl, Zacchia, and Zeichner (1981) interviewed people who had participated in research involving deception, shock, and alcohol. Of these participants, 19% reported being bothered by some part of the study. Of those, 4% were bothered by the deception; most were bothered by the consumption of alcohol and the speed with which it was consumed. In another investigation, 464 participants were asked their opinions of the research projects in which they had been involved (Smith & Richardson, 1983). Participants who had experienced deception in research projects reported greater educational benefits and enjoyment of those experiences than did participants who had not experienced deception.

Those who study participants' reactions to research suspect that debriefing is an important step in making participants feel positive toward an experience that involved deception. In a replication of Milgram's obedience study, only 4% of debriefed individuals wished that they had not participated in the study, but approximately 50% of those who had not been debriefed wished they had not participated (Ring, Wallston, & Corey, 1970).

In some research, however, debriefing itself may be unethical. In research where participants act cruelly or prejudicially, it may be better not to point out their behavior in a debriefing. For example, imagine that a person on crutches stumbles in front of you and drops some books and, for whatever reason, you choose not to assist the person. It may be more damaging to learn that your behavior was observed and recorded than it would be to simply go on your way without realizing you were part of a research project.

Perhaps deception in research is more of a problem for researchers and ethicists than for the participants of the investigations. And perhaps that is how it should be, for the goal of ethical treatment of research participants is that they not be discomforted by the procedures of the investigations. Maybe the evidence that participants are not distressed by the deception they face in research suggests that researchers have been successful at minimizing the negative effects of deception.

This discussion should not be construed as an argument in favor of the use of deception in research. Ideally, deception should be avoided; some would say that its use is never justified. However, considering that roughly 44% of psychological research with human participants in the past has involved deception (Leavitt, 1991), we should not expect that the use of deception will stop in the near future. It is important, though, that those who oppose deception in research remain vocal, for they help to ensure that researchers make a diligent effort to minimize the negative effects of deception on participants in psychological research.

Concept Question 2.1

How strictly do you define deception? Is deception used when a participant is misled about the purpose of a study—for instance, if the participant is told that its purpose is to investigate how well a small child likes a toy but it is really to assess the interactions between a mother and a child? Is deception used when a participant is not given full information about the purpose of a project—for example, if the participant is told that a study's purpose is to investigate natural language usage while actually it is to identify the use of swear words in conversation?

Ethical Treatment of Animal Participants

During the early 1980s, psychological research with animals as participants accounted for approximately 7% of all research published by the APA (Miller, 1985). Brink and his colleagues (1995) found that, at last count, animal research accounted for 14% of the articles published in the *Canadian Journal of Psychology*. Historically, the results of animal research have played a central role in the development of psychology. Ivan Pavlov's research on classical conditioning, Edward Thorndike's instrumental-conditioning research, and B. F. Skinner's operant-conditioning research provided the foundations for our current understanding of animal and human learning.

Although quite specific requirements and regulations protect the welfare of animal research participants, animal-rights supporters have been quite vocal and active in recent years. Often, they try to bring to public attention what is perceived as—and sometimes is—the mistreatment of animals in unnecessary or poorly conducted research. Some members of animal-rights groups feel justified in breaking into laboratories to destroy equipment and data and to "liberate" animals. In 2002, James Jarboe of the Federal Bureau of Investigation's counterterrorism office reported that the Earth Liberation Front and Animal Liberation Front organizations had committed more than 600 criminal acts since 1996, with an estimated cost of $43 million in damages (Schabner, 2002).

Animal-rights supporters express a range of views about the value of animal research. Some only want to make certain that the animals are treated humanely and that no unnecessary research is conducted. Others will not be satisfied until there is a total ban on animal research (Erikson, 1990). In response to such challenges, many researchers have catalogued the advances and benefits made as a direct result of animal research. In psychology, Neal Miller (1985) asserts that the results of animal research underlie, among much else, advances in psychotherapy; behavioral medicine; rehabilitation of neuromuscular disorders; understanding and alleviation of the effects of stress and of constant pain; drug treatment for anxiety, psychosis, and Parkinson's disease; knowledge about drug addiction and relapse; treatment of premature infants in incubators; understanding of the relationship between aging and memory loss; and the treatment of anorexia nervosa.

Animal-rights activism has encouraged scientists to work with animals in a humane manner and to develop alternative methods that do not require the use of animals (Erikson, 1990). Organizations like the National Institute of Environmental Health Sciences (2000) have developed panels to encourage the development and approval of alternative testing methods, such as developing tests like Corrositex, which uses a synthetic skin to show the effects of corrosive chemicals. Partly as a reaction to public concern for the ethical treatment of animal participants, the APA (1981, 1996) developed a set of guidelines for animal researchers to use in their research.

In summary, the **APA principles for the care and use of animals** require that the animals be treated humanely; that treatments involving pain, stress, or privation be used only when absolutely necessary; and that surgical procedures be performed using anesthetics and techniques to avoid infection and minimize pain. The personnel that interact with the animals must be well-trained and must be supervised by a psychologist who is trained and experienced in the care of laboratory animals. And, of course, the animals must be treated in accordance with local, state (or provincial), and federal laws. For more information, see the APA's Web site: http://www.apa.org/science/anguide.html.

The U.S. Department of Agriculture is responsible for regulating and inspecting animal laboratory facilities. In addition to inspections, the Animal Welfare Act of 1990 requires institutions to establish institutional animal care and use committees. These committees are similar to IRBs for human research, and must review proposals for animal research at the institution (Erikson, 1990).

In reaching their decisions, these committees may consult the *Guide for the Care and Use of Laboratory Animals*, published by the National Institutes of Health (1996). This guidebook, based on information across the sciences, supplies information and recommendations about all aspects of laboratory animal care. For example, it provides guidelines about the environmental needs of numerous species. Rats weighing between 100 and 200 grams, for instance, should have a cage 7 inches high with 23 square inches of floor area. In addition, the laboratory should be kept at 64° to 79°F with a relative humidity between 30% and 70%. Information of this sort can be very useful to animal care and use committees as they meet their goal of assuring humane housing and treatment of animals.

Animal research has played an important historical role in the development of psychology as a discipline and continues to contribute to psychological science and human betterment. Not all psychologists, however, are in favor of animal research; the debate continues within our own discipline. (For both sides of the issue, see Baldwin, 1993 and Bowd & Shapiro, 1993.) Only time will tell what role animal research will play in the future of psychology.

ETHICS AND THE
REPORTING OF RESEARCH RESULTS

Another important area of ethical concern for researchers is how the results of a research project are presented. Basically, what a reader wishes to know is that the article represents a research project that actually occurred, that it occurred in the manner described, and that the results were accurately reproduced in the article. Unfortunately, some individuals take shortcuts in the research process or attempt to present research results in a manner that more closely fits their original expectations.

During the past few decades, more attention and publicity has been focused on **scientific misconduct** than in the past, in part because several cases of fraud in government-funded research have been uncovered. In 1988, Stephen Breuning, a once-respected research psychologist and former authority on the treatment of mental retardation with tranquilizers and stimulants, plead guilty to two counts of fraud. He was charged with taking federal grant money for research and falsifying results (Bales, 1988). More recently, research linked to Columbia University and published in the *Journal of Reproductive Medicine* that suggested a relationship between prayer and pregnancy was investigated for possible scientific misconduct, primarily because one of the coauthors turned out to be a convicted con-man (Gershman, 2004). Scientific misconduct does not occur only in psychology-related research either. Recently, researchers in other fields have come under scrutiny (Munro, 2004; Stein, 2005).

Scientific misconduct is not a new phenomenon. Isaac Newton is said to have purposely adjusted his data to make a rival look worse, and Gregor Mendel is suspected of having tampered with his data on inherited characteristics since some of his results are suspiciously perfect (Roman, 1988). Freud has also come under suspicion of having distorted facts to better fit his theory (Raymond, 1991). In psychology, there have been widely publicized accusations of scientific misconduct against Sir Cyril Burt, who investigated intelligence and heredity in the early twentieth century (Roman, 1988). After his death, critics suggested that Burt not only fabricated data, but also invented participants and research assistants. Burt's defenders responded that some of the charges against him were totally unfounded (at least one of the supposedly imaginary research assistants actually did exist) and that, at worst, Burt was somewhat sloppy with his statistics (Eysenck, 1977; Jensen, 1983; but see also McAskie, 1979). We will probably never know for sure whether Burt's results are error-filled as a result of unintentional mistakes or purposeful misconduct.

Scientific misconduct can occur in a number of ways. A researcher can fabricate data, as is alleged of Breuning and Burt. Or a researcher can alter data from actual studies, as Newton and Freud are suspected of doing. There is general agreement that altering and fabricating data are serious breaches of ethics, but gray areas emerge when discussing the proper way to make research findings public. Some researchers will publish many articles from one large set of data; they break the project into what is sometimes called the "least publishable unit." This practice has been portrayed as an inappropriate way for researchers to gain prestige and a waste of journal space that could be used to present new research. Others argue that it is a legitimate response to the limitations that journals impose on the number of pages per article. Also, tenure and promotion in the academic world is often dependent on publishing research articles; thus, a researcher's job may depend on publishing multiple papers on one topic.

Another bone of contention in psychology is that some researchers present results to the popular press before they are published in the professional press. Problems can arise here, because the popular press does not submit the research for quality review by a panel of professionals prior to publication. Also, the popular press does not usually understand the research thoroughly and can misrepresent it to the public. The counterargument is that the review process is too slow and that the public has a right to know about potential research breakthroughs as soon as possible (Grisso et al., 1991).

Authorship and the order of authorships can also be a point of contention in psychology. Quite often a research paper has more than one author. According to the APA, the order of authorship in psychology is determined by the relative contributions made by the authors. If a student did most of the thinking, organizing, and writing, the student should be first author, even if his or her professor is a bigwig in psychology. Note, however, that these guidelines, while true for psychology, are not the same in all disciplines. In mathematics, for example, authors are usually listed alphabetically.

The APA (2002) has developed a set of ethical standards for reporting and publishing scientific information. Despite some well-publicized cases, there is no evidence to suggest that scientific misconduct is on the rise. In general, researchers are conscientious and honest; they present research as it was done and present results as they occurred. Unfortunately, it is the rare case of misconduct that the public usually hears about.

Ethics and the Sponsorship of Research

Research can be very expensive, and it is not uncommon for researchers to receive grants from either the government or private industry to fund their projects. However, funding by an outside source brings up another area in which an individual's sense of ethics can be compromised.

An organization that funds a project may expect to apply the results of that research toward their own interests. For example, NASA funds research on motion sickness so that it can apply the results to the motion sickness experienced by some astronauts. Because it is sometimes difficult to foresee how the results may be used, the APA suggests that researchers familiarize themselves with an organization's mission and how the organization has used the results of previous research (APA, 1982). When conducting research for organizations, researchers may feel pressure to produce particular results, as in this example:

> I design, analyze and write up research reports that identify the advantages of one medium over the other media. Yet with large expenditures for the research, I feel constrained to report *something*. But there is a limit to how many unpleasant findings I come up with. Finally, I have to find some truthful positives or I start looking for another job. (Pope & Vetter, 1992, p. 403)

A last ethical issue that researchers should be aware of is that knowledge is a double-edged sword. For every new piece of information that can be used for good ends, we also gain knowledge that can be used for bad ends. For example, information on how to undermine stereotyping also provides information on how to instill it. If we know how to make material easier to read and more comprehensible, we can also use that understanding to purposely make material difficult and opaque. Knowledge of animal behavior can be used to teach a dog to sit or to teach it to attack.

We tend to believe that misuse of scientific information could only occur in science fiction. Yet, there are some who believe that one instance occurred during the early twentieth century. Henry Goddard, a psychologist, used the newly developed intelligence test to assess the intelligence of Jews, Italians, Poles, and Russians. The testing was done in English, regardless of the language spoken by the immigrant. Some scholars have suggested that these data and data on the intelligence test scores of Army draftees (Brigham, 1923) were instrumental in convincing Congress to enact this country's strictest immigration law, the Immigration Act of 1924 (Sieber & Stanley, 1988; but see also Snyderman & Herrnstein, 1983, who dispute the link between IQ testing and the Immigration Act of 1924).

There are no guidelines for how to deal with the dilemma that knowledge can be used to help and to hinder. Each individual must make his or her own decision as to whether to research an area despite the possible consequences.

SUMMARY

Research in psychology can be a rewarding endeavor for the researcher, the participants, the consumers of the research, and the beneficiaries of advances in science, but only when that research is conducted and reported in an ethical manner.

Psychological researchers are guided in their ethical decision making by laws and the APA guidelines for the ethical treatment of human and animal research participants. But ultimately, it is the researcher's conscience that determines whether the research is conducted and reported ethically.

Given the thousands of colleges, universities, and other institutions in the United States and around the world at which psychological and other research is conducted, it is encouraging that so few complaints of unethical treatment are made. By and large, scientists respect the dignity of their participants and their disciplines.

IMPORTANT TERMS AND CONCEPTS

American Psychological
   Association (APA)
anonymous
APA ethical principles
   in the conduct of research
APA principles for the
   care and use of animals
confederate
confidentiality

debriefing
deception
free consent
informed consent form
institutional review boards (IRBs)
minimal risk
privacy
risk
scientific misconduct

EXERCISES

1. Define informed consent and free consent and describe a situation in which informed consent might be given but free consent might be impossible to obtain.

2. Consider a situation in which the researcher is studying the relationship between personality types and tendencies toward violence. The participants are told that the study is about something else entirely, but during the course of the study they are provoked by a confederate posing as another research participant regarding an issue they feel strongly about until the participant reacts strongly, perhaps even violently.

   a. From the researcher's perspective, why might this be considered an acceptable, even important, study to conduct?

   b. From an IRB's perspective, what concerns might they have about the study?

   c. From the participant's perspective, why might he or she feel good or bad about having participated in this study?

   For each of the following questions, explore your own feelings about the situations described and the issues addressed. There are no right or wrong answers to ethical questions. Don't focus on what you think you should say, but rather try to discern your own attitudes. You may wish to share your answers with others—if you do, the diversity of opinions that you hear may surprise you.

3. You are a member of an IRB reviewing the following proposal. A researcher would like to determine how much of a person's casual conversation is composed of slang and figurative expressions. The results of this research would add to the body of knowledge of language comprehension and would also aid those teaching and learning English as a foreign language. To collect data on this topic, the researcher would like permission to tape-record conversations at restaurants without the participants' knowledge. The participants would all be strangers to the researcher, the conversations would be coded for slang and figurative expressions only, and then the tapes would be destroyed. The participants would never know that they had been involved in this study.

   a. What questions would you ask the researcher?

   b. What alternative procedures might you suggest?

   c. Would you require changes in the proposal? If so, what would they be?

   d. What APA ethical principles are, or are in danger of, being violated by this project?

   e. Would you allow this project to be conducted? Why or why not?

4. With advances in medicine, more people are surviving closed head injuries and strokes. These individuals suffer brain damage as a result

of some external or internal trauma. In order to study the effect of a drug that might benefit these individuals, research using animals is proposed. You are on the institutional animal care and use committee for the drug company that is proposing this research. An unpleasant aspect of the research is that the animals—in this case, cats—must suffer brain damage for the drug to be tested. Brain damage would be induced under a general anesthesia; a small predetermined part of the brain would be destroyed surgically.

a. As a member of the animal use committee, what questions would you ask the researcher? Would you allow this research to be conducted? If not, why not? If so, would you ask the researcher for any modifications or additions to the procedure?

b. Consider your own personal feelings about animal research. Do you feel the type of research described here is necessary? Would you feel comfortable about conducting this type of research? Would your feelings be different if the animals involved were rats instead of cats? If so, why? If not, why not?

5. An acquaintance approaches you about conducting a survey to assess racist attitudes in your community. The organization that this individual represents agrees that you may publish the results under your name, but also intends to use the results in its own advertisements and literature.

a. Considering your own personal views, what information would you wish to know about this organization?

b. You discover that the organizations' philosophies are in agreement with your own, but they have distorted research results in the past to fit their own needs. Given this information, would you still be willing to conduct their research? Why, why not, or with what conditions?

ANSWERS TO CONCEPT QUESTIONS AND ODD-NUMBERED EXERCISES

Note: There will often be more than one correct answer for each of these questions. Consult with your instructor about your own answers.

Concept Question 2.1

No single answer is correct for this question. For some students the definition of deception will be very clearly defined, for others there will be a large gray area between truth and deception. Some might find it unacceptable to "lie" to the mother about the purpose of the study or to suggest that the purpose is to study the child's reaction to the toy while the mother and child interaction is the true focus. Others will find this to be a perfectly acceptable situation. Still others might find it acceptable only if the mother was told the truth immediately after participating.

Similarly, students may vary in their opinion of the situation in which general terms are used to describe a more specific focus (the participants are told they are studying natural language usage while the investigators are particularly interested in swearing). Students who are more sensitive to the use of swear words might find this to be an inappropriate situation. It could be interesting to see if they would feel the same way if the study was actually focused on something more innocuous, such as the use of idioms.

Exercises

1. Informed consent is agreement to participate in a study after learning all the relevant information about the potential risks and benefits. Free consent is agreeing to participate without any expectation that participation will affect the person's situation in any manner. Students in a psychology class may give informed consent to participate in a study being conducted by their professor, but they might not be giving free consent if they think participating will help their grades.

3. One possible set of answers is as follows.

   a. Would the conversations be videotaped or audiotaped? Will the researcher ever see the participants? How many people will listen to the tapes? What happens if someone who is not a stranger to the researcher sits at the table?

   b. Could conversations be audiotaped in a laboratory setting where participants have given their informed consent?

   c. To assure anonymity, the researcher must not be able to see the participants.

   d. Sections 8.02 and 8.03.

   e. I would probably allow this study because the participants are only at minimal risk; anyone could eavesdrop in a restaurant.

5. a. I would need to know if the organization's views are aligned with mine. I would not want to help an organization that is actively working against a cause I believe in. However, others might feel that conducting the research and publishing the results would be an effective way of countering the organization's arguments and perspective.

   b. I probably would not conduct their research, because I wouldn't want my name associated with their reputation for distorting results, but again, others might be eager to counter the organization head on.

3

The Research Process

The scientific method is the process by which scientists, including psychologists, collect information and draw conclusions about their disciplines. In this method, observations are made systematically and objectively, so that the results will be as meaningful as possible.

When using the scientific method in psychology, the researcher often tries to determine the effect of some factor on some type of behavior. In other words, the researcher wants to know if a change in an independent variable will cause a change in a dependent variable.

It is important to be precise and concrete when designing a study using the scientific method. This precision and clarity allows the researcher to more readily foresee pitfalls, ambiguity, and confounds that could render the results meaningless.

One important way to avoid confounds and ambiguity in research is by carefully defining all of the important concepts. Perhaps a researcher is interested in the effect of stress on work efficiency. The researcher plans to study this effect by inducing stress in half of the participants and then measure all of the participants' performance on some task. The first step is to define the terms "stress" and "work efficiency." Dictionary definitions are not precise enough for a researcher's needs. What is required is an **operational definition**—a definition that tells the reader exactly what was done to produce a phenomenon or to measure some variable. In this example, the researcher needs to explain how stress will be induced and exactly how performance will be measured. The researcher may intend to induce stress in one group of participants by telling them that they will be videotaped as they give an impromptu speech. This information about the videotaped speech serves as the operational definition for stress in this experiment; it describes the precise procedures used to induce stress. The operational definition of work efficiency must be equally precise. Perhaps our researcher will measure work efficiency by the number of anagrams from a list of 10 that are solved during a 3-minute interval. This operational definition of work efficiency tells the reader what task was performed, for how long it was performed, and what measurement was made. Together, these operational definitions of what was induced and what was measured supply considerable information about the research project.

An operational definition should be so clear that a person who is not familiar with the topic under investigation can understand the definition without additional information. A good operational definition is such that an individual can come back a day, a week, or a year later and still understand it and use it in the same manner. By clearly specifying how the behavior is to be recorded, the operational definition makes it more likely that consistent results will be obtained.

An operational definition, of course, has to be appropriate. Informing participants that they will be videotaped while giving an impromptu speech may be an excellent stress inducer when the participants are typical adults who find public speaking stressful. This same operational definition would be of little value, however, if the participants are all actors, motivational speakers, or college professors—people who are used to speaking in public and tend not to find it especially stressful.

Concept Question 3.1

Which of the following is the most complete operational definition?

a. Learning defined as the amount of information retained after a period of time.

b. Learning defined as the number of correct responses on a 25-question multiple choice test that covers material presented in a lecture.

c. Learning defined as studying for an exam for 30 minutes.

d. Learning defined as a relatively permanent change in behavior that occurs because of experience.

RELIABILITY AND VALIDITY

Reliability is a key concept in research. Just as a reliable vehicle will start each time the ignition key is turned, a reliable measure is consistent. In other words, different researchers who use the same procedure to measure the same phenomenon should obtain the same results if the procedure is reliable. When used with comparable participants, a reliable operational definition should yield similar results each time.

Validity is the extent to which a measurement technique measures what it purports to measure. An operational definition is likely to yield valid results if it corresponds closely to what is to be measured. Thus, measuring work efficiency by the number of anagrams completed in 3 minutes may be a valid measure if the results are meant to generalize to work based on written language. The same measurement technique would probably be an invalid measure if it were meant to generalize to physical labor because anagram solving and physical labor are not very closely related.

Internal Validity and Confounds

A specific type of validity that is important in scientific research is internal validity. **Internal validity** is the extent to which the design of an experiment ensures that the independent variable, and not some other variable or variables, caused the measured difference in the dependent variables. In other words, an internally valid study has no problems that would confound the results. A **confound**, as described in chapter 1, is a factor that yields alternative explanations for a study's results and thus limits its internal validity. Internal validity is maximized by eliminating confounds. Experienced researchers automatically watch for some common confounds and design their studies so that these confounds are avoided or controlled. For example, an inexperienced researcher may wish to compare performance on a simple task under two temperature conditions: warm and cool. One research assistant is responsible for the cool condition, and another is responsible for the warm condition. If performance is found to be better in the cooler condition, it might be because the temperature had an effect on behavior, or it might be that the research assistants affected the participants' behavior in some manner. Perhaps one research assistant was more neatly dressed than the other and the participants with the neater assistant took the project more seriously. This would be a confound called an **experimenter effect**. An experienced researcher might foresee this problem and avoid it by using only one assistant or by keeping both assistants but having each collect half their data in the warm condition and half in the cool condition.

Researchers must also ensure that the study is not confounded by **demand characteristics**. Demand characteristics are the cues participants use to determine what is expected of them in a study. Suppose that to study the effect of mood on sense of wellness, a researcher induces either a positive or a negative mood and then asks the participant some questions about how healthy he or she feels. A participant in this study might very well perceive that the researcher expects mood to affect the responses and may try to help the researcher by responding as the researcher expects. To avoid this problem, the researcher would want to take special steps to dissociate the two parts of the study, perhaps by having a confederate act as if the questions about health are for a different study entirely.

There are numerous other potential confounds; each can threaten the internal validity of a study. We'll discuss more threats to internal validity in later chapters, especially chapters 5 and 6.

External Validity

Another important goal of research projects is external validity. **External validity** is the generalizability of the results of an investigation beyond the specific participants, measures, and site of the research. For example, a study with results that generalize to all English-speaking adults has greater external validity than a study with results that generalize to English-speaking college students. There is no rule of thumb, however, about how externally valid a study needs to be. Many useful research ideas come from studies with little external validity. Any investigation needs to have some external validity, though; an experiment with results irrelevant beyond the particular participants in the study is of little or no value.

The controls needed to create an internally valid study can sometimes limit the external validity of the study. For example, suppose an investigator wishes to research the effect of hypnosis on pain tolerance. In an experimental group, each participant will be hypnotized and given the suggestion that he or she cannot feel pain; then, each participant will submerge his or her arm in a bucket of ice water. Participants in the control group will not be hypnotized, but each person will also submerge an arm in the ice water. The dependent variable is the length of time that each participant keeps his or her arm in the water.

The investigator is aware that factors other than the independent variables could possibly affect the outcome of this study—these are called **extraneous variables**. In the present case, the sex of the experimenter and the sex of the participants are extraneous variables. The sex of the experimenter might affect how long the participant is willing to tolerate the pain of the ice water. For instance, male participants may withstand the pain for a longer period of time in front of a male experimenter than in front of a female. Also, male participants may feel honor-bound to sustain pain longer than would female participants. How should the researcher deal with these problems? Should both male and female experimenters be used? The sex of the experimenter could be balanced across the control and experimental groups, and the researcher could also make certain that half of the people in each group are tested by a member of the same sex and half by a member of the opposite sex. Should both male and female participants be involved in the study, or should it be limited to only one sex? Using both male and female participants and male and female experimenters increases the external validity of the experiment, but complicates the design of the study and requires more participants and more time for the study to be conducted. There is no correct answer to this problem. Some researchers will choose greater external validity, while others will opt for a simpler, quicker study.

The external validity of a study can also be affected by the manner in which the participants are selected for the project. In research, we talk about selecting a sample of participants from a larger population. A **population** is all of the organisms (usually people, sometimes animals) to which the researcher wishes to be able to generalize the research results. A **sample** is a subset of the population; the goal is for the sample to represent the population. The larger the population represented by the sample of participants, the greater the external validity of the study. An effective procedure is to identify participants from a population by random selection. In **random selection**, all members of the population are equally likely to be chosen. This procedure maximizes the probability that the sample is representative of the population, as long as a sufficient number of participants are chosen. Choosing five people from 5,000 possible participants is not likely to yield a sample that is representative of the population.

More often than not, participants are not selected randomly; instead, they come from a readily available pool of potential volunteers, such as college students. It is very common for researchers to solicit volunteers from introductory psychology classes. This type of sample is called a **convenience sample** (or an **accidental sample**). In convenience sampling, participants are not randomly chosen, but instead happen to be in the right place at the right time. Once a group of volunteers has been identified, the participants are assigned to different experimental conditions (the different levels of the independent variable). The most common way of assigning the participants to the conditions is by **random assignment**. Random assignment is the use of a procedure—perhaps as simple as flipping a coin—such that each participant is equally likely to be assigned to any of the conditions. Notice how this differs from random selection. Random selection describes how participants are chosen from the population; random assignment describes how participants are assigned to experimental conditions.

Does convenience sampling automatically reduce external validity? It depends on the research. If a researcher is investigating the political concerns of 18- to 22-year-olds, then using only college students of that age range will limit the external validity of the study; the results cannot be generalized to 18- to 22-year-olds who do not attend college. On the other hand, research into physiological or perceptual processes, which are assumed to be pretty much the same whether an individual is in college or not, would be likely to have reasonable external validity even if the participants were exclusively college students. Finally, the external validity of a study is open to testing. We simply repeat the work in a different context to see if the results can be generalized.

Careful and precise planning is necessary when conducting research by the scientific method. Only by planning ahead and thinking critically can a researcher avoid design flaws and make choices that will maximize a study's internal and external validity. Actually, designing projects devoid of confounds can be something of a brain teaser; for me, it makes up half the fun of doing research.

HYPOTHESES

The other half of the fun in research is learning new things by testing your ideas. Suppose that a researcher is interested in the relationship between summer programs and the intelligence of grade-school children. In particular, this researcher wishes to know whether those who participate in a summer program where students can pick from among a number of intellectual topics are smarter than most people. This is the research question. On the basis of this question, the researcher forms one or more hypotheses (or predictions). In this case, the researcher may hypothesize that the IQ scores of students in the summer program will be higher than those of the population in general. This is the researcher's hypothesis.

To be precise, two hypotheses are involved because there are two sides to every question: what the researcher expects and what the researcher does not expect. One of these hypotheses is called the **null hypothesis** (represented by H_0), and the other is called the **alternative** (or **research**) **hypothesis** (represented by H_1 or sometimes H_A). The null hypothesis is the prediction that there is no difference between the groups being compared. We would expect the null hypothesis to be correct if the population from which the sample is taken is the same as the population with which it is being compared. In our example, if the students in the summer program are actually a representative sample of the general population, the students' IQ scores will be roughly equivalent to the IQ scores of the general population. The null hypothesis is typically what the researcher does not expect to find; a researcher does not usually predict the null hypothesis.

The alternative hypothesis is the prediction the researcher makes about the results of the research. It states that there is a difference between the scores of the groups being compared. In other words, it states that the sample is not representative of that particular population's scores, but instead better represents some other population's scores. There are two types of alternative hypotheses. In one type, the researcher simply predicts that the two groups being compared will differ, but does not predict the direction of that difference—the researcher does not predict which group will score higher or lower. This is called a **two-tailed hypothesis**. To clarify why it is said to be two-tailed, consider the normal curve in figure 3.1. In the middle of the curve is the population mean; in the case of the IQ example, that would be 100. If a sample mean (an average of the sample members' IQ scores) were much higher than 100, it would fall far to the right of the mean, up in the positive tail of the distribution. If a sample mean were much lower than 100, it would fall far to the left of the mean, down in the negative tail of the distribution. If a researcher simply predicts that a sample mean will be different from the population mean and does not predict whether it will be higher or lower, the researcher is predicting that it will fall in one of the two tails of the distribution. Thus, an alternative hypothesis that does not predict the direction of the difference is called a two-tailed hypothesis.

Figure 3.1   The normal distribution of IQ scores

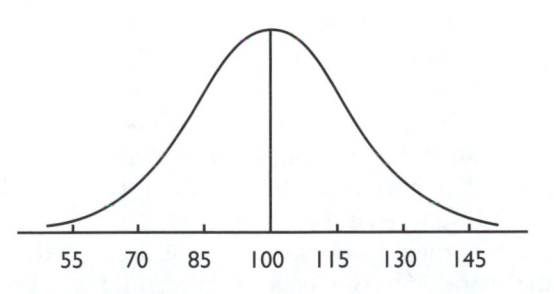

| 55 | 70 | 85 | 100 | 115 | 130 | 145 |

As you may have guessed, if the researcher predicts the direction of the difference—for example, if the researcher predicts that the mean IQ of college students will be higher than the population mean—this is a **one-tailed hypothesis**. The researcher predicts in which tail of the distribution the sample mean is expected to fall. In our example, the alternative hypothesis is that the students in the summer program will have IQ scores greater than those of the general population. (What would the two-tailed alternative hypothesis be? What would the other one-tailed hypothesis be?)

Concept Question 3.2

A researcher hypothesizes that a sample of families from the Midwest differs in size from the national average family size. What are the null and alternative hypotheses?

HYPOTHESIS TESTING

Although scientific research is designed to determine if the alternative hypothesis is supportable, hypothesis testing actually involves testing the null hypothesis, not the alternative hypothesis. If the difference between the groups being compared is so large that the difference is unlikely to have been caused by chance, then the groups being compared are unlikely to represent the same population and the null hypothesis is *rejected*. If the null hypothesis is rejected, the alternative hypothesis is *supported*. On the other hand, if the difference between the groups is so small that the difference is not unlikely to have occurred simply by chance, we fail to reject the null hypothesis. If the null hypothesis is *not rejected*, the alternative hypothesis *cannot* be supported.

In our example, the researcher has predicted that the mean IQ scores of summer-program students will be greater than the population mean of 100. This is a one-tailed alternative hypothesis. The null hypothesis is always that there is no difference between the groups being compared. In this case, the null hypothesis is that the sample mean will be no different from the general population mean. If we collect our data and find a mean that is greater than 100 (the mean IQ for the general population) by more than could reasonably be expected by chance, then we can reject the null hypothesis. When we do this, we are saying that the null hypothesis is wrong. Because we have rejected the null hypothesis and because the sample mean is greater than the population mean, as was predicted, we support our alternative hypothesis. In other words, the evidence suggests that the sample of summer-program students represents a population that scores higher on the IQ test than the general population.

On the other hand, if we collect our data and the mean IQ score does not differ from the population mean by more than could reasonably be expected by chance, then we fail to reject the null hypothesis and also fail to support our alternative hypothesis.

Errors in Hypothesis Testing

Researchers carefully design their studies so that they answer their research questions by either supporting or failing to support their alternative hypotheses. However, because researchers are not omniscient, it is possible to reject the null hypothesis when it really is true. A researcher may conclude that two populations differ when in fact they do not. Another possible error is to find no difference in a study when a difference between the populations truly exists.

For any research problem there are two possibilities: either that the null hypothesis is correct and there is no difference between the populations or that the null hypothesis is false and there is a difference between the populations. The researcher, however, never knows the truth. Look at figure 3.2. Along the top is the truth (which the researcher can never know), and along the left side are the researcher's two decision choices, to reject the null hypothesis or to fail to reject it. This allows four possible outcomes—two ways for the researcher to be correct, and two ways to be wrong.

The two ways to be correct are straightforward. First, the researcher can reject the null hypothesis when, in reality, it is false; that is, the researcher finds a true difference between the groups being compared. Second, the researcher might fail to reject the null hypothesis when, in fact, the null hypothesis is true. In this case, the researcher would not detect a difference between the groups being compared and, in reality, there is no difference between the groups.

The two possible errors are to reject the null hypothesis when it is true (a **Type I error**) and to fail to reject the null hypothesis when it is false (a **Type II error**).

Thus, the Type I error is to find a difference between the groups being compared that does not truly exist in the population. Regardless of how well designed a study might be, a difference is sometimes detected between sample groups that does not reflect an actual difference in the populations. For example, we might find that the mean IQ score of our sample of summer-program students is higher than that of the general population. But perhaps our sample of summer-program students just happened to be bright students, and there truly isn't a difference between the IQ scores of the overall population of summer-program students and the general public. Because a difference was identified that does not truly exist, we have made a Type I error. To the extent that the results of a study have immediate ramifications—for instance, if important changes to the curriculum are made on the basis of IQ scores—Type I errors can be very serious indeed.

Figure 3.2   The four possible research outcomes

	THE TRUTH	
	The null hypothesis is true	The null hypothesis is false
THE DECISION		
Reject H_0	Type I error (α)	Correct $(1 - \beta)$
Fail to reject H_0	Correct $(1 - \alpha)$	Type II error (β)

The Type II error is to fail to detect a difference between the sample groups when a difference truly exists between the populations. We would have made a Type II error if our sample of summer-program students did not have a mean IQ score significantly greater than the mean IQ for the general population when, in fact, the population of summer-program students did have a higher IQ than the general population. Our study would have failed to detect a difference that actually exists. This can happen for a number of reasons. Perhaps our sample included the less intelligent of the summer-program students. Perhaps our IQ test was administered in a nonstandard way that caused greater variation in the scores than if it had been conducted in the standard way. Still another possibility is that we included too few students in our sample to detect the difference.

Type II errors are often seen as less serious than Type I errors. If a difference truly exists but is not identified in one research project, continued research is likely to detect the difference. On the other hand, a Type I error is seen as something to be avoided. The results of applied research affect policy and practice in many areas of our life, such as education, medicine, and government. The results of basic research further our body of knowledge and move along the development and advancement of theory that affects applied research. Researchers set their standards high to avoid making Type I errors, to avoid finding differences between comparison groups that don't actually exist in the populations. We need to keep the odds that advances in research and any changes in policy or practice are based on real results, not erroneous results.

An analogy with the U.S. justice system may clarify the significance of Type I and Type II errors. Consider the case of a person accused of a crime. The null hypothesis is that an accused person is innocent; the accused person is no different from the general population. The alternative hypothesis is that the accused is guilty; the accused person is different from the general population, a deviant. In the United States, it is considered a more serious error to convict an innocent person than to acquit a guilty person; that is, it is more serious to find a difference that does not exist (a Type I error) than to fail to find a difference that really is there (a Type II error).

Concept Question 3.3

A researcher collects information on family size and concludes, on the basis of the data, that Midwestern families are larger than the average family in the United States. However, unbeknownst to the researcher, the sample includes several unusually large families, and in reality, Midwestern families are no larger than the national average. What type of error was made?

The Probability of a Type I Error

The probability of making a Type I error is called **alpha (α)**. The acceptable alpha level is typically chosen by the researcher; in the social and behavioral sciences, it has traditionally been set at .05. In other words, researchers in the social and behavioral sciences are willing to accept a 5% risk of making a Type I error. With alpha set at .05, a difference between the groups that is large enough for us to reject the null hypothesis will occur by chance only 5 times out of 100 when the null hypothesis is true. A difference this large is said to be a **significant difference**.

Let's consider our summer-program example again. The normal distribution in figure 3.3 represents the sampling distribution of IQ scores in the general public. (The **sampling distribution** is the distribution of sample means, as opposed to a distribution of individual scores.) If the null hypothesis is true, the mean IQ score for the sample of summer-program students will be included as part of this distribution. However, if the alternative hypothesis—that the population mean IQ of the summer-program students is greater than the mean for the general population—is correct, the mean for our sample better represents a different distribution. To determine whether the population mean of the summer-program students is greater than or equal to the population mean of the general public, we compare our sample mean to the population mean of the general public. If our sample mean is so great that it falls in the top 5% of the sampling distribution for the general public, we infer that there was only a 5% chance of our sample mean being drawn from that population. Having chosen α = .05, we then reject H_0 and support H_1. The 5% of the distribution that is shaded in figure 3.3 represents α, and is called the **region of rejection**. If a score falls within the region of rejection, the null hypothesis is rejected.

Figure 3.3   The region of rejection for a one-tailed hypothesis

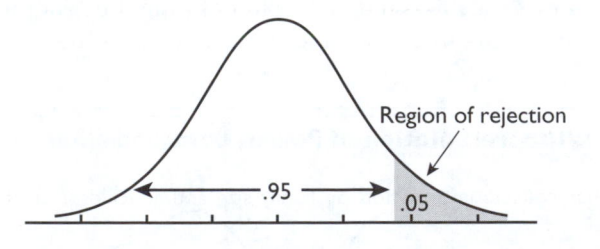

In our example, the alternative hypothesis was one-tailed. With a one-tailed hypothesis, the region of rejection lies at one end of the distribution. For a two-tailed hypothesis, the region of rejection is split equally between the two tails—2.5% in one tail and 2.5% in the other tail when α

= .05 (figure 3.4). If our sample mean is so great that it falls in the top 2.5% of the sampling distribution for the general public, or it is so small that it falls in the bottom 2.5% of the sampling distribution, then we infer that there was only a 5% chance (5% because the two regions of rejection add up to 5% of the distribution) of our sample mean being drawn from that population. Having chosen $\alpha = .05$, we then reject H_0 and support H_1.

Figure 3.4   Regions of rejection for a two-tailed hypothesis

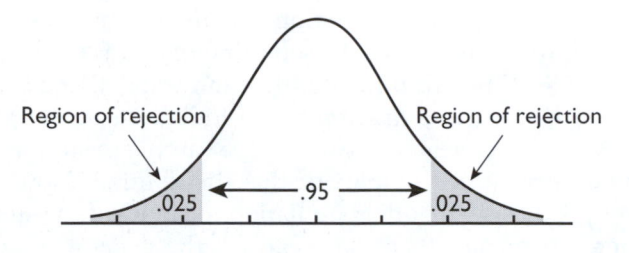

The Probability of a Type II Error

The probability of making a Type II error is called **beta (β)**. Beta is a measure of the likelihood of *not* finding a difference that truly exists. The opposite of β is called **Power** and is calculated as $1 - \beta$. Power is the likelihood of finding a true difference. In general, researchers want to design studies that are high in Power and have a low β. However, β, α, and Power are interconnected, as an examination of figure 3.5 makes clear.

In figure 3.5, the distribution on the left represents the distribution of sample means when the null hypothesis is correct. The distribution on the right represents the distribution of sample means when the alternative hypothesis is correct. In terms of our summer-program example, the distribution on the left is the distribution of mean IQ scores for the general public; this distribution would include the sample of summer-program students if they are not significantly different from the general public. The distribution of sample means on the right represents the mean IQ scores

Figure 3.5   A representation of Power, beta, and alpha

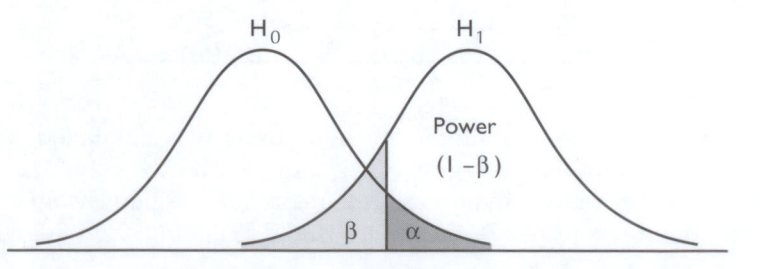

of the population of summer-program students if they do score significantly higher than the general public.

The darker shaded area labeled "alpha" is the top 5% of the null hypothesis distribution. If our sample's mean is so large that it falls within the top 5% of the null hypothesis distribution, then we say that it is unlikely to belong to that distribution, and we reject the null hypothesis.

The lighter shaded area of the alternative hypothesis distribution (to the left of alpha) represents beta. This is the probability of making a Type II error. If a mean is too small to land in the region of rejection, but actually does belong to a separate population, then it will fall within the beta region. The researchers will fail to reject H_0, even though it is false, and thus will make a Type II error. Whenever possible, a researcher attempts to increase the Power of a project, in order to increase the likelihood of rejecting a false null hypothesis.

Consider figure 3.5 again. Power can be increased by reducing beta (imagine moving the line delineating beta and alpha to the left), and beta can be reduced by increasing alpha (moving the line delineating beta and alpha to the left). Often, however, increasing alpha is not a realistic option. Only rarely will a researcher—and perhaps more importantly, the researcher's colleagues—trust the results of a study where alpha is greater than .05. A relatively simple way for a researcher to increase the Power of a study is to increase the sample size. The larger the size of the samples in a study, the easier it is to find a significant difference using statistical tests. Statistically, a small difference may indicate a significant difference if many participants were involved in the study. If the same small difference is based on only a few participants, the statistical test is more likely to suggest that the results could have happened just by chance.

Why We Don't Accept the Null Hypothesis

You may be wondering why we keep saying that we *fail to reject the null hypothesis*, instead of simply stating that we accept the null hypothesis. If we reject the null hypothesis, we know it is because our finding was relatively unlikely to occur by chance alone. But, if we do not reject the null hypothesis, what does that mean? The null hypothesis says there is no significant difference between our sample mean and the population mean. If we do not reject the null hypothesis, does that mean that our sample's scores are equal to the population's scores? Not necessarily. By failing to reject the null hypothesis, we have failed to find a significant difference, but that does not mean we have found an equality. There can be a number of reasons for failing to find a difference—that is, for failing to reject the null hypothesis. It could be because we made a Type II error. Perhaps our method of data collection was not sensitive enough to detect the difference, or we needed a larger sample to detect the difference consistently. Perhaps, simply by chance, our sample was such that its mean was not significantly different from the population's score, or perhaps a confound in our study caused our results to come out differently than expected. Any of these reasons and more could cause a Type II error and make us fail to reject the null hypothesis when it is false. Of course, there is also the possibility that we failed to reject the null hypothesis because the null hypothesis is actually true. How can we tell if the null hypothesis is true or if we have made a Type II error? We can't, and for this reason it is risky to accept the null hypothesis as true when no difference is detected. Similarly, it is risky to predict no difference between our sample and the population. If we find no difference, we cannot know by this one study if it is because our prediction was accurate or because we made a Type II error.

If a researcher does reject the null hypothesis, how much does that support the alternative hypothesis? Support for the alternative hypothesis means that the identified difference was so large as to be unlikely to have occurred by chance. If the difference didn't occur by chance, why did it occur? Explaining the difference is the researcher's task. One researcher may believe that summer-program students are smarter than the general public, while another researcher may think that the summer program serves to increase students' IQ scores. On the basis of their beliefs, both of these researchers are likely to predict that the mean IQ score for a sample of summer-program students will be greater than 100. Suppose that both researchers collect and analyze some data, and both find results that are consistent with their predictions. Each researcher can be sure that only 5 times out of 100 would the mean of the summer-program students' IQ scores be significantly greater than the population mean by chance. However, neither can be totally confident that his or her explanation for the results is correct. Rejection of the null hypothesis and support of the alternative hypothesis lend confidence to the results found, but not to the explanation given. The explanation may or may not be correct; it is vulnerable to all of the subjectivity, wishful thinking, and faulty reasoning that humans are heir to. The best explanation will emerge only after other carefully designed investigations have been conducted.

HOW TO DO SCIENCE

Conducting scientific research, like any project, involves a series of steps. In general, the steps are the same for any scientific research project, only the specifics differ from project to project. These steps are outlined in figure 3.6.

The first step is to identify the topic to be studied. At first this can be somewhat difficult, not because there are so few topics to choose from, but because there are so many.

One way to begin is to think about courses you have had in psychology and related fields. What courses were your favorites? Thumb

Figure 3.6   The steps in conducting scientific research

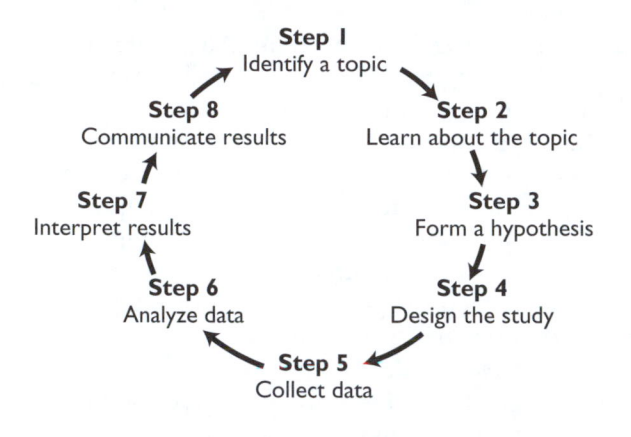

through your old introductory psychology textbook. Which chapters did you find most fascinating? Another approach is to consult with faculty or other students who are conducting research. Often, there are more projects that need to be done than any single person has time to address. Choose a topic to research that you find particularly interesting; research is a time-consuming task and can become tedious if you aren't especially curious about the questions you have asked.

Once you have identified a topic, the second step is to learn about what has already been done in the area. The library is your primary source for this information. The results of previous research on your topic may be found in whole books or in book chapters. Research journals publish descriptions of individual research projects, but they also publish review articles, which describe the results of many projects. (For more information about journal articles and literature searches, see appendix C.) Courses and textbooks can also serve as sources of information about an area. Less frequently considered, but often very worthwhile, is actual correspondence with the experts and researchers in a field. These individuals can provide valuable information about details and nuances of their work that would be unavailable elsewhere.

The impetus for specific research projects may appear during your review of the area. Perhaps you find the results of one study doubtful and wish to replicate it. Maybe you'd like to try to detect a particular phenomenon under a different set of circumstances. You might decide to combine ideas from two different studies or to conduct the next in a series of projects. The only way to learn from others' experiences is to discover what others have done.

The third step is to focus on a specific research question and form a hypothesis. This entails narrowing your focus from a general area of research to a specific question that you want to answer. Your predicted answer to the research question is the hypothesis. Hypotheses can be derived from theory or from previous research or may simply reflect curiosity about a topic.

Perhaps you have been learning about the research conducted on eating disorders and, during the same time period, you learned about operant conditioning in one of your psychology classes. You might wonder if operant conditioning can be used to modify eating behaviors by using positive reinforcement to increase eating. A hypothesis needs to be precisely stated in a testable manner; therefore, this hypothesis needs to be honed some. Perhaps it develops into the following statement: Participants who receive positive reinforcement contingent upon eating will consume more food than do participants who receive no positive reinforcement. As you learn more about research, you'll see that the research question and hypothesis guide how a study is designed.

The fourth step involves designing your study so that the results will either support or refute your hypothesis. This is when you decide exactly how you will make your observations. Here you must operationally define your terms. Continuing with our eating-behaviors example, the terms "positive reinforcement contingent upon eating" and "consume more food" need to be operationally defined. Maybe positive reinforcement will be defined as complimentary statements about the participant's hair and clothing made within one second after the participant eats a potato chip. Having thus defined the food as potato chips, we might measure the consumption of potato chips in grams. The research design implied in this hypothesis involves an experimental group (which receives the positive reinforcement) and a control group. Many other types of research designs can be used to test hypotheses; each has its own advantages and disadvantages. The choice of research design often reflects a balance between the benefits and pitfalls of the design, the practical concerns of the particular situation, and personal preference.

Many other specific decisions about your study must also be made during this stage. Who will be the participants in your study? How many will you need? Will they be tested together, in small groups, or individually? How will the potato chips be presented? Will the same experimenter interact with all of the participants? Where and when will this experiment take place? How long will it take? Should the participants be asked to refrain from eating for some amount of time prior to the study? When will the participants be told the true purpose of the study? As the questions are answered and the experiment begins to take shape, it is important to keep a wary eye out for potential confounds. The challenge is to design your study so that the results either clearly support or fail to support your hypothesis.

The fifth step in conducting scientific research is to actually make your observations and collect your data according to the procedures prescribed in your research design. Here is where attention to detail during the design stage pays off. It is often unwise to change the procedures after a study is underway, as this makes it more difficult to interpret the results. However, even the most experienced researchers are occasionally surprised by problems that arise while the data are being collected, and sometimes this means scrapping the project and redesigning the study. Surprises are not necessarily bad, though, for with every surprise comes a bit of new information and perhaps the seed of new research efforts.

In the sixth step, the data that have been collected are summarized and analyzed to determine whether the results support the hypothesis. This process is called **statistical analysis**. By using statistical analysis, you can determine how likely or unlikely it is that your results are due to chance and with how much confidence you can state that your results reflect reality.

The seventh step involves interpreting the results of the statistical analyses and drawing conclusions about your hypotheses. Here you determine the implications of your results in relation to the topic you focused on in step 1.

Finally, the eighth step is to communicate your research results to others. In psychology, this is done a number of ways, including conference presentations and publications. Psychology conferences are an important venue for presenting research. Many, but not all, conferences review submitted projects and allow the authors of the best projects to present their work. Other conferences allow all members of the sponsoring organization to present research. Also, numerous student conferences allow undergraduates to present research to their peers from other institutions. All of these types of conferences provide excellent opportunities to gain up-to-date information, to meet with people who are researching an area in which you are interested, and to become enthused and inspired to conduct research.

Probably the most prestigious way to communicate research results is by publishing an article in a scholarly journal. Other researchers review the proposed article and provide the journal editor and author with feedback about how to improve the project and/or manuscript; they also provide their opinion about whether the article should be published. (Appendix C relays more information about this topic.) A published research article has been read by a number of professionals and typically (but not always) represents excellent research work.

Regardless of whether a research project results in a publication or presentation, doing research inevitably provides the researcher with new information, new insights, or simply new questions. Then the cycle begins again, as a new research project begins to grow in the researcher's mind.

SUMMARY

Conducting scientific research involves being precise about what is studied and how it is studied so that confounds can be avoided. An important step is to carefully define all important terms using operational definitions. Operational definitions differ from dictionary definitions in that they describe the exact procedures used to produce a phenomenon or measure some variable.

A good study not only has clearly defined terms but also provides consistent results. The production of consistent results is called reliability. As important as reliability is validity. Validity is the extent to which a measurement tool or technique measures what it purports to measure. A study that is not valid and/or is not reliable is of no use to the researcher.

When a study is designed well, so as to provide reliable and valid data for which there is only one explanation, then the study is said to have good internal validity. Internal validity can be threatened by the existence of confounds such as experimenter effects or demand characteristics. If the results of a study may be generalized beyond the original set of participants, it is said to have strong external validity.

One way to increase the external validity of a study is by choosing a sample carefully. Random selection maximizes the probability that the sample is representative of the population. However, convenience sampling is used more often and is typically followed by random assignment of participants to different experimental conditions.

Much research in psychology and the other sciences is based on hypothesis testing. The null hypothesis states that there is no effect of the independent variable on the dependent variable. If two groups are being compared, the null hypothesis states that there will be no significant difference between the two groups.

The alternative hypothesis is typically the researcher's prediction. The researcher might predict that the independent variable will cause an increase in the dependent variable—that would then be the alternative hypothesis. This particular example would be a one-tailed hypothesis, because it predicts the direction of the difference. A two-tailed hypothesis predicts a difference but does not predict its direction.

The researcher actually tests the null hypothesis. If the researcher finds strong enough evidence, he or she will reject the null hypothesis and thus support the alternative hypothesis. Without strong evidence, the researcher fails to reject the null hypothesis.

The null hypothesis is rejected, or is not rejected, on the basis of probabilities. If the probability is strong enough, the researcher will reject the null hypothesis. If in reality the null hypothesis is true, however, the researcher has made a Type I error. If the researcher fails to reject the null hypothesis when it is actually false, the researcher has made a Type II error. Researchers never know if they have made one of these errors, but they do take measures to reduce the probability of doing so. The most straightforward way to reduce the probability of a Type II error without increasing the probability of a Type I error is to increase the number of participants in the study.

Conducting research is not a linear task, but instead tends to be circular; the results of one study affect the way in which the next study is designed and interpreted.

IMPORTANT TERMS AND CONCEPTS

alpha (α)	population
alternative (or research) hypothesis	Power
	random assignment
beta (β)	random selection
confound	region of rejection
convenience (or accidental) sample	reliability
	sample
demand characteristics	sampling distribution
experimenter effect	significant difference
external validity	statistical analysis
extraneous variables	two-tailed hypothesis
internal validity	Type I error
null hypothesis	Type II error
one-tailed hypothesis	validity
operational definition	

EXERCISES

1. A researcher wishes to look at the effect of stress on fidgeting. What terms need to be operationally defined? What are some possible operational definitions?

2. What is the difference between reliability and validity? Can a study be valid and not reliable? Can a study provide reliable data but not valid data?

3. Suppose I have conducted a study in which participants were asked to perform a mood induction task that created a happy, sad, or neutral mood. The participants were then asked to complete a questionnaire about their sense of wellness. Why might demand characteristics be a problem in this study? How could demand characteristics affect the results?

4. A researcher wants to create a random sample of students at Smart U. A friend suggests that the researcher walk across campus and approach every third person she encounters. Is this a random sample? If not, what type of sample is it? Can you develop a procedure to create a random sample?

5. What is the difference between a null hypothesis and an alternative hypothesis?

6. I want to investigate the effect of chocolate on mood. One group of participants eats a chocolate bar before completing a mood scale; the other participants complete the mood scale without first eating chocolate. I

expect that those who have eaten chocolate will have higher mood scores. What is the null hypothesis and what is the alternative hypothesis? Is the alternative hypothesis one-tailed or two-tailed?

7. A researcher finds a significant difference on the speed of reading between participants who have drunk a caffeinated drink and those who haven't. What type of error is this person at risk of making?

ANSWERS TO CONCEPT QUESTIONS AND ODD-NUMBERED EXERCISES

Note: There will often be more than one correct answer for each of these questions. Consult with your instructor about your own answers.

Concept Question 3.1

Option (b) is the best example of an operational definition since it defines learning in terms of how it is being measured; option (a) does not define "information" or "period of time"; option (c) does not define "studying"; option (d) is a dictionary definition, not an operational definition.

Concept Question 3.2

The null hypothesis is that families in the sample from the Midwest do not differ in size from the national average family size. The alternative hypothesis is that the family size of the Midwest sample will be either bigger or smaller than the national average, but not equivalent to it. (This is a two-tailed hypothesis.)

Concept Question 3.3

The researcher has made a Type I error by identifying a difference that doesn't actually exist.

Exercises

1. How is "fidgeting" going to be defined? How will "stress" be defined? An operational definition of stress might be to give a 3-minute extemporaneous videotaped speech. Fidgeting could be defined as the number of times the participant touches his or her face. There are many other possible ways to define stress and fidgeting.

3. The participants are likely to realize that I am looking at the effect of mood on wellness and might think that I expect to find that people in a depressed mood will have lower wellness scores than do people in a happy or neutral mood; therefore, those in a depressed mood might actually report themselves as having a lower sense of wellness than they actually do; similarly, people in a happy mood might report that they feel more well than they really do.

5. A null hypothesis is the prediction that there is no difference between the groups being compared. The null hypothesis is true if the population that the sample is from is the same as the population with which it is being compared.

An alternative hypothesis is the prediction that there will be a difference between the groups being compared (one group will have a score greater than, less than, or significantly different from the other group).

7. A Type I error. She may have found a difference that doesn't truly exist between the populations of people who have drunk caffeinated drinks and people who haven't.

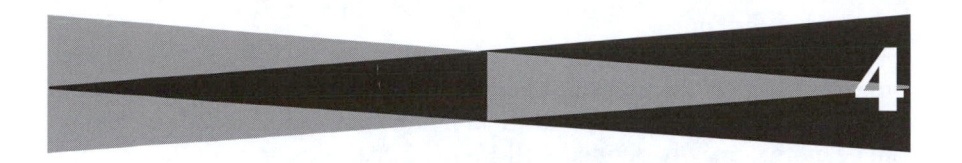

The Role of
Statistics in Research

Statistics are the tools researchers use to organize and summarize their data. If you collect memory test scores from 100 participants, you have 100 numbers. Little useful information can be gleaned from 100 individual numbers; they need to be organized. It might be useful to know what the highest and lowest scores are (the range), what the most common score is (the mode), or what the middle score is (the median). Certain statistical tests can help determine if one group of participants scored significantly better on a test than another. The term "significantly" means that the difference is of such a magnitude that it is unlikely to have occurred by chance alone.

Statistics are used to make generalizations from a sample to an entire **population**. A population is all of the individuals to whom a research project is meant to generalize. A population can be as broadly defined as all of the people in the world, or even all living organisms; or the population can be more narrowly defined—all 18- to 22-year-olds or all of the psychology majors at a particular school. Typically, a researcher cannot test all of the members of a target population. Instead, only a small percentage of that population—a **sample** of the members—can be tested. This sample is meant to represent the entire population so that if we identify a characteristic of the sample—for example, that the men in the sample are taller than the women—we can be fairly confident that this characteristic holds true for the entire population. Statistics help us determine how confident we can be that a characteristic of our sample can be generalized to the population.

Let's assume that a researcher has conducted a memory experiment, and the mnemonic (memory technique) group performs better than the control group. Perhaps the participants in the mnemonic group recall an average of 18 out of 20 words, and the control group recalls an average of 16 out of 20 words. At this point, the researcher has not yet supported the alternative hypothesis that mnemonic instructions lead to better memory performance, even though 18 is greater than 16. The researcher does know that the *sample* of participants in the mnemonic group outperformed the *sample* of participants in the control group, but does not know at this point if the same difference can be expected between the *populations*. The researcher should consider using some statistical techniques to answer that question.

This chapter offers a nontechnical introduction to some statistical concepts. The purpose is to familiarize you with some of the terms and ideas used in organizing and analyzing data statistically so that you will have a basis for understanding research that you encounter as part of your studies, in your work, or in the media.

SCALES OF MEASUREMENT

In most jobs, satisfactory work depends on using the right tools. In research, this means choosing the right statistical tool; unless the most appropriate statistical technique is employed, the research results might be misleading. The first step toward choosing the right statistical technique is to identify the type of data being analyzed.

In psychology, researchers assume that anything that exists—be it a physical characteristic, such as your height, or a psychological construct, such as extroversion—exists in some amount, and that amount can be measured. **Measurement** involves systematically assigning numbers to objects, events, or characteristics according to a set of rules (Stevens, 1951). Rating how happy you feel today on a scale of 1 to 10 is a type of measurement. It entails identifying a characteristic, your happiness, and quantifying the amount of happiness you are experiencing. The rules used in this example are that the number you assign to your happiness must be between 1 and 10, where 1 refers to a lack of happiness and 10 refers to an abundance of happiness.

Not all measurement systems are equivalent. Some measurements can be mathematically manipulated—for instance, by adding a constant or by taking the square root of each number—but still keep its primary characteristics. Other systems are very intolerant of any mathematical manipulation; adding a constant or taking the square root renders the data meaningless. Measurement systems can be assigned to one of four scales of measurement that vary by the level of mathematical manipulation they can tolerate. These four scales of measurement (also called levels of measurement) are the nominal, ordinal, interval, and ratio scales.

Nominal Scale

The **nominal scale** of measurement merely classifies objects or individuals as belonging to different categories. The order of the categories is arbitrary and unimportant. Thus, participants might be categorized as male or female, and the male category may be assigned the number 1 and the female category assigned the number 2. These numbers say nothing about the importance of one category as compared to the other. The numbers could just as well be 17.35 and 29.46. Other examples of nominal scales of measurement are numbers on basketball players' jerseys or the numbers assigned by the Department of Motor Vehicles to the license plates of cars. Numbers, when used in a nominal scale of measurement, serve as labels only and provide no information on the magnitude or amount of the characteristic being measured.

Ordinal Scale

An **ordinal scale** differs from a nominal scale in that the order of the categories is important. A grading system with the grades A, B, C, D, and F is an ordinal scale. The order of the categories reflects a decrease in the amount of the stuff being measured—in this case, knowledge. Note, however, that the distance between the categories is not necessarily equal. Thus, the difference between one A and one B is not necessarily the same as the difference between another A and another B. Similarly, the difference between any A and B is not necessarily the same as the difference between a B and a C.

Rank-order data is also measured on an ordinal scale. An observer may rank-order participants according to attractiveness or a researcher may ask tasters to rank-order a number of crackers according to saltiness. When your eyesight is tested and you are asked to choose which of two lenses results in a clearer image, you are being asked to provide ordinal data. Again, when data are rank-ordered, a statement is being made about the magnitude or amount of the characteristic being measured, but the intervals between units need not be equivalent. If seven people are rank-ordered on attractiveness, the difference in attractiveness between the first and second person is not necessarily the same as the difference between the second and the third. The first and second persons may both be very attractive, with only the smallest difference between them, while the third person might be substantially less attractive than the second.

Interval Scale

The **interval scale** of measurement is characterized by equal units of measurement throughout the scale. Thus, measurements made with an interval scale provide information about both the order and the relative quantity of the characteristic being measured. Interval scales of measurement, however, do *not* have a true zero value. A true zero means that none of the characteristic being measured remains. Temperature measurements in degrees Fahrenheit or in degrees Celsius (also called centigrade) correspond to interval scales. The distance between degrees is equal over the full length of the scale; the difference between 20° and 40° is the same as that between 40° and 60°. In neither scale, however, is there a true zero; zero simply represents another point on the scale, and negative numbers are possible and meaningful. Because there is no true zero on these scales, it is inappropriate to say that 40° is twice as warm as 20°. In other words, ratios cannot be computed with interval scale data.

There is a controversy among psychological researchers regarding interval and ordinal scales in relation to rating. Suppose that a participant is asked to rate something on a scale with particular end points, such as 1 to 7 or 0 to 5. For example, a person might be asked the following rating question:

How satisfied are you with your friendships?

1	2	3	4	5	6	7	8	9	10
very dissatisfied								very satisfied	

The end numbers usually have labels, but the middle numbers sometimes do not. The controversy arises as to whether the ratings should be considered ordinal data or interval data. What has never been ascertained is whether the scales that people use in their heads have units of equal size. If the units are equal in size, the data could be regarded as interval data; if they are unequal, the data should be regarded as ordinal data. This is a point of contention because interval data often permit the use of more powerful statistics than do ordinal data.

There is still no consensus about the nature of rating scale data. In some research areas, ratings tend to be treated cautiously and are considered ordinal data. In other areas—such as language and memory studies, where participants may be asked to rate how familiar a phrase is or how strong their feeling of knowing is—ratings tend to be treated as interval data. The particular philosophy of any particular area of study is possibly best ascertained from previous research in that area.

Ratio Scale

The **ratio scale** of measurement provides information about order; all units are of equal size throughout the scale, and there *is* a true zero value that represents an absence of the characteristic being measured. The true zero allows ratios of values to be formed. Thus, a person who is 50-years-old is twice as old as a person who is 25. Age in years is a ratio scale. Each year represents the same amount of time no matter where it occurs on the scale; the year between 20 and 21 years of age is the same amount of time as the year between 54 and 55.

As you may have noticed, the scales of measurement can be arranged hierarchically from nominal to ratio. Staring with the ordinal scale, each scale includes all the capabilities of the preceding scale plus something new. Thus, nominal scales are simply categorical, while ordinal scales are categorical with the addition of ordering of the categories. Interval scales of measurement involve ordered categories of equal size; in other words, the intervals between numbers on the scale are equivalent throughout the scale. Ratio scales also have equal intervals but, in addition, begin at a true zero score that represents an absence of the characteristic being measured and allows for the computation of ratios.

Importance of Scales of Measurement

The statistical techniques that are appropriate for one scale of measurement may not be appropriate for another. Therefore, the researcher must be able to identify the scale of measurement being used, so that appropriate statistical techniques can be applied. Sometimes, the inappropriateness of a technique is subtle; at other times, it can be quite obvious—and quite embarrassing to a researcher who lets an inappropriate statistic slip by. For example, imagine that ten people are rank-ordered according to height. In addition, information about the individuals' weight in pounds and age in years is recorded. When instructing the computer to calculate arithmetic averages, the researcher absentmindedly includes the height rankings along with the other variables. The computer calculates that the average age of the participants is 22.6 years, that the average weight of the group is 155.6 pounds, and that the average height is 5'5". Calculating an average of ordinal data, such as the height rankings in this example, will yield little useful information. Meaningful results will only be obtained by using the statistical technique appropriate to the data's scale of measurement.

Concept Question 4.1

On what scale of measurement would each of the following data be measured?

a. The number of dollars in one's wallet.

b. The rated sweetness of a can of soda.

c. Whether one responds yes or no to a question.

d. Height measured in inches.

e. The gender of individuals.

f. Weight measured as light, medium, and heavy.

TYPES OF STATISTICAL TECHNIQUES

Having recognized the type of data collected, the researcher needs also to consider the question that he or she wants to answer. You can't tighten a screw with a hammer, and you can't answer one research question with a statistical test meant for a different question.

Let's consider three questions that a researcher might ask:

1. How can I describe the data?

2. To what degree are these two variables related to each other?

3. Do the participants in this group have different scores than the participants in the other group?

These three questions require the use of different types of statistical techniques. The scale of measurement on which the data were collected determines more specifically which statistical tool to use.

Describing the Data

When a researcher begins organizing a set of data, it can be very useful to determine typical characteristics of the different variables. The statistical techniques used for this task are aptly called **descriptive statistics**. Usually, researchers use two types of descriptive statistics: a description of the average score and a description of how spread out or close together the data lie.

Averages

Perhaps the most commonly discussed characteristic of a data set is its average. However, there are three different averages that can be calculated: the mode, the median, and the mean. Each provides somewhat different information. The scale of measurement on which the data are collected will, in part, determine which average is most appropriate to use.

Let's consider a researcher who has collected data on people's weight measured in pounds; hair color categorized according to 10 shades ranging from light to dark; and eye color labeled as blue, green, brown, or other. This researcher has measured data on three different scales of measurement: ratio, ordinal, and nominal, respectively. When describing the eye colors of the participants, the researcher will need to use a different statistic than when describing the participants' average weight.

To describe the eye colors of the participants, the researcher would use the **mode**. The mode is defined as the score that occurs most frequently. Thus, if most of the participants had brown eyes, brown would be the modal eye color. Sometimes a set of data will have two scores that tie for occurring most frequently. In that case, the distribution is said to be **bimodal**. If three or more scores are tied for occurring most frequently, the distribution is said to be **multimodal**.

In our example, hair color is measured on an ordinal scale of measurement, since we have no evidence that the ten shades of hair color are equally distant from each other. To describe average hair color, the researcher could use the mode, the median, or perhaps both.

The **median** is defined as the middle point in a set of scores, the point below which 50% of the scores fall. The median is especially useful because it provides information about the distribution of other scores in the set. If the median hair color was the eighth darkest hair category, then we know that half of the participants had hair in categories 8 to 10, and that the other half of the participants had hair in categories 1 to 8.

Finally, our researcher will want to describe the participants' average weight. The researcher could use the mode or the median here, or the researcher may wish to use the **mean**. The mean is the arithmetic average of the scores in a distribution; it is calculated by adding up the scores in the distribution and dividing by the number of scores.

The mean is probably the most commonly used type of average, in part because it is mathematically very manipulable. It is difficult to write a formula that describes how to calculate the mode or median, but it is not difficult to write a formula for adding a set of scores and dividing the sum by the number of scores. Because of this, the mean can be embedded within other formulas.

The mean does, however, have its limitations. Scores that are inordinately large or small (called **outliers**) are given as much weight as every other score in the distribution; this can affect the mean score, which will be inflated if the outlier is large and deflated if the outlier is small. For example, suppose a set of exam scores is 82, 88, 84, 86, and 20. The mean of these scores is 72, although four of the five people earned scores in the 80s. The inordinately small score, the outlier 20, deflated the mean. Researchers need to watch out for this problem when using means. Nevertheless, the mean is still a very popular average. The mean can be used with data measured on interval and ratio scales. It is sometimes used with numerical ordinal data (such as rating scales), but it cannot be used with rank-order data or data measured on a nominal scale.

The mode, median, and mean are ways of describing the average score among a set of data. They are often called **measures of central ten-**

dency because they tend to describe the scores in the middle of the distribution (although the mode need not be in the middle at all).

Concept Question 4.2

A researcher observes cars entering and leaving a parking lot and records the gender of the driver, the number of people in the car, the type of car (Ford, Chevrolet, Mazda, etc.), and the speed at which the car drives through the lot (measured with a radar gun in mph).

a. For each type of data measured, what would be an appropriate average to calculate (mode, median, and/or mean)?

b. One driver traveled through the parking lot at a speed 20 mph higher than any other driver. Which type of average would be most affected by this one score?

Another important characteristic of a set of data is the degree to which the scores are close to the average or are spread out. Statistics that describe this characteristic are called **measures of dispersion**.

Measures of Dispersion

Although they can be used with nominal and ordinal data, measures of dispersion are used primarily with interval or ratio data.

The most straightforward measure of dispersion is the **range**. The range is the number of possible values for scores in a discrete data set or the number of intervals of scores covered by a data set taken from a continuous distribution. In a discrete data set, fractions of scores are not possible, such as the number of times a sample of women have been pregnant; as they say, you can't be a little pregnant—she either is or she isn't. In a continuous distribution set, fractions of scores are possible, such as the heights of people in a sample; for some that extra half inch is very important. The range is computed by subtracting the lowest score from the highest score and adding 1:

$$Range = Highest - Lowest + 1$$

We add 1 so that the range will include both the highest value and the lowest value. If a researcher had measured weights of 110, 115, 129, 176, 194, and 207, the range would be

$$207 - 110 + 1 = 98$$

This sample of scores covers 98 pounds from the lightest to the heaviest weights.

The range tells us over how many scores the data are spread, but it does not give us any information about how the scores are distributed over the range. It is limited because it relies on only two scores from the entire distribution. But it does provide us with some useful information about the spread of the scores and it is appropriate for use with ordinal, interval, and ratio data.

A more commonly used measure of dispersion is the **standard deviation**. The standard deviation may be thought of as expressing the average distance that the scores in a set of data fall from the mean. For example, imagine that the mean score on an exam was 74. If the class all performed about the same, the scores might range from 67 to 81; this set of data would have a relatively small standard deviation, and the average distance from the mean of 74 would be fairly small. On the other hand, if the members of the class performed less consistently—if some did very well, but others did quite poorly, perhaps with scores ranging from 47 to 100— the standard deviation would be quite large; the average distance from the mean of 74 would be fairly big.

The standard deviation and its counterpart, the **variance** (the standard deviation squared), are probably the most commonly used measures of dispersion. They are used individually and also are embedded within other more complex formulas. To calculate a standard deviation or variance, you need to know the mean. Because we typically calculate a mean with data measured on interval or ratio scales, standard deviation and variance are not appropriate for use with nominal data.

Learning to calculate standard deviation and variance is not necessary for the purposes of this book (although it is presented in appendix A). The underlying concept—the notion of how spread out or clustered the data are—is important, however, especially in research where two or more groups of data are being compared. This issue will be discussed a little later in the chapter.

Concept Question 4.3

The weather report includes information about the normal temperature for the day. Suppose that today the temperature is 10 degrees above normal. To determine if today is a very strange day or not especially strange, we need to know the standard deviation. If we learn that the standard deviation is 15 degrees, what might we conclude about how normal or abnormal the weather is today? If the standard deviation is 5 degrees, what does that suggest about today's weather?

Measures of Relationships

Often a researcher will want to know more than the average and degree of dispersion for different variables. Sometimes, the researcher wants to learn how much two variables are related to one another. In this case, the researcher would want to calculate a **correlation**. A correlation is a measure of the degree of relationship between two variables. For example, if we collected data on the number of hours students studied for a midterm exam and the grades received on that exam, a correlation could be calculated between the hours studied and the midterm grade. We might find that those with higher midterm grades tended to study more hours, while those with lower midterm grades tended to study for fewer hours. This is described as a **positive correlation**. With a positive correlation, an increase in one variable is accompanied by an increase in the other variable. With a **negative correlation**, by contrast, an increase in one variable is accompanied by a decrease in the other variable. A possible negative correlation might occur between the number of hours spent watching television the night before an exam and the scores on the exam. As the number of hours of viewing increase, the exam scores decrease.

A mathematical formula is used to calculate a correlation coefficient, and the resulting number will be somewhere between −1.00 and +1.00. The closer the number is to either +1.00 or −1.00, the stronger the relationship between the variables is. The closer the number is to 0.00, the weaker the correlation is. Thus, +.85 represents a relatively strong positive correlation, but +.03 represents a weak positive correlation. Similarly, −.91 represents a strong negative correlation, but −.12 represents a relatively weak negative correlation. The *strength* of the relationship is represented by the absolute value of the correlation coefficient. The *direction* of the relationship is represented by the sign of the correlation coefficient. Therefore, −.91 represents a *stronger* correlation than does +.85.

A particular type of graph called a **scattergram** is used to demonstrate the relationship between two variables. The two variables (typically called the x and the y variables) are plotted on the same graph. The x variable is plotted along the horizontal x-axis, and the y variable is plotted along the vertical y-axis. Figure 4.1 is a scattergram of the hypothetical data for number of hours studied and midterm exam scores.

Each point on figure 4.1 represents the two scores for each person. To calculate a correlation there must be pairs of scores generated by one set of participants, not two separate sets of scores generated by separate sets of participants. Notice that the points tend to form a pattern from the lower left corner to the upper right corner. This lower left to upper right pattern is an indication of a positive correlation. For a *negative* correlation, the points show a pattern from the top left corner to the bottom right corner. Furthermore, the more closely the points fall along a straight line, the stronger the correlation between the two variables. Figure 4.2 presents several scattergrams representing positive and negative correlations of various strengths.

Several types of correlations can be calculated. The two most common are Pearson's product-moment correlation (more often called Pearson's r) and Spearman's rho (for which the corresponding Greek symbol is ρ). Pearson's r is used when the two variables being correlated are measured on interval or ratio scales. When one or both variables are measured on an ordinal scale, especially if the variables are rank-ordered, Spearman's rho is appropriate. Other correlation coefficients can be calculated for situations when, for example, one variable is measured on an

Figure 4.1   Scattergram representing pairs of midterm exam scores and numbers of hours spent studying for the exam

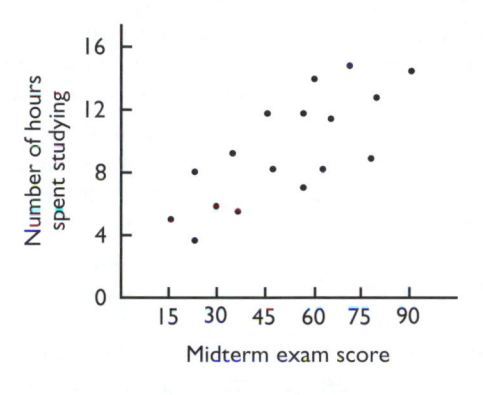

Figure 4.2   Scattergrams representing correlations of different strengths and directions

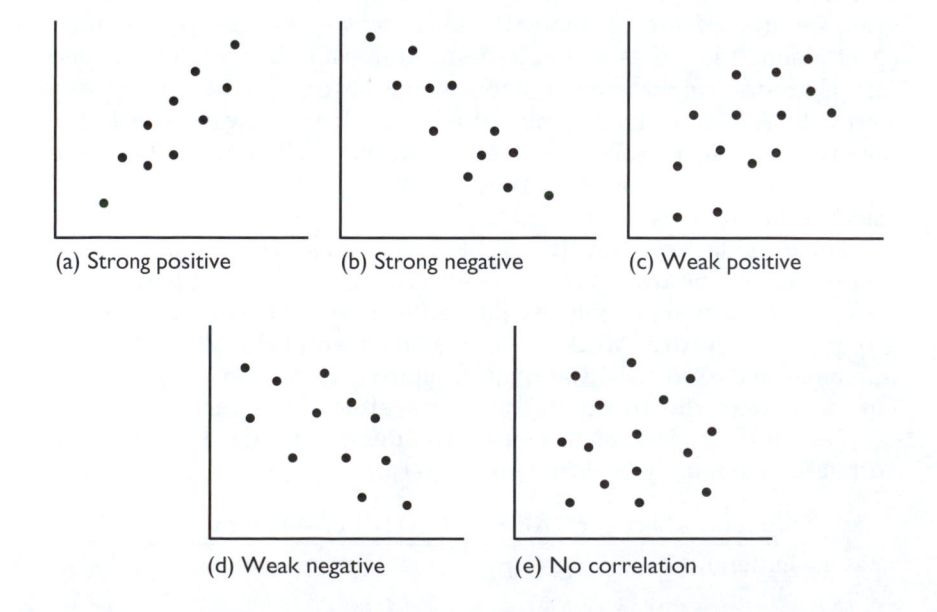

interval or ratio scale and the other is measured on a nominal scale with only two options (such as yes or no, male or female). Most statistical textbooks discuss these coefficients. Regardless of the specific correlation coefficient being calculated, however, the statistical tool is used to measure the degree of relationship between two variables.

Comparing Groups

A very common type of research project compares the performance of one group of participants to that of a separate group. For example, one group of individuals who tend to experience migraine headaches might be given a new drug meant to reduce the frequency of headaches, while a control group receives a placebo. All of the participants might then be asked to report the number of migraine headaches experienced during a 3-month period. (When you have a minute, consider the ethical ramifications of this study. When would it be acceptable to withhold effective medication from a sample of migraine-headache sufferers?)

Assume the IRB found this study to be valuable and data were collected. Suppose that, for the experimental group (the participants receiving the new drug), the mean number of headaches is 3.5, while the control group's rating is 5.7. The researcher can see that, in general, the participants in the experimental group had fewer headaches than those in the control group, but the researcher needs to determine if the difference between the experimental and control groups is both large enough and consistent enough to suggest that the *populations* represented by those samples would show the same effect.

One way to determine if the results can be generalized to the population is to create a ratio of the differences among the scores *between* the groups to the differences among the scores *within* each group. Any differences among the scores within a group—for example, within the experimental group—might be attributable to how severe each headache was to start with, how sensitive the individuals are to pain, how conscientiously they record their headaches, and so on. Taken together, these differences are referred to as the **error variance**, which can be measured with the standard deviation we discussed earlier.

The same factors—severity of headache, sensitivity to pain, motivation—may also be responsible for differences in the scores between the groups. However, there will also be a difference in the scores between the groups if the new drug works better than the placebo. In other words, any difference in the scores between the groups will be due not only to the difference between the drug and placebo, but also to error variance.

The ratio of the differences between the groups and the differences within the group may be written in the form:

$$\frac{\text{Differences between groups}}{\text{Differences within group}} = \frac{\text{Effect of IV + Error variance}}{\text{Error variance}}$$

If the independent variable (IV) has little or no effect, the ratio will be approximately equal to 1. But, if the independent variable does have an effect on the scores, the ratio will be considerably greater than 1. How much greater than 1 must the ratio be to be *significant*—that is, to suggest that the results can be generalized to the population? That depends on the sizes of the samples. The number of people who participate in the study will determine the ratio needed to reject the null hypothesis and support the alternative hypothesis. The more participants involved, the smaller the ratio needs to be.

The concept of a ratio of between-groups differences to within-group differences is used for all of the statistical techniques that compare groups when data are measured on an interval or ratio scale. However, different research designs call for different statistical tests. For example, a researcher who wishes to compare two groups would probably use a statistical test called a *t*-test. If the researcher needs to compare three or more groups, the test to use would probably be one called **analysis of variance (ANOVA)**. To make life a little easier for statisticians, tables of numbers have been developed so that, for any particular statistical test and sample size, the researcher can see how large the ratio of the **between-groups variance** and the **within-group variance** must be in order to reject the null hypothesis. Some of these tables appear in appendix B.

When data are not measured on an interval or ratio scale of measurement, we need to use different types of statistical tests—**nonparametric tests**. A **parameter** is a characteristic of a population. Most statistical tests comparing groups using interval or ratio data are called **parametric tests**, because the user makes assumptions about the parameters of a population. The researcher assumes, for instance, that the *sample* standard deviation is a fairly accurate estimate of the *population* standard deviation. Nonparametric tests, however, do not generally require that assumptions be made about the underlying population of scores. They allow the researcher to use data measured on nominal, ordinal, interval, or ratio scales. On the other hand, they are often less powerful than parametric tests and thus usually need larger differences to reject the null hypothesis. Table 4.1 presents various research situations and the type of statistical technique that might be appropriate in each, including several nonparametric tests.

An important step in designing research is to determine what statistical techniques are appropriate to answer the research questions before data are collected. A very common mistake of novice researchers is to design a research project, collect the data, and then discover that there is no appropriate way to analyze the data.

Statistics provide an important set of tools that researchers may use to describe their data and to test their hypotheses. The field of statistics is a subdiscipline of mathematics, but you need not be a mathematician to use statistics, just as you need not be a physicist to drive a car. The concepts presented in this chapter and the techniques illustrated in appendix A are enough for you to start doing scientific research in psychology.

Table 4.1   Some Appropriate Statistics for Different Situations and Scales of Measurement

Statistical Technique	Scales of Measurement			
	Nominal	**Ordinal**	**Interval**	**Ratio**
1. Averages	mode	mode, median	mode, median, mean	mode, median, mean
2. Measures of dispersion		range	range, s.d.,[a] variance	range, s.d., variance
3. Correlations	φ (Phi) coefficient	Spearman's ρ	Pearson's r	Pearson's r
4. Single group compared to a population	χ^2 Goodness-of-Fit	χ^2 Goodness-of-Fit	z-test, single-sample t	z-test, single-sample t
5. Two separate groups	χ^2 ToI[b]	χ^2 ToI	Wilcoxon's rank-sum, χ^2 ToI	Wilcoxon's rank-sum, χ^2 ToI, independent-samples t
6. Three or more groups	χ^2 ToI	χ^2 ToI	ANOVA, Kruskal-Wallis	ANOVA, Kruskal-Wallis
7. One group tested twice			Mann-Whitney U, dependent-samples t	Mann-Whitney U, dependent-samples t

[a] Standard deviation
[b] χ^2 test of independence

SUMMARY

Researchers use statistics to help them test their hypotheses. Often, statistics are used to generalize the results from a sample to a larger population.

Which type of statistical technique is used depends on the scale of measurement on which the data are collected. Data measured on a nominal scale are classified in different categories. Order is not important for nominal data, but it is for data measured on an ordinal scale of measurement. The data measured on an interval scale of measurement are also ordered but, in addition, the units of measurement are equal throughout the scale. The ratio scale of measurement is much like the interval scale, except that it includes a true zero, which indicates a zero amount of the construct being measured.

The scale of measurement for the data and the question being asked by the researcher determine what statistical technique should be used. When describing data, descriptive statistics are used. These include averages and measures of dispersion.

There are three ways to measure an average: the mode, the median, and the mean. The mode is the most frequent score; the median is the central score; and the mean is the arithmetic average of the data set.

Measures of dispersion provide information about how clustered together or spread out the data are in a distribution. The range describes the number of score values the data are spread across. The variance and standard deviation provide information about the average distance the scores fall from the mean.

A researcher might also ask if two variables are related to each other. This question is answered by calculating a correlation coefficient. The correlation coefficient is a number between −1.00 and +1.00. The closer the coefficient is to either −1.00 or +1.00, the stronger the correlation is. The negative and positive signs indicate whether the variables are changing in the same direction (a positive correlation) or in opposite directions (a negative correlation).

Finally, a researcher may wish to compare sets of scores in order to determine if an independent variable had an effect on a dependent variable. A number of statistical techniques can be used to look for this difference. The appropriate technique depends on a number of factors, such as the number of groups being compared and the scale of measurement on which the data were collected.

If data at the ratio or interval level were collected, the statistical techniques that look for differences between groups have the same underlying logic. A difference between groups is considered to exist when the variation among the scores *between* the groups is considerably greater than the variation among the scores *within* the group.

When data are measured on ordinal or nominal scales, other statistical techniques can be used; these tend to be less powerful than those used for data on ratio and interval scales, though.

Statistical techniques are necessary to test research hypotheses once data have been collected. Knowledge of this field is essential for research psychologists.

IMPORTANT TERMS AND CONCEPTS

analysis of variance (ANOVA)	median
between-groups variance	mode
bimodal	multimodal
correlation	negative correlation
descriptive statistics	nominal scale
error variance	nonparametric tests
interval scale	ordinal scale
mean	outliers
measurement	parameter
measures of central tendency	parametric tests
measures of dispersion	population

positive correlation   standard deviation
range   *t*-test
ratio scale   variance
sample   within-group variance
scattergram

EXERCISES

1. Give two examples of variables corresponding to each of the scales of measurement.

2. a. If a researcher measures height in inches, what averages might be calculated?

   b. If a researcher measures height by assigning people to the categories short, medium, and tall, what averages might be calculated?

3. a. If a researcher measures weight in pounds, what measures of dispersion could be calculated?

   b. If a researcher measures weight in ounces, what measures of dispersion could be calculated?

   c. If a researcher measures weight by assigning each person to either the skinny, medium, or heavy category, what measures of dispersion could be calculated?

4. Which correlation is stronger: −.87 or +.55?

5. What is the difference between a positive and a negative correlation? Provide an example other than the one in the chapter.

6. A researcher studying the effect of a speed-reading course on reading times compares the scores of a group that has taken the course with those of a control group. The researcher finds that the ratio of the variation between the groups to the variation within the group is equal to 2.76. A colleague does a similar study and finds a ratio of between-groups variation to within-group variation of 1.32. Which ratio is more likely to suggest a significant difference between reading groups?

ANSWERS TO CONCEPT QUESTIONS AND ODD-NUMBERED EXERCISES

Note: There will often be more than one correct answer for each of these questions. Consult with your instructor about your own answers.

Concept Question 4.1
a. ratio
b. ordinal or interval
c. nominal
d. ratio
e. nominal
f. ordinal

Concept Question 4.2

a. For gender, the mode; for the number in the car, the median and/or mode; for the type of car, the mode; for the speed, the mean, median, and/or mode.

b. The mean.

Concept Question 4.3

If the standard deviation is 15, a day that is 10 degrees above the normal temperature is not an unusually warm day; however, if the standard deviation is 5, a day that is 10 degrees above the normal temperature is twice the average distance from the mean (roughly), and thus is an unusually warm day.

Exercises

1. Nominal: license plate numbers, eye color. Ordinal: ordered preference for five types of cookies, class rank. Interval: degrees Fahrenheit, money in your checking account (assuming you can overdraw). Ratio: loudness in decibels, miles per gallon. There are of course any number of other correct answers.

3. a. range, standard deviation, and variance

   b. range, standard deviation, and variance

   c. range

5. A positive correlation describes a relationship in which two variables change together in the same direction. For example, if the number of violent crimes increases as crowding increases, that would be a positive correlation. A negative correlation describes a relationship in which two variables change together in opposite directions. For instance, if weight gained increases as the amount of exercise decreases, that would be a negative correlation.

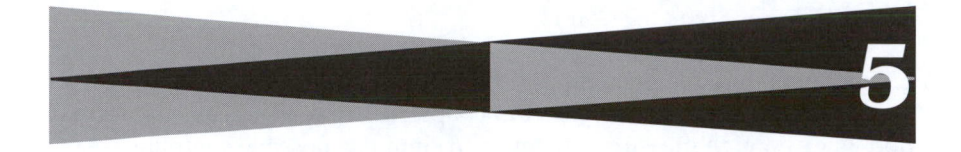

Introduction to Experimentation and the Between-Groups Design

EXPERIMENTS VERSUS CORRELATIONAL STUDIES
    Equivalent Groups
    Control over Extraneous Variables
INTERNAL VALIDITY AND CONFOUNDS
    Experimenter Bias and Demand Characteristics
    Instrumentation Effects
    Subject Mortality
    Comparable Treatment of Groups
    Sensitivity of the Dependent Variable
SUMMARY

EXPERIMENTS VERSUS CORRELATIONAL STUDIES

Not all research projects in psychology can rightly be called experiments. **Experiments** are investigations in which the researcher manipulates an independent variable to see if there are any differences in the dependent variable among equivalent groups of participants. The great advantage of experiments is that, when performed correctly, they yield causal information about the effect of the independent variable on the dependent variable.

A study in which the groups of participants aren't equivalent (for example, because participants weren't randomly assigned to the groups), but an independent variable is manipulated, is called a quasi-experiment. Quasi-experiments, which are discussed in chapter 10, may yield causal information when enough measures are taken to eliminate possible confounds.

An investigation that explores the effect of a subject variable on a dependent measure is referred to as a **correlational study**. Correlational studies do not yield causal information; they do, however, identify relationships between the subject variable and the dependent variable. To clarify the difference between a correlational study and a true experiment, consider the following example.

A researcher interested in the effect of alcohol on reaction time throws a large party, where both alcoholic and nonalcoholic beverages are available. After several hours, the researcher measures the blood alcohol levels (BAL) of the partygoers and identifies a group of sober people and a group of people with a BAL of .10. The researcher measures the reaction times of all of these people and finds that the sober people have faster reaction times than do those with the elevated BAL. The researcher, however, cannot assume that this difference in reaction time between the sober and intoxicated groups is attributable to the alcohol. The researcher did not randomly assign the individuals to specific levels of the independent variable; the participants, in essence, assigned themselves to either the sober or the intoxicated condition.

Although the researcher may note a relationship between reaction time and BAL, he or she cannot assume a causal relationship. One possible explanation is that the participants who chose to become intoxicated had slower reaction times before the party began than did the participants who chose to remain sober. Can you think of any other possible explanations? This investigation is not an experiment; it is a correlational study.

Now consider an alternative investigation. The experimenter assigns people to two groups such that each person is equally likely to be in either group. One group receives drinks containing alcohol, and one group receives a **placebo**—an inert treatment that has no effect on the dependent variable. In this case, the placebo might be a drink—such as grapefruit juice—that tastes as if it could have alcohol in it, but does not. The participants' reaction times are then measured. Any differences between the groups can now be attributed to the effect of the alcohol. This study is an experiment.

In this experiment, there are two groups of participants. A two-group experiment is a simple example of a **between-groups research design**. Research designs are general plans for setting up a research project. In a between-groups design, the performance of participants in one or more groups is compared with the performance of participants in another group. In an experiment, the groups are made up of very similar participants and are treated in the same manner, except in relation to the independent variable. Thus, the people in the alcohol and no-alcohol conditions are told the same information and tested under the same circumstances. The only difference is that one group consumes alcohol and the other group does not.

Sometimes, one group of participants in an experiment is called the control group, and the other is the experimental group (or the treatment group). The control group is usually in what might be considered the more natural condition. Here, the no-alcohol group would be considered the control group. Both groups are measured on the same dependent variable; in this case, their reaction times are measured. If the control group and experimental group differ on the dependent measure, it is assumed that the difference is *caused* by the difference in the independent variable. If the experimental group has slower reaction times than the control group, it is assumed that the alcohol consumed by the experimental group caused this difference.

Two requirements must be met for an experiment to yield causal results: The groups being compared must be equivalent before the independent variable is introduced; and the design must be free of other potential confounds that would provide alternative explanations for the results. Meeting one or the other of these requirements is not sufficient for making causal statements about the results; both requirements must be met. Designing an experiment so that causal inferences can be made requires careful planning and full consideration of all the factors that might affect the dependent variable.

Equivalent Groups

At the beginning of the experiment, the control and experimental groups must be equivalent so that any changes noted between the groups can be attributed to the independent variable and not to initial group differences. The preferred way of obtaining equivalent groups of subjects is by **random assignment**. When participants are randomly assigned to one of two groups, each participant is equally likely to be assigned to either of the groups, and any characteristics that may affect the dependent variable are therefore distributed randomly between or among the experiment's groups. Simple techniques for random assignment are to flip a coin, draw names or numbers from a hat, or to take numbers from a random-numbers table. For example, people allotted an odd number from the random-numbers table might be assigned to one group, and even numbers might be assigned to the other. (Do you remember the difference between random selection and random assignment? If not, you might look back at chapter 3.)

Researchers do not choose who will be in each group, nor do participants choose which group they would like to be in. To do so would leave the study vulnerable to **selection bias**, that is, it increases the risk of obtaining nonequivalent groups. We all have biases, and they can affect our behavior intentionally or unintentionally. Researchers avoid this risk by using random assignment.

Random assignment allows the researcher to be reasonably confident that the groups are equivalent. It does not guarantee that the groups will be equivalent in all ways, but any differences between the groups will be caused by chance; they will not be systematic. Therefore, if the groups are large enough, such differences are likely to have little or no effect on the experiment.

Random assignment yields the best results with larger samples; equivalence among the groups increases as they become more representative of the population—that is, as they get larger. See concept question 5.1 for an exercise that should yield greater clarification.

Concept Question 5.1

Randomly assign two pennies, two dimes, and two nickels to the heads group or the tails group by flipping each coin. Note how different the groups are in size and in characteristics (number of pennies, nickels, and dimes in each group). Now randomly assign more coins of each type. As your sample size gets larger, do your groups become more similar or less similar?

Sometimes, instead of relying on random assignment to balance the effects of extraneous variables, a researcher uses a technique called **matching** to be sure that the experimental groups are equivalent on one important characteristic. Matching involves identifying pairs (or triplets, quadruplets, and so on) of participants who measure similarly on a characteristic that is related to the dependent variable and then randomly assigning each of these participants to separate experimental conditions. The challenge for the researcher who wishes to use matching is to determine what characteristic to match on and how to measure that characteristic. The characteristic, of course, must be related to the outcome of the research. Let's revisit the experiment on reaction time and alcohol consumption. Suppose the researcher notes that the pool of participants includes some tennis players with superb reaction times. The researcher is concerned that, even with random assignment, more of the tennis players may be assigned to one condition than the other and that their natural abilities may affect the results. The researcher decides to use matching instead and to match all of the participants on reaction time. This is done by **pretesting** each participant with a reaction time test. A pretest is a test given before the independent variable is manipulated. When matching, the ideal pretest is the same task that will be used in the experiment. This isn't always possible, however; sometimes, introducing the participants to the task before the study makes the task too easy to complete during the study or otherwise confounds the results. In such cases, a similar but not identical task would be used. The least-preferred alternative is to pretest with a general test that is correlated with the dependent variable but is not especially similar to it.

Matching can be a useful technique, especially when a researcher has access to relatively few participants and can't depend on random assignment alone to yield equivalent experimental conditions. However, matching is not without its problems. It can be difficult or impossible to find adequate matches for each participant; consequently, some participants might need to be dropped from the study. By dropping participants, the researcher reduces the extent to which the sample is representative of the general population and increases the risk of a Type II error. More importantly, matching ensures that the experimental conditions are equivalent on only this one characteristic; the researcher hopes that all other characteristics that might affect the results are balanced by the use of random assignment. Despite these flaws, matching is preferable to the use of random assignment alone in certain situations.

Finally, a note should be made regarding the appropriate statistical procedures when groups have been matched. In matching, two or more groups are being compared. However, many researchers feel that the statistical tests used to measure the differences should be the same as those used to look for differences in performance when a single group of participants is tested two or more times. For more information about why this is so, you should consult a statistics textbook.

When the independent variable is a subject variable, the experimenter cannot randomly assign participants to different conditions. Consequently, the experimenter cannot manipulate this independent variable. For instance, a comparison of the replies of males and females to a question on sexual harassment can be very informative, but any difference in the replies between the genders cannot be assumed to be caused by gender. Other factors that correlate with gender—such as past experiences, socialization, or awareness of gender roles—may actually be causing the difference in replies.

A commonly occurring type of between-groups correlational study is called **cross-sectional design**. A cross-sectional design is typically used to look at differences between different age-groups. For instance, a researcher might be interested in how liberal or conservative voters of different ages rate themselves. The researcher might query voters who are 20-years-old, 40-years-old, 60-years-old, and 80-years-old. Perhaps the results suggest that the age-groups differ on their ratings on a liberal/ conservative scale. The researcher may hypothesize several reasons for this difference, including the varying environmental experiences of age-groups or even that the results suggest a developmental trend. Because the groups are not necessarily equivalent, however, the researcher cannot draw causal conclusions from the study.

Although they do not provide causal information, correlational studies are important contributors to the body of psychological knowledge;

they provide the only way to study many important issues, such as gender differences or the effects of early child abuse on development. In fact, many of the most interesting psychological questions are about the influence of subject variables on behavior. Thus, the contributions of correlational studies should not be underestimated. Moreover, when interpreting the results of a correlational study, it is always appropriate to suggest *possible* causal explanations for the results, and sometimes only one causal explanation is plausible. Only true experiments, however, yield results that can be causally interpreted with confidence.

Concept Question 5.2

Researchers identified individuals who regularly saved money and other individuals who rarely, if ever, saved money and asked both groups to rate their marital satisfaction. They found that those who saved money were more satisfied with their marriages and concluded that saving money causes this increase in satisfaction.

Are the researchers' conclusions well-founded? Are there other explanations for the results? How might the researchers design an experiment that would test their hypothesis that saving money affects marital satisfaction?

Control over Extraneous Variables

As we have seen, in order to draw a causal conclusion from the results of an experiment the experimenter must begin with equivalent groups. In addition, the experimenter must be able to control variables that could affect the outcome of the study. Variables that can affect the dependent variable are called **extraneous variables**. If an extraneous variable is present for one group in an experiment, but not (or not to the same degree) for the other, we cannot conclude that the change in the independent variable caused a difference in the dependent variable. It could be that differences between the groups on the dependent variable were caused by the change in the extraneous variable, by the change in the independent variable, or by both.

When extraneous variables change along with the independent variable, they provide alternative explanations for the results of the study. In that case, we say that we have obtained **confounded results**. For instance, suppose a researcher is studying the effects of noise on memory performance. The participants are randomly assigned to either the noise condition or the no-noise condition. Each participant puts on a set of headphones, through which those in the noise condition hear static and those in the no-noise condition hear nothing. After putting on the headphones, the participants in the no-noise condition study a list of 25 words for 2 minutes and those in the noise condition study a *different* list of words for 2 minutes. When the researcher tries to interpret the results, he or she encounters a problem: Is the difference in performance between the noise and no-noise conditions a result of the independent variable (noise), or a result of the difference between the lists, or a combination of the two? The researcher can't tell. To avoid this problem, the experimenter must plan ahead, identify potential confounds, and control their effects.

One way to control an extraneous variable is to hold it constant across all groups. That means that all groups in the study will have the same level of the extraneous variable. If gender is identified as an extraneous variable when studying the effect of room temperature on productivity, this extraneous variable could be controlled by limiting the study to participants of one gender; in this way, gender cannot change between room-temperature conditions, and any difference in productivity cannot be attributed to gender. An alternative approach is to balance gender within the study; that is, to ensure that the genders occur in similar proportions within each group. If the control group is 60% male and 40% female, then the experimental group should also be 60% male and 40% female.

It is important that extraneous variables be controlled by some means. Otherwise, the results of the experiment will be muddled, and the researcher will be unable to draw meaningful conclusions.

INTERNAL VALIDITY AND CONFOUNDS

Internal validity is the extent to which the design of an experiment ensures that the independent variable, and not some other variable or variables, caused a measured difference to the dependent variable. In other words, an internally valid study has no extraneous variables or other problems that would confound the results. As we have already seen, a **confound** is an extraneous variable or other flaws in the research design that yield alternative explanations for the results and thus limit a study's internal validity. Internal validity, therefore, is maximized by eliminating confounds. Experienced researchers automatically watch for some common confounds and design their studies so that these confounds are avoided or controlled. Let's take a look at several common confounds.

Experimenter Bias and Demand Characteristics

A researcher who has spent considerable time conceptualizing, developing, planning, and undertaking an experiment hopes that the results will be meaningful and useful. However, the researcher may unconsciously (or even consciously) affect the results of the experiment. The researcher may reinforce certain responses by the participant and ignore others or, when coding data, may consistently code ambiguous data so that they comply with the hypothesis being tested. When the researcher's expectations affect the outcome of a study, this confounding variable is called **experimenter bias**.

Participants in a study are not blank slates; they develop their own hypotheses about the purpose of the study and how the experimenter wants them to behave. Often these hypotheses are based on information provided by the experimenter, as well as by the setting of the experiment and by any rumors the participants may have heard about the study. These cues are called **demand characteristics**; if they are too powerful, they can control the outcome of an experiment. For instance, an experiment to identify the effects of alcohol on mood might include three groups of participants: those who have drunk enough alcohol to raise their BAL to .10; those who have drunk enough to raise their BAL to .05; and those who have not had any alcohol. If the participants in the first two groups know they are drinking alcohol, this knowledge itself might affect how they behave and rate their moods. The researcher would not know whether the moods of those in the alcohol conditions were the result of the alcohol or the participants' ideas about how they should feel after drinking alcohol.

Clearly, a researcher wishes to prevent both demand characteristics and experimenter bias from affecting the outcome of an experiment. This can often be accomplished by using a single-blind or a double-blind procedure. In a **single-blind procedure**, either the participants do not know which experimental condition they are in or the experimenter does not know. In a **double-blind procedure**, neither the experimenter nor the participants are aware of the experimental conditions to which particular participants have been assigned.

In the experiment on alcohol and mood, participants who know that they are in one of the alcohol groups might report being more relaxed than they actually feel; those who know they are in the control group might report feeling more tense than they are. If the participants are unaware of the group to which they have been assigned, the effects of the demand characteristics will be greatly diminished.

It may be just as important to keep the experimenter blind to the condition of the participant. The experimenter who expects alcohol to have a relaxing effect may be more likely to perceive relaxed behavior or to elicit responses from the participants who drank the alcohol that they are more relaxed. The experimenter may subtly reinforce responses consistent with his or her expectations or may simply act more relaxed with those in the alcohol groups than with those in the control group.

By using a double-blind procedure, in which neither the participant nor the experimenter knows whether the participant is in an experimental or control condition, the effects of both demand characteristics and experimenter bias can be minimized or eliminated.

Instrumentation Effects

Another threat to the internal validity of an experiment is called an **instrumentation effect**. An instrumentation effect occurs when the instrument used to measure the dependent variable changes in accuracy over time. Instrumentation effects can occur when mechanical equipment is used; for example, a measuring device may become less accurate with use. In addition, such effects may be introduced by the observer. The set of criteria adopted at the beginning of a series of observations may change somewhat as the observer becomes more experienced. The criteria may become more relaxed, or more stringent. Perhaps the observer becomes fatigued and less accurate over time. When the measuring device fails to measure in the same manner across participants, an instrumentation effect can be expected.

Subject Mortality

After volunteering to participate in an experiment and providing informed consent before it begins, some people quit part way through. This is known as **subject mortality** (or **subject attrition**).

Subject mortality can be categorized as either systematic or nonsystematic. **Nonsystematic subject mortality** occurs when participants leave a study (or their data cannot be used) for reasons unrelated to the experiment itself. For example, a participant may quit because the study is taking more time than expected, or a participant's data may be excluded because of equipment problems during the experimental session. Nonsystematic subject mortality is more of an annoyance than a threat to internal validity.

In the case of **systematic subject mortality**, the participants who quit are distributed unevenly among the various groups. This is a threat to the internal validity of the experiment, because the groups of participants that remain may no longer be equivalent. Suppose that smokers are asked to participate in an experiment investigating a new way to quit smoking. The participants are randomly assigned to either the experimental group, which receives nicotine-releasing patches to wear, or the control group, which is to quit cold turkey. The groups of participants are relatively equivalent; they include some people who are highly motivated to quit, some who are moderately motivated, and some who are only appeasing friends and family. Many of the low-motivation participants volunteered for the study because they thought they'd have the opportunity to try the nicotine patches. Upon finding that they have been assigned to the cold-turkey control group, they lose interest in the study and quit. Now the groups are no longer equivalent; while the experimental group still contains people of various levels of motivation, the control group has lost many of the low-motivation participants and consists primarily of those highly motivated to stop smoking.

Comparable Treatment of Groups

To maximize the internal validity of an experiment, the researcher must treat the experimental groups as similarly as possible, except for the manipulation of the independent variable. In other words, the experimenter must ensure **comparable treatment of groups**.

When an experiment involves individual testing of many participants, reliance on a single experimenter can often be too time-consuming. However, the internal validity of the experiment will be impaired if different experimenters test the different experimental groups. For example, if one experimenter tests the participants in the control group and one experimenter tests the participants in an experimental group, the experimenter becomes an extraneous variable that covaries with the independent variable. In other words, the use of two experimenters in this manner confounds the results; any difference between the groups could be a result of the change in the independent variable or the different experimenters.

This does not mean that all studies must be conducted by a single experimenter. Instead, the effect of the experimenter must be distributed evenly across the experimental conditions, which can be achieved by ensuring that all the experimenters are equally involved with all the experimental groups. For example, in a study with three experimental conditions and two experimenters, each experimenter would test half of the participants in each of the three groups. When experimenters are balanced across groups, any differences in the experimenters that might affect the dependent variable occur in both the experimental and control groups.

The experimenter needs to be alert to the confounding effect of other variables that covary with the independent variable. Examples may include the time of day that the groups are tested, the way the experimenter is dressed, the weather conditions, the day of the week, the point during the academic term, and many more. If any variable is considerably different for one group than for the others, the experimenter should consider the possibility that the results have been confounded. With some foresight, however, the effect of extraneous variables can be distributed across conditions.

Sensitivity of the Dependent Variable

Balancing potential confounding variables will maintain the internal validity of an experiment, but it may cause another problem. Because balancing allows an experimenter to distribute the effect of an extraneous variable across the experimental conditions, it also tends to increase the amount of error variance in the study. As we saw in chapter 4, **error variance** is the natural, random fluctuation in scores caused by factors other than the independent variable. The greater the amount of error variance in a study, the more difficult it is to identify consistent differences in performance between groups. The ratio of between-groups variance to within-group variance is small when error variance is great. (You might review parts of chapter 4 if you need to.) For example, suppose that a researcher is studying the effect of caffeine on cognitive abilities. Half of the participants drink a caffeinated beverage before solving a series of puzzles; half drink a decaffeinated beverage. To finish the study in half the time, the researcher uses two test rooms. Half of the participants in each of the conditions are tested in a room that happens to have a large window; half are tested in a room that has no windows. Whether the room has windows might affect the participants' performances, but this effect will be spread across both the caffeine and no-caffeine conditions and will be seen only as error variance among the scores. However, this increase in error variance can be a problem. Greater error variance means that a greater and more consistent difference between the group scores is required before the effect of caffeine can be regarded as statistically significant. Therefore, distributing the effect of an extraneous variable across conditions can actually make it more difficult to reject the null hypothesis, because it increases the error variance among the data.

This increase in error variance may be taken into account by including it as an additional independent variable in the experiment. A study with two or more independent variables is called a factorial design (see chapter 7) and can be used to investigate the effect of an otherwise extraneous variable. When it is not feasible to include the extraneous variable as another independent variable (perhaps because several independent variables have already been included in the design), the researcher needs to consider carefully whether the increased error variance will be problematic. If that is the case, a preferable solution may be to control the variable by holding it constant at one level instead of balancing it on two or more levels across groups.

When designing an experiment, the researcher must not only minimize error variance but also pay attention to the **sensitivity of the dependent variable**. It is important to choose a dependent variable that will be sensitive enough to detect differences between the experimental conditions. An insensitive measure will fail to detect a difference between the experimental groups even when there is one. For example, measuring the weights of premature and full-term infants to the nearest ounce instead of the nearest gram may not be sensitive enough to detect differences between the groups.

Sometimes an insensitive measurement tool will tend to yield mostly high scores or mostly low scores. When a dependent variable yields scores near the top limit of the measurement tool for one or all groups, the experimenter is said to have found a **ceiling effect**. Similarly, if the dependent variable yields scores near the lower limit of the measurement tool for one or all groups, the experimenter has found a **floor effect**. Ceiling and floor effects are not desirable. If the experimental group and control group recall approximately the same number of words, and neither group recalls many words at all (or recalls all of the words), the task was probably too difficult (or too easy) for both groups, and any effect of the independent variable cannot be determined.

Concept Question 5.3

A researcher investigates the effectiveness of a new diet program. Participants wishing to lose weight are randomly assigned to either the control group or the diet-program group. The control participants are told to try to lose weight on their own. The diet-program group is provided with educational material, complete menus, and free diet-program foods. After one month, each participant is weighed and the number of pounds lost is recorded.

What potential confounds might affect the results of this study? What improvements would you propose?

SUMMARY

Experiments are the cornerstone of the scientific method. The primary advantage of experiments over other types of research is that they yield causal results; that is, the researcher can conclude that any change in the dependent variable was caused by the manipulation of the independent variable.

The most common type of experiment uses two or more separate groups of participants; this is called a between-groups design. However, not all studies using between-groups designs are experiments. If the independent variable cannot be manipulated but can only be chosen, it is called a subject variable and cannot be studied within an experiment. For subject variables, the between-groups design yields correlational studies, which simply demonstrate relationships among variables.

When developing a research project on the basis of a between-groups design, the researcher must maximize the study's internal validity by avoiding confounds. Confounds cause the results of the research to be ambiguous. Common confounds include nonequivalent groups, selection bias, experimenter bias, demand characteristics, instrumentation effects, and subject mortality.

Careful choice of a dependent variable is essential to a successful research project. The variable chosen must be sensitive enough to demonstrate an effect of the independent variable. Experimenters should avoid floor and ceiling effects, which occur when all participants tend to score very low or very high, respectively.

IMPORTANT TERMS AND CONCEPTS

between-groups research design	floor effect
ceiling effect	instrumentation effect
comparable treatment of groups	internal validity
confound	matching
confounded results	nonsystematic subject mortality
correlational study	placebo
cross-sectional design	pretesting
demand characteristics	random assignment
double-blind procedure	selection bias
error variance	sensitivity of the dependent variable
experimenter bias	single-blind procedure
experiments	subject mortality (or subject attrition)
extraneous variables	systematic subject mortality

EXERCISES

1. To compare two methods for teaching statistics, an instructor taught the statistics course using a lecture/discussion format during the fall semester but adopted a self-paced, independent-study approach in the spring semester. Each class was given the same final exam, and the results suggested that the students in the self-paced class performed better than those in the lecture/discussion class. The instructor concluded that the superior performance of the self-paced class was caused by the teaching technique and decided to teach statistics in this manner from then on.

   a. Was this a true experiment or a correlational study? Explain.

   b. Are there any confounds and alternative explanations for these results?

   c. Design a better study to test this instructor's question.

2. To discover whether males or females spend more money in an average week, two students solicit information from a random sample of males and females on their campus. They find that males spent more money than females. Why is this a correlational study and not an experiment? Is it possible to test this question using a between-groups design?

3. A drug company has developed a new antihistamine and wishes to compare it to the leading over-the-counter brand. Design a between-groups experiment that compares these two antihistamines. Be sure to operationally define your independent and dependent variables, and of course avoid confounds.

4. A researcher wishes to know if people are more likely to save money that they have earned, that they have worked for but didn't expect to receive, or that they have found. Design a between-groups experiment that will test this question.

5. What is the difference between controlling for an extraneous variable and balancing it? What are the advantages and disadvantages of each?

6. For each confound presented in the chapter, give an example of a study where this confound is a problem and provide a way to improve the study.

7. In an experiment, I measured the time required to read ambiguous and nonambiguous sentences. Because participants in both groups had difficulty reading the sentences from a computer screen, each sentence had a reading time of approximately 1 second. What do I call this problem?

ANSWERS TO CONCEPT QUESTIONS AND ODD-NUMBERED EXERCISES

Note: There will often be more than one correct answer for each of these questions. Consult with your instructor about your own answers.

Concept Question 5.1

Your heads and tails groups should become increasingly more similar as your sample sizes become larger. In other words, the number of pennies, dimes, and nickels in each group might be quite different when you only have two of each type of coin in your study, but as the number of coins increase the number of pennies, nickels, and dimes in each group should become closer and closer to the same number.

Concept Question 5.2

The research conclusions are not well-founded. The researchers conducted a correlational study and found a relationship between saving money and marital satisfaction, but they do not have enough evidence to conclude that saving money caused marital satisfaction. It may be that being satisfied in marriage makes it easier to save money, or that both saving and marital satisfaction are related to some third variable—perhaps a personality characteristic such that some individuals tend to be satisfied in their marriages and also tend to save money.

The researchers might design an experiment in which they randomly assign couples to the savings group and the spending group. The couples in the savings group would agree to save 10% of their income each month for six months, while those in the spending group would agree not to save any money for six months. At the end of the six months, the marital satisfaction of each couple would be measured, and the overall satisfaction of each group would be compared.

Concept Question 5.3

This study might be susceptible to nonsystematic mortality effects, experimenter bias, and demand characteristics, as well as other confounds. The researcher might want to pinpoint an aspect of the diet program that he or she wishes to assess—such as the complete menus—and then vary the groups on only this factor. Otherwise, participants who know they are in the control group may be less motivated to continue in the study or less motivated to lose weight since they might think that the researcher expects them to show little change. Also, the person who weighs the participants should not know the condition to which each person has been assigned.

Exercises

1. a. Correlational study. The participants were not randomly assigned to the teaching technique conditions.

   b. The students in the spring semester may have been smarter than those in the fall course; the instructor may have been more inspiring using the self-paced technique; the students in the self-paced class may have tried harder because of the demand characteristics of the situation.

   c. Ideally, students would be randomly assigned to the different teaching techniques. Also, it would be good to have more than one instructor in the experiment, with each instructor using both techniques.

3. In this study, I would investigate the effect of the new antihistamine and the highest-selling brand of antihistamine on the participants' rated feelings of wellness. Each participant would be randomly assigned to either the new-drug condition or the leading-brand condition; the participants, however, would not know to which condition they had been assigned. The research assistants conducting the experiment would also be unaware of the conditions to which the participants had been assigned. The participants would take the medication and then be exposed to a wide array of allergy-provoking pollens. After one hour, the participants would rate how well they felt on a scale of 1 (not feeling well at all) to 10 (feeling very well).

5. Controlling for an extraneous variable requires limiting the variable to only one level. For instance, a researcher might have the opportunity to use two rooms to conduct some research, but there is a distinct possibility that the room itself could affect the outcome (for example, if one has a window and the other doesn't). The researcher could control this extraneous variable by conducting the entire study in one room. Balancing an extraneous variable involves spreading the potential effect of the extraneous variable across the experimental conditions. The researcher might use both rooms to conduct the research, but he or she should be sure that participants from every condition in the study participate in each room. The researcher must avoid having all the participants from one condition in one room and all the participants from the other condition in the other room.

7. A ceiling effect.

The Within-Subjects Design

In many experiments, separate groups of participants receive different treatments, or levels of the independent variable, and the researcher looks for differences *between* the groups on the dependent variable. That is a description of a between-groups design. But in a between-groups design the experimental groups differ not only on the independent variable, but also on a number of uncontrolled variables, and this contributes to the error variance. The greater the error variance, the more difficult it is to detect a significant effect for the independent variable.

Researchers can reduce the amount of error variance in a study in a number of ways, such as by carefully controlling extraneous variables, as discussed in chapter 5. Another way the error variance can be reduced is by using the same participants in all of the experimental conditions. For example, if a researcher were interested in the effect of color on mood, participants might be asked to complete a mood-rating task after sitting in a blue room for 15 minutes. On another day, the same participants might sit in a red room for 15 minutes and then again complete the mood-rating task. In this case, the researcher can search for changes in the dependent variable (mood) that can be attributed to the independent variable (room color) by looking for changes *within* the participants' data. An investigation in which each participant receives each level of the independent variable at least once is called a **within-subjects design.**

TYPES OF WITHIN-SUBJECTS DESIGNS

Two important types of within-subjects designs are the pretest-posttest design and the repeated-measures design. In a **pretest-posttest design**, one group of participants is tested two or more times using the same measurement tool, once before and once after the independent variable is manipulated in some way. For example, a researcher may wish to investigate the effect of exercise on mood by having participants rate their moods before and after a moderate workout. The participants' mood ratings involve a pretest (a rating prior to the exercise) and a posttest (a rating after the exercise). Pretest-posttest designs typically involve only two test scores per participant; a **repeated-measures design**, as the name suggests, involves multiple measurements per participant.

A type of within-subjects design related to the repeated-measures design is called a **longitudinal design**. This type of study involves, like the repeated-measures design, testing participants multiple times, but a longitudinal design looks for changes that occur over time, thus, its duration can often be months or years, sometimes decades. My son, as an infant, toddler, and pre-schooler, was a participant in a longitudinal study that focused on language development. Beginning as an infant, followed by intervals of several months and then yearly, I would complete numerous questionnaires addressing his language and comprehension skills as well as his health. Just recently I received a follow-up survey to one I'd taken 10 years ago on walking, fitness, and health issues. From the question asking for the name and address of someone who would know my whereabouts in 10 years I suspect they are planning to continue this study for at least another decade.

Longitudinal studies are often combined with cross-sectional studies in which several groups differing in age (or another factor that varies with time) are tested at one time (see chapter 5). Used together, these designs can give a fuller picture than either design can alone.

Not all within-subject designs require multiple testing of the participants. Studies in which a researcher is measuring an effect using two or more types of stimuli or materials may also be within-subjects designs and may only require a single testing situation. For instance, suppose a researcher is interested in individuals' recall of concrete and abstract words. Participants are asked to study a single list of 20 words (10 concrete nouns and 10 abstract nouns) for 3 minutes and then given a recall test. The researcher will calculate two scores for each person: the number of concrete nouns recalled and the number of abstract nouns recalled. The researcher will compare the number of concrete words recalled with the number of abstract words recalled. Because each participant has more than one score (although he or she was only tested once) this investigation is a type of repeated-measures design.

BENEFITS OF THE WITHIN-SUBJECTS DESIGN

Within-subjects designs are very popular among researchers for some very good reasons. Typically, within-subjects designs require fewer participants than between-groups designs; they often take less time; subject variables remain constant across the experimental conditions; and, relatedly, the error variance is reduced, so that the test is more powerful. Let's consider these factors in more detail.

Fewer participants are needed because the participants perform in each of the experimental conditions. Suppose that a study involves two levels of an independent variable and the researcher wishes to have 12 participants in each level. Therefore, 24 participants would be required for a between-groups design, or 12 in each group. If a within-subjects design can be used, however, only 12 participants will be needed, because each person will participate in both experimental conditions.

In some types of research, such as perceptual research, the participants' task takes so little time—perhaps less than a second—that the participant can perform in each experimental condition not just once but numerous times. In this case, each participant's data can be analyzed as a miniature experiment; the researcher not only can look for differences among the experimental conditions, but is also able to determine whether there are significant differences in performance among the participants.

An important advantage of the within-subjects design is the low level of error variance, which results in a more powerful test of the effect of the independent variable. A researcher using a powerful design has a relatively low likelihood of making a Type II error—that is, they are unlikely to fail to find a significant difference that actually exists. A within-subjects design is more powerful than a between-groups design because, typically, the same participants perform in all of the experimental conditions. In other words, the participants serve as their own control group; this reduces the amount of error variance between the conditions.

Consider two experiments on sleep deprivation and cognitive abilities. The first experimenter chooses a between-groups design. One sample of participants sleeps for 8 hours in a sleep lab and, upon awakening, performs the digit-span test (a memory test in which the participants must repeat increasingly long lists of numbers, half the time in the order presented and half the time in reverse order). A second sample of participants sleeps for only 4 hours in the sleep lab and, like the previous group, performs the digit-span test upon awakening.

Suppose that the mean score on the digit-span is lower for the 4-hour group than for the 8-hour group. However, when the researcher conducts the appropriate statistical test, the null hypothesis cannot be rejected. Why might this be? It is possible that there really is no difference in digit-span performance between the two groups, but it's also possible that the researcher has made a Type II error—that a difference exists between the populations, but it was not detected using this design. As we know, a Type II error is more likely when there is substantial error variance among the scores. Although the two experimental conditions vary in number of hours slept, the participants in each group also vary in other ways. Some of the participants can perform well with relatively little sleep, others can't function without at least 9 hours of sleep. Some of the participants could be morning people, while others are more alert in the evenings. Some have slept well in the lab, others found the lab distracting and slept poorly. All of these factors and more would contribute to the error variance, both within each group of participants and between the groups; and an increase in error variance restricts our ability to detect a significant difference between the means.

Our second researcher chooses to test the same hypothesis using a within-subjects design. In this study, each participant sleeps in the lab on two occasions, for 8 hours on one occasion and for 4 hours on the other. (Half the people sleep 4 hours the first night, and half sleep 8 hours the first night.) As in the previous study, the participants take the digit-span test each morning upon awakening.

This is a more powerful experiment than the first, and thus the researcher is less likely to make a Type II error. Although the participants still vary on how much sleep they need, whether they slept well or poorly, and whether they perform better in the morning or evening, these subject variables affect only the variance within each condition. Because the same participants are in both conditions, the subject variables are held constant. In addition, the inferential statistical tests used with within-subjects designs account for the variance caused by each subject and subtract that from the error variance. Usually, the amount of error variance that remains is rather small.

Because of their power and efficiency, within-subjects designs are very popular and useful to researchers. But they are not without their flaws and are not suitable for all research problems.

Concept Question 6.1

A researcher wants to conduct a study that has three conditions. The researcher wants 20 scores in each condition. If each participant receives each condition once, how many participants would be needed for a within-subjects design? How many would be needed for a between-groups design?

DISADVANTAGES OF THE WITHIN-SUBJECTS DESIGN

If within-subjects designs were flawless, no one would use a between-groups design. But a number of problems detract from the value of the within-subjects design. For example, within-subjects designs are susceptible to confounds caused by demand characteristics; carryover effects, such as practice or fatigue from doing the same task a number of times; and side effects of events that occur during the course of the study. Let's take a look at these problems.

Having agreed to be in a study, a participant tries to determine what is expected of her or him and typically tries to cooperate. A participant derives information about what is expected from cues called **demand characteristics**. Because participants in a within-subjects design perform in all of the experimental conditions, they have a greater opportunity to determine the purpose of the investigation, which can lead to a deliberate change in behavior. Therefore, a within-subjects design is especially susceptible to the disabling effects of demand characteristics. For instance, if a researcher asks participants to rate their moods before and after moderate exercise, the participants probably will not only realize that the researcher wants to know if exercise affects mood, but will suspect that the researcher expects to find that their moods are elevated after exercise. Purposely or not, the participants might modify their mood ratings so as to be consistent with what they think the researcher wants. The researcher can't know whether the results reflect the participants' true moods or are the effect of demand characteristics.

One way to minimize the likelihood of demand characteristics is to hide the true reason for the experiment. For example, the researcher might request information on a number of topics before and after exercise. The participants might be asked how secure their finances are or what their favorite foods are, as well as being asked to rate their moods. As a result, the participants may be less certain about the purpose of the study and less likely to change their behavior in a consistent manner.

Other problems may arise in a within-subjects design if the participants are required to perform the same task repeatedly. When participants perform a task numerous times, their performance on earlier trials might affect their performance on later trials. This is called a **carryover effect**. If the task is difficult enough, through repetition the participant's performance may improve; this type of carryover effect is called a **practice effect**. On the other hand, if required to do the task often enough, the participant may become tired or merely bored. The type of carryover effect in which performance declines with repetition is referred to as a **fatigue effect**. Changes caused by practice or by fatigue can confound a study unless special care is taken to distribute their potential effects among the experimental conditions by counterbalancing the order of the conditions—for example, by alternating the order of tasks—or, if several types of materials are presented, by presenting them in a random order.

Carryover effects and demand characteristics can confound the results and render a study uninterpretable. Yet, these potential confounds can usually be foreseen, and the researcher can take measures to eliminate them. Sometimes, however, an unexpected problem during the study confounds the results. In some within-subjects designs, participants are asked to remain in the study for a considerable amount of time—days, weeks, or even years. If an event occurs during the course of the investigation that affects the participants' performance on the dependent measure, a **history effect** is present. A history effect is the result of an event that occurs outside the experiment at the same time that the independent variable is being changed.

Imagine a study addressing the effects of caffeine on anxiety levels. The participants, college students, are asked to monitor their coffee intake and anxiety levels for a month. Each week, they are given a supply of ground coffee. The coffee is either decaffeinated, partially decaffeinated, or contains caffeine, but (to avoid demand characteristics) is provided in unmarked canisters. However, in designing the study, the researchers were unaware that the week that some of the participants were provided with caffeinated coffee was also the week of most midterm exams. As the researchers expected, the anxiety scores during the weeklong consumption of caffeinated coffee were higher than those during the other weeks, but they cannot know whether the elevation in the scores was caused by the coffee, the exams, or both.

Another problem is that when participants are tested over a considerable period, their scores may change simply because of the passage of time rather than any effect of the independent variable. Such a change in performance is called a **maturation effect**. Maturation refers to any changes in behavior caused by the passage of time—for example, by growing older or just by growing hungrier (Campbell & Stanley, 1963).

When participants are tested repeatedly, their experience on a previous test is likely to affect the results of their next test; this is called a **testing effect**. People who repeat standardized tests such as the Graduate Record Exam or an intelligence test find that their scores are higher the second time. This is not because they have gotten smarter between testings; rather, they have a better idea of what to expect, what the questions will be like, how to pace themselves, and so on. This effect is also seen in personality testing and, to some degree, in tests of prejudice and social attitude (Campbell & Stanley, 1963). In research, a testing effect can make a small difference look larger; if the expectation is that scores will decrease, a testing effect can leave the researcher with no significant difference.

When the likelihood of any of these confounds—history, maturation, and testing effects—is substantial, the only way to assess their impact may be to redesign the study as a between-groups design, with a control group.

Occasionally, you will read about a study where people who scored very high (or very low) on a test participated in some type of treatment and were then retested. Lo and behold, the participants' scores changed, and the mean for the sample moved closer to the population mean. Studies of this type look impressive to the layperson inexperienced in research design. But frankly, their results may be due in large part to a natural phenomenon called **regression toward the mean**.

In regression toward the mean, people with extreme scores, when retested, spontaneously have less extreme scores; this may occur with no treatment whatsoever. It is related to our old foe, error variance. Each score reflects both the true score—the score that would be recorded in the purest of situations—and some error variability. If someone scores extremely high on an IQ test, it is most likely in part because the person is very intelligent (this component reflects his or her true score) and in part because the person was feeling alert, wasn't hungry, wasn't distracted, and was able to give his or her full attention to the test. In other words, all of the other little things that affect performance on a test were in this person's favor. Now, if that person retakes the test (or a different form of the test) a few weeks later, chances are that the extraneous variables won't all be quite so favorable. The person is no less intelligent, but the score is likely to decrease. This decrease is natural regression toward the mean.

Unfortunately, research that is confounded by regression toward the mean is occasionally published. Suppose that volunteers are given a test of some type—perhaps a body-image distortion test—and those with the highest scores are asked to participate in a research project. The project involves a new treatment to decrease body-image distortion, in which the participants are presented with pictures of models who are of normal size—that is, not especially slim. After looking at these pictures, the participants are retested, and their scores on body-image distortion are now lower. With this design, there is no way to determine whether the scores decreased because of the treatment, because of regression toward the mean, or because of both. In chapter 10, we will discuss research designs called quasi-experimental designs that avoid regression toward the mean, so that studies of this type, with some modifications, can provide useful data. Also, not all scores are equally susceptible to regression toward the mean. How much a person wins in the lottery is likely to be very susceptible to regression, but how much a person weighs is not likely to regress much at all over a short period of time.

Finally, within-subjects designs cannot be used to study the effect of subject variables for the simple reason that a participant can't experience one level of a subject variable in one testing session and then experience a different level at another session. You cannot be short today and then tall tomorrow, or male at 2:00 AM and female at 2:05 AM.

Although within-subjects designs are not foolproof, most of their flaws can be avoided, or minimized, with some forethought. The result can be a very powerful and efficient approach to a research question.

Concept Question 6.2

In a study, participants are asked to read sentences from a computer screen so that their reading speed may be measured. Some of the sentences contain ambiguous words. In the second half of the study, the sentences are preceded by a short paragraph that provides additional context for the ambiguous words. The researcher finds that participants read the sentences preceded by context more rapidly than they read those without context. What might be confounding the results of this study?

COUNTERBALANCING

Presenting experimental conditions to all participants in the same order can create confounds, and these confounds can make research results worthless. However, confounds can be avoided through counterbalancing. **Counterbalancing** involves presenting the experimental conditions to participants in different orders so that carryover effects (sometimes referred to as order effects) can be controlled. This counterbalancing is accomplished by developing either a complete within-subjects design or an incomplete within-subjects design.

Complete Within-Subjects Design

In a **complete within-subjects design**, all the participants perform in each experimental condition several times until they have each received all possible orders of the conditions. This means that the data from any one participant can be interpreted as a miniature research project. Together, data from several participants demonstrate that any effect noted is reliable and generalizable.

Because all possible orders are experienced by each participant, any effects that might be associated with presenting conditions in a specific order, including practice effects, are counterbalanced by presenting the conditions in the opposite order to the same participant.

ABBA Counterbalancing

The simplest complete within-subjects design involves only two experimental conditions, which we will refer to as conditions A and B.

For a complete within-subjects design, each participant experiences condition A followed by B and B followed by A; therefore, this technique is called **ABBA counterbalancing**. The ABBA sequence can be repeated as many times as necessary. For example, with three iterations the participant would experience the conditions in the following order: ABBAAB-BAABBA. By presenting the A condition both first and last, this technique controls for practice effects; thus, any advantage or disadvantage condition A may have by being first in the order is counterbalanced because it also occurs last in the sequence.

The ABBA technique is very useful if practice affects performance linearly—that is, if performance gradually improves or gradually deteriorates. If performance is not linear—for instance, if it increases sharply and then remains steady—the ABBA technique may be a poor choice for counterbalancing. If performance increases sharply at the beginning of testing, the first condition in the test would be at such a distinct disadvantage that its repetition at the end could not remedy the situation. In such cases, researchers will often present a number of practice trials until the participant reaches a steady state of performance, and then begin the ABBA technique. Examples of a linear and nonlinear practice effect are shown in figure 6.1.

Figure 6.1   Graphs of linear and nonlinear practice effects

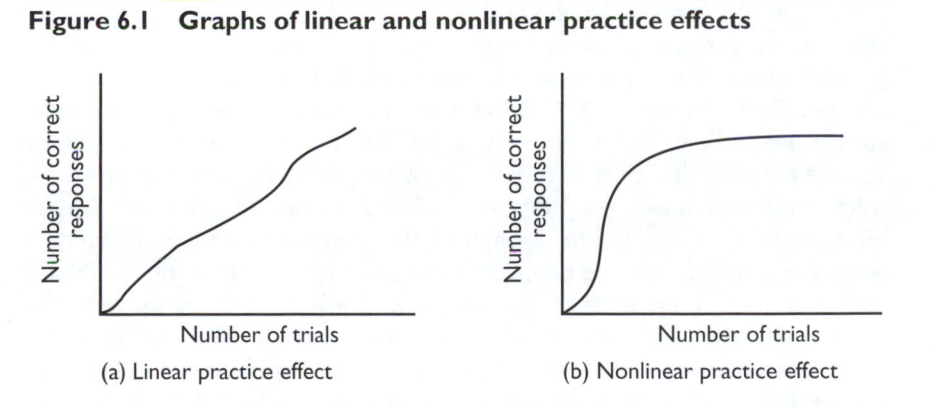

(a) Linear practice effect   (b) Nonlinear practice effect

In the ABBA technique, the conditions are presented in a standard order. This may be a problem if the participants realize that an ABBA order is being used and anticipate which condition is next. For example, a participant who knows that the next task involves responding as quickly as possible to a word on the screen may respond more rapidly than if he or she weren't anticipating the task. This is analogous to a false start in a race when runners anticipate the gunshot after "get ready... get set. ..." The runners are responding to their knowledge and not to the gunshot and, as a result, they actually start running before the gun goes off. If the participant is likely to know what condition is occurring next, and if this information can affect performance, the ABBA technique should not be used.

Block Randomization

An alternative to the ABBA technique is called **block randomization**. In block randomization, blocks of conditions are presented in random order. A block of conditions consists of a single presentation of each of the conditions in the study—each block is a unique ordering of the conditions. Thus, if there are three conditions (A, B, and C) in a study, the possible blocks are: ABC, CBA, BAC, CAB, ACB, and BCA. These blocks are then presented to each participant numerous times in a random order. The blocks are presented a sufficient number of times such that each condition occurs about equally often in each ordinal position. In other words, A is first, second, and third about equally often; B is first, second, and third about equally often; and C is first, second, and third about equally often. If there were three conditions and block randomization were used, each participant might receive the conditions in the following order: ABC BCA BCA CBA CAB BAC ACB. Enough blocks must be presented to let randomization do its job and counterbalance for practice effects. Using only a few blocks won't suffice.

To make block randomization a little clearer, let's consider an example. Suppose a researcher is conducting an experiment to determine the effect of background color on reading speed. There are three conditions. In the first condition, participants read white letters against a black background (B); in the second condition, they read white letters against a blue background (BL); and in the third condition they read white letters against a green background (G). Each participant will participate in each color condition numerous times, and these color conditions will be organized in blocks. In any block, each of the three conditions is presented once; for example, in one block, the presentation of letters on the black background is followed by the presentation of letters on the green background and then by the presentation of letters on the blue background. Altogether, there are six combinations of the three conditions. Each participant will receive a block of the three conditions followed by more randomly chosen blocks of conditions. Box 6.1 presents a possible order for the participants in this study. The blocks are numbered 1–6. By choosing numbers 1–6 from a random-numbers table, the researcher can establish a random order for the blocks, so that each condition is presented 12 times and all of the possible sequences of the conditions are used at least once.

Block randomization is useful for creating a complete within-subjects design in a case where there are more than two conditions and participation in each condition is not especially time-consuming. With three conditions, there are six possible ways to order these conditions; it is quite reasonable to ask participants to commit to a study that involves six

---

Box 6.1

A Possible Random Order of Blocks for a Three-Condition Study Using Block Randomization

Blocks

(1) *B BL G*   (2) *B G BL*   (3) *BL G B*
(4) *BL B G*   (5) *G BL B*   (6) *G B BL*

Random Order of Blocks
1 2 5 3 6 2 3 1 5 5 4 3

---

orders of three conditions if testing does not take much time. However, if the experiment involves four conditions, the number of possible orders increases to 24; with five conditions, the number of possible orders is 120. It is still conceivable to ask participants to judge five stimuli presented in 120 different orders if the task takes no more than a few seconds. But, if the time commitment required of a participant per condition is too long to expect them to give their best for the duration of the study under a complete within-subjects design, it might be worth considering an incomplete within-subjects design.

Incomplete Within-Subjects Design

Often, the participant cannot be expected to remain in the study for as long as the block randomization technique would require, and the ABBA technique may not be appropriate either. In these situations, an **incomplete within-subjects design** is used. In such designs, each participant receives a unique order of the conditions at least once, but does not receive all possible sequences of the conditions. With an incomplete within-subjects design, the number of participants needs to be sufficient to counterbalance potential fatigue and practice effects.

One incomplete within-subjects technique is called **random order with rotation**. In this technique, the experimental conditions are ordered randomly, and the first participant receives this order. The first condition is then moved to the last place in this sequence and all of the other conditions are shifted up one, producing a new order that the second participant receives. Then, all the conditions are moved one place forward again (the condition that was in first place is shifted to last place), with the resulting order used for the third participant. This rotation continues until each condition has occupied each position in the sequence. For example, if four conditions exist in an experiment (ABCD), the first participant receives a random ordering of these conditions, such as BCAD. The second participant receives CADB; the third participant receives ADBC; and the fourth participant receives DBCA. The next rotation leads us back to the original random ordering, BCAD.

Because there are four conditions in our example, there are four orderings of the conditions. The number of participants chosen for this study should then be a multiple of four so that each condition appears in each ordinal position (first, second, third, or fourth) an equal number of times across the study. Thus, a researcher designing a study with four conditions would want to have 4, 8, 12, 16, 20, or more participants, as long as the total is evenly divisible by four.

How many participants is optimum for a particular experiment depends on the strength of the effect being studied and the sensitivity of the dependent measure. Fewer participants are required to study a strong effect using a sensitive dependent measure than to study a weak effect on the basis of a relatively insensitive dependent measure. In other words, the former study has more Power and is thus less likely to lead to a Type II error. In the latter study, the probability of making a Type II error can be reduced by increasing the number of participants.

The balanced Latin square (or simply **Latin square**) technique may also be used to counterbalance practice effects in an incomplete within-subjects design. In this technique, the researcher presents each condition in each ordinal position and also presents each condition before and after each other condition. The number of orderings necessary is equal to the number of conditions in the study; thus, if each order is written on a separate line, a square is formed.

Setting up a Latin square can be something of a brain teaser. Some people enjoy the challenge, others find it frustrating and tiresome. One solution for a Latin square involving four conditions is as follows:

ABCD
BDAC
CADB
DCBA

There is a procedure that I present at the end of the chapter for creating Latin squares that can be used with any even number of conditions, but it's nearly as cumbersome as figuring out the square from scratch.

The Latin square comes out square when there is an even number of conditions. When there is an odd number of conditions a rectangle is constructed with twice as many orderings (thus, a 5-condition study needs 10 different orders of the conditions to complete counterbalance for order and position relative to the other conditions). While it can be a trick to create it is a useful technique for counterbalancing practice and fatigue effects.[1]

---

[1] In practice, any incomplete counterbalancing that completely controls for position is often called a Latin square, although it doesn't actually meet all of the criteria.

Concept Question 6.3

Can you create a solution for a study with six conditions?

As in designs based on a random order with rotation, the number of participants chosen for a Latin square design should be a multiple of the number of conditions. Again, the precise number of participants depends on the Power of the study.

Thus, incomplete and complete within-subjects designs allow the researcher to conduct an efficient investigation while controlling for practice and fatigue effects.

Sometimes, however, carryover effects cannot be dealt with by counterbalancing. Imagine a memory researcher who wishes to test the effectiveness of a mnemonic technique involving imagery. The researcher can introduce participants to the control condition (simple memorization without instruction), instruct them in the use of the mnemonic, and then conduct the mnemonic condition. However, the researcher cannot expect to get the same results if the participants first experience the mnemonic condition and then the control condition. The participants cannot unlearn the imagery mnemonic and, once they have learned something that works, why would they not use it in the control condition? Of course, the researcher could instruct the participants not to use the mnemonic, but this presents obvious demand characteristic problems. Telling someone not to make an image is much like telling someone not to think of a pink elephant. (I bet you thought of one.) In some circumstances, using a within-subjects design will lead to unavoidable confounds, and in that case the study needs to be redesigned on the basis of a between-groups design.

SUMMARY

In this chapter, we discussed the within-subjects design. In a within-subjects design, participants are involved in all of the experimental conditions. The advantage of the within-subjects design is that it reduces error variance and thus can provide a more powerful statistical test of a hypothesis than a between-groups design.

Within-subjects designs are not without their pitfalls, however. The design may be susceptible to confounding caused by demand characteristics. Or, because the participant performs the same task in a number of experimental conditions, often many times in a row, carryover effects such as practice or fatigue effects may be encountered. Carryover effects occur whenever participants' experience in one condition affects their performance in another condition. If carryover effects are present, interpretation of the data may be impossible, and a between-groups design might be more appropriate. Another potential problem, especially when testing is carried out over a relatively long period of time, is that an event occurring outside of the experiment may affect the participants' performance on the dependent measure; this is called a history effect. Finally, unless carefully developed, a study based on a within-subjects design may be susceptible to regression toward the mean. In this confound, apparent changes in the dependent measure scores are actually the result of a natural tendency for extreme scores to become less extreme with retesting.

A researcher can avoid many potential confounds by designing the study carefully and counterbalancing the order of presentation of the experimental conditions. In a complete within-subjects design, all of the

A Procedure for Creating a Latin Square

There is a general solution for creating a Latin square with an even number of conditions. Let's consider an example with 8 conditions that we'll label with the letters of the alphabet: A B C D E F G H. To establish the first row we follow this pattern:

first condition, second condition, last condition, third condition, second-to-last condition, fourth condition, third-to-last condition, fifth condition (this pattern could be continued for situations with more than eight conditions).

For this example the first row is:

ABHCGDFE

Remember that each condition is labeled alphabetically. To create the second ordering, each letter of the alphabet is replaced by the next letter in the alphabet, so A becomes B, B becomes C, C becomes D, etc. For the last condition, in this case H, the H becomes an A. So, the second row becomes:

BCADHEGF

Drawn together the rows look like this:

ABHCGDFE
BCADHEGF

Perhaps you can sense a pattern developing here. You continue increasing each letter by one alphabetically (except for the final condition, H, which reverts to the first condition, A) and you do this for each row. Perhaps more easily, you can begin to write this small portion of the alphabet vertically in each column. Thus, the first column becomes ABCDEFGH. The second column has started as B, then C, and continues as DEFGHA. Either way, eventually, you will have a full square:

ABHCGDFE
BCADHEGF
CDBEAFHG
DECFBGAH
EFDGCHBA
FGEHDACB
GHFAEBDC
HAGBFCED

participants receive all possible orders of the conditions. Such designs include ABBA counterbalancing and block randomization. In an incomplete within-subjects design, each participant receives all of the conditions, but not in all of the possible orders. Such designs include random order with rotation and the Latin square.

IMPORTANT TERMS AND CONCEPTS

ABBA counterbalancing
block randomization
carryover effect
complete within-subjects design
counterbalancing
demand characteristics
fatigue effect
history effect
incomplete within-subjects design
Latin square

longitudinal design
maturation effect
practice effect
pretest-posttest design
random order with rotation
regression toward the mean
repeated-measures design
testing effect
within-subjects design

EXERCISES

1. A researcher is developing an idea for a research project in which satisfaction ratings on three types of cars are compared. The participants will drive a car for 20 minutes and then rate the car on a satisfaction scale. The researcher wishes to have 18 satisfaction ratings for each car.

   a. How many participants would be needed for a between-groups design? How many participants would be needed for a within-subjects design?

   b. Assuming that the participants don't wish to participate for much more than an hour, explain how you would design this investigation on the basis of a within-subjects design while controlling for order effects. Would you be using a complete or an incomplete within-subjects design?

   c. Determine an order of the vehicles for each of the participants if the researcher uses an incomplete within-subjects design.

2. Students at a university have the option to live in a residence hall that aims to promote wellness and to provide a healthy environment, physically, mentally, socially, and spiritually. A researcher has collected scores on a wellness survey at the start of the fall semester and at the end (before final exams). The researcher finds that participants' scores are higher at the end of the semester and concludes that the aims of the residence hall are being fulfilled. What confounds and alternative explanations for the results can you identify?

3. A university is trying to help students who are on academic probation because of their low grades. These students receive tutoring and take a

special study skills course. Their grades tend to be higher at the end of the next grading period. The university uses this information as evidence that the special strategies work. Suggest an alternative explanation.

4. A researcher wishes to learn whether college students use more slang when speaking with a person their own age than when speaking with an older person. Design a within-subjects experiment to test this hypothesis.

5. A researcher is designing a study on the basis of a within-subjects design with four levels of the independent variable. The researcher wants to use an incomplete within-subjects design where each participant experiences each level of the independent variable once. What is the minimum number of participants required for this study, and what order of the independent variables will each participant receive?

6. A researcher for a cookie company asks participants to taste four types of cookies. To avoid order effects, this researcher uses random order with rotation. Create a possible set of orders for the first four participants.

ANSWERS TO CONCEPT QUESTIONS AND ODD-NUMBERED EXERCISES

Note: There will often be more than one correct answer for each of these questions. Consult with your instructor about your own answers.

Concept Question 6.1

The researcher would need 20 participants for a within-subjects design. The researcher would need 60 participants for a between-groups design.

Concept Question 6.2

This study is confounded by practice effects. The reason why the participants read the sentences preceded by context more rapidly may be that they have already had practice in reading sentences from the computer screen.

Concept Question 6.3

One solution for a Latin square with six conditions is as follows:

ABCDEF
BDFACE
CFBEAD
DAEBFC
ECAFDB
FEDCBA

Exercises

1. a. For a between-groups design, 54 participants; for a within-subjects design, 18 participants.

   b. I would have each participant drive and rate each car. To control for order effects, I would vary the order of the cars and three participants would receive each order of the cars. This is an incomplete within-subjects design.

c. The orders for an incomplete within-subjects design might be: ABC, ACB, BCA, BAC, CAB, CBA.

3. Perhaps the students matured during the year and would have been better students even without the special program. Perhaps their experiences in other classrooms helped them learn to be better students (a history effect). These students may also be showing reactivity; they changed their behavior simply because they were observed, not because the tutoring and special study skills course were effective. They may also be showing regression toward the mean since these extreme scores are moving toward the mean.

5. The researcher will need a minimum of four participants, although a greater number would be preferable. Ideally, this number should be divisible by four, in order to counterbalance order effects equally across conditions. A Latin square design could be used for this study (but so could a random order with rotation design). For each set of four participants, the order of the conditions could be as follows:

ABCD
BDAC
CADB
CDBA
DCBA

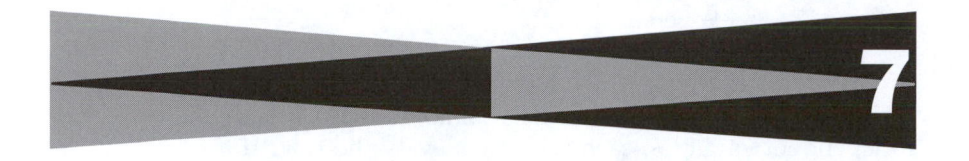

Factorial Designs

Suppose a researcher is interested in the effect of positive or negative feedback ("you did great" versus "your performance was not up to expectations") on a person's confidence about performing certain tasks. In particular, the researcher wants to determine if receiving positive or negative feedback affects how well women think they would perform on a mathematics test or a reading comprehension test. The researcher predicts that negative feedback will be more damaging to women's self-confidence regarding the mathematics test than to their self-confidence regarding a reading task. This prediction actually includes two hypotheses: (a) that the negative feedback will have a deleterious effect on self-confidence (as compared with positive feedback) and (b) that this effect will be stronger for self-confidence measures related to math than for those related to reading.

How will the researcher test these hypotheses? The researcher could carry out a series of experiments, for instance, one to test the effects of negative reinforcement on math, one to test the effects of positive reinforcement on math, one to test the effects of negative reinforcement on reading, and one to test the effects of positive reinforcement on reading. This is a laborious undertaking, however. At least four experiments would be needed, each with two conditions. If there were ten participants in each condition, the researcher would need to solicit the assistance of 80 volunteers. A less cumbersome approach to testing this hypothesis is to develop and conduct one slightly more complex experiment.

In previous chapters, we have discussed the design of studies with one independent variable. In the situation described here, there are two independent variables, each with two levels: the type of feedback (positive or negative) and the type of test (mathematics or reading). Sometimes, however, researchers need to simultaneously test the effect of two (or more) independent variables on a dependent measure[1] and determine if the effect of each independent variable is the same for each level of the other independent variable. For example, the researcher in our example predicts that the effect of negative feedback will be stronger in relation to a mathematics test than in relation to a reading test.

This type of design, in which the effect of two or more independent variables (also called **factors**) on a dependent variable is assessed, is called a **factorial design**. In a factorial design, several hypotheses are tested simultaneously. The effect of each independent variable (or factor) on the dependent measure is determined while disregarding the other factor or factors; this is called the **main effect**. In our example, the researcher would investigate the main effects for the type of reinforcement and for the type of test. In addition, the researcher often wishes to determine how the effect of each independent variable differs at each level of the other independent variables. This is referred to as the **interaction effect** between the factors.

In our example, the researcher might find that, overall, the women in the study perform significantly better on the reading test than on the mathematics test. This would be a significant main effect for the type of test. If, overall, the participants performed significantly better when they received positive feedback than when they received negative feedback, this would be a main effect for the type of feedback. The researcher might also find an interaction between the type of feedback and the type of test. For instance, it may be that the type of feedback has very little effect on the reading test performance but has a considerable effect on the mathematics test performance.

USING A FACTORIAL DESIGN

In our example, the researcher is interested in the effect of feedback (positive and negative) on confidence judgments, as well as the effect of feedback on the confidence judgments regarding different types of tests (math and reading). To carry out this study, the researcher might randomly assign participants to one of four conditions.

- In the *positive feedback/math* condition, the participants complete a short mathematics exercise and receive positive feedback about

---

[1] Actually, research studies can also involve more than one dependent variable; these types of studies require multivariate analyses, which are described in more advanced statistical textbooks.

their performance. They are asked to judge how well they would do on a longer test of the same type.

- In the *positive feedback/reading* condition, the participants complete a short reading exercise and are then given positive feedback about their performance. These participants are asked to judge how well they would do on a longer reading test.

- In the *negative feedback/math* condition, the participants receive negative feedback about their performance on the short math exercise before being asked to judge how well they'd perform on a longer test.

- In the *negative feedback/reading* condition, the participants receive negative feedback about the results of the reading exercise before providing their confidence judgments.

Of course, the researcher wants to keep constant as much as possible among the experimental conditions and so avoids introducing extraneous variables that might confound the results. Designing an investigation on the basis of a factorial design requires the same attention to detail and avoidance of confounds as does designing a study with a single independent variable. In this particular study, the experimenter might be concerned about demand characteristics. Will the relationship between the type of feedback and confidence judgments be so obvious that the participants guess what the researcher expects and behave accordingly? The researcher might need to make special efforts to minimize the effect of any demand characteristics. One possibility might be to have the participant complete a number of tasks and make a number of different types of judgments, so that the relationship between the confidence judgment and feedback would be less obvious. Another possibility is to initially carry out a smaller version of the study with just a few participants (a **pilot study**) and to ask them what they think the purpose of the investigation is. It's possible that what seems transparent to the researcher is opaque to the participants and that no one will identify the purpose of the study.

Imagine that the study has been carried out, and the researcher finds the following means in each condition:

| | | **Feedback** | |
		Positive	Negative
Test	Reading	90.0	85.0
	Math	80.0	60.0

When considering the results, statistical analyses would need to be conducted to ascertain which effects are and are not statistically significant. Using these means, the researcher can identify possible significant interactions and main effects. For example, the difference in confidence between the positive and negative feedback conditions for the reading test is only 5 points, while this same difference for the math test is 20 points. In addition, the difference between math and reading under positive feedback is 10 points, but the difference between math and reading after receiving negative feedback is 25 points. That these differences are so disparate suggests that the effect of feedback is not consistent across the two tests; it appears to have a stronger effect on confidence in mathematics than on confidence in reading. In other words, there is an interaction between type of test and type of feedback; the type of feedback affects the dependent variable differently depending on the type of test. A graph of these means is presented in figure 7.1.

Figure 7.1   Graph of the means illustrating the effect of type of feedback and type of test on self-confidence

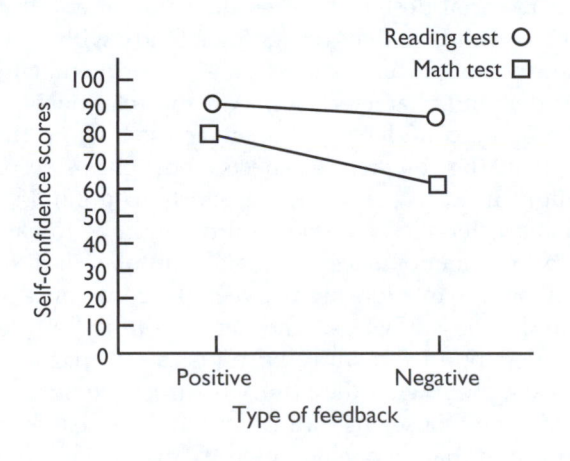

The researcher may also wish to identify the potential main effects. This is done by comparing the **marginal means**. The marginal means are computed for each level of an independent variable, disregarding the other independent variables. Let's consider the means again, now with the marginal means also included:

		Positive	Feedback Negative	Marginal means
	Reading	90.0	85.0	87.5
Test				
	Math	80.0	60.0	70.0
Marginal means		85.0	72.5	

The mean for the positive feedback conditions was 85 points, whereas the mean for the negative feedback conditions was 72.5 points. Perhaps this indicates that the participants were more confident, in general, after receiving positive feedback. Statistical analysis would be needed to determine if the difference is statistically significant.

The mean for the mathematics conditions was 70 points, 17.5 points less than the mean confidence judgments for the reading conditions (87.5 points). This might suggest that participants were generally more confident in reading than in mathematics; again, statistical analysis would be needed to determine if these means are statistically different. Graphs of these main effects are presented in figure 7.2. By the way, as in figure 7.2, line graphs are typically used to depict main effects when the independent variable is continuous—that is, when it is theoretically possible to experience something that falls between the units on a scale. In this case, it is theoretically possible to receive feedback that is between positive and negative, such as neutral feedback. Bar graphs are used to depict main effects when the independent variable consists of discrete categories, as for the math and reading tests.

Factorial designs are most commonly analyzed using a statistical procedure called **analysis of variance (ANOVA).** The results of ANOVA tell the researcher which main effects and/or interaction effects are statistically significant.

Figure 7.2   Graphs of the main effects for the type of feedback and the type of test

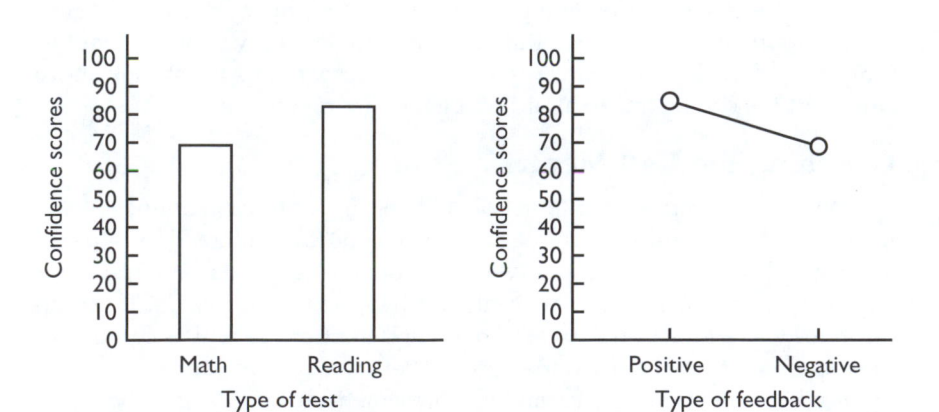

Interpreting Main Effects

A significant main effect means that, in general, there is a difference (or differences) among the means of that particular independent variable. An important point to remember is that the main effects ignore all other factors included in the study. If there is no interaction between the significant factor and any other factor, the main effect can be generalized to each level of the independent variable. But, if there is a significant interaction between the independent variable and some other factor, the main effect may not be consistent across all levels of the independent variable, and interpretation of the main effect must be made with care.

Suppose a researcher induces a happy or a sad mood in a group of men and women to determine how mood affects males' and females' desire for chocolate (as measured on a 20-point scale). The researcher finds the following means:

| | | Mood | | |
		Happy	Sad	Marginal means
Sex	Male	10.0	8.0	9.0
	Female	10.0	16.0	13.0
Marginal means		10.0	12.0	

According to the marginal means, females rated their desire for chocolate at 13 points on average, whereas males rated this desire at 9, on average. It might be tempting to conclude that females desire chocolate more than males do, but a closer look at the means suggests that this is an overgeneralization. In fact, when happy, males and females had an equivalent desire for chocolate; only when they were sad did the females' desire for chocolate exceed the males'. This difference was in part because the females' desire for chocolate increased but also because the males' desire for chocolate decreased when they became sad. It is very important not to jump to conclusions based on main effects; researchers must look more closely at the cell means to avoid overgeneralizing the results.

Graphing the Cell Means

When interpreting an interaction, the researcher must examine the cell means. An important step in interpreting a significant interaction is to create a graph of the means involved. The dependent variable—desire for chocolate in our last example—is always assigned to the y-axis. To graph our two-way interaction between mood and gender, we will assign one of the independent variables to the x-axis. There is no particular rule to determine which independent variable is presented on the x-axis; I typically assign the one with the greater number of levels, so that there are fewer lines in my graph, one for each level of the second independent variable. The means for each level of the second independent variable are then plotted on the graph and connected by means of a line. Both possible **graphs of the cell means** for the study on mood, gender, and chocolate are presented in figure 7.3. The graphs differ in terms of which independent variable is represented on the x-axis, but both represent the same information.

Figure 7.3   Line graphs of interaction between mood and gender on desire for chocolate

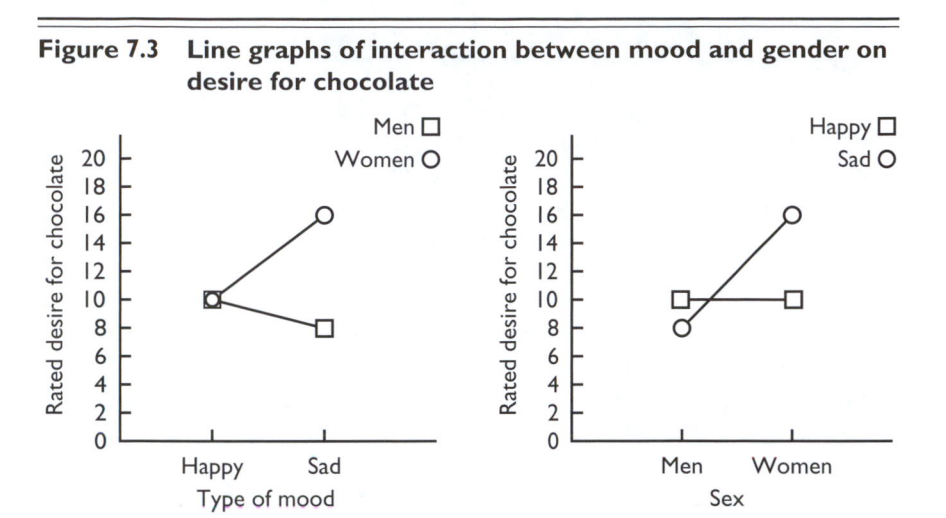

Notice that, in the graphs of the means, the lines representing each mood or each gender are not parallel. When an interaction is statistically significant, the lines will not be parallel (although not necessarily intersecting as they are here). (Note that, however, in some cases where the lines aren't parallel, the interaction still isn't statistically significant.) If means are graphed and the lines are nearly parallel, we infer that an interaction between the two variables is not present—that is, that the effect of one independent variable is consistent across the levels of the other. Some possible graphs of means are illustrated in figure 7.4. Some of these graphs suggest an interaction between the variables (some also suggest main effects), and some do not.

Figure 7.4   Various possible graphs of means

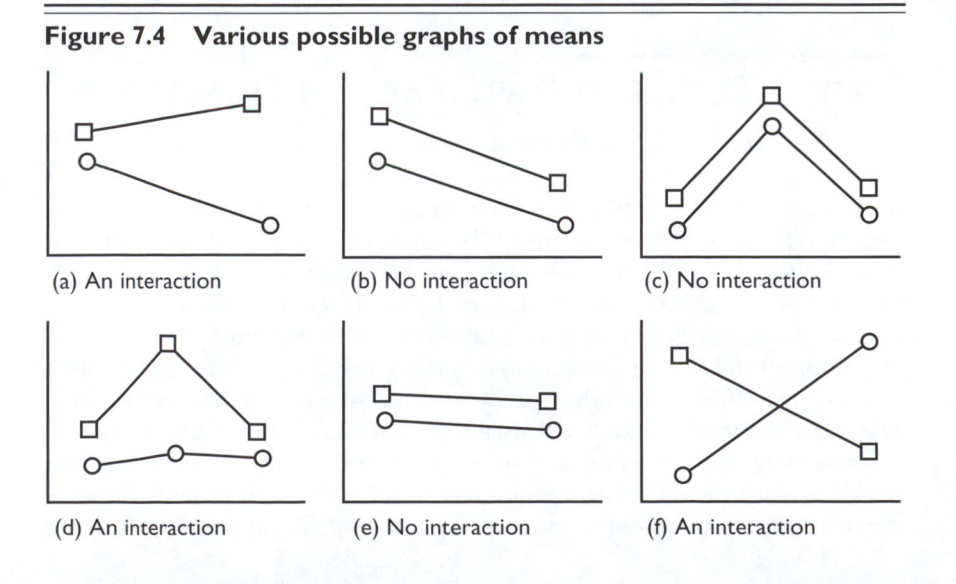

A researcher designs a study in which two independent variables are manipulated. The participants sit in a driving simulator that represents an automobile with either a manual or an automatic transmission. In addition, the simulator either includes or does not include a cellular telephone. The participants simulate driving while maintaining a conversation with the researcher's assistant, who is either sitting as a passenger in the simulator or talking with the participant on the cellular phone. The researcher measures the amount of time that passes before the participant makes a dangerous driving error (as operationally defined by the researcher). Look at the accompanying graph of the cell means from this study and describe the results in several sentences.

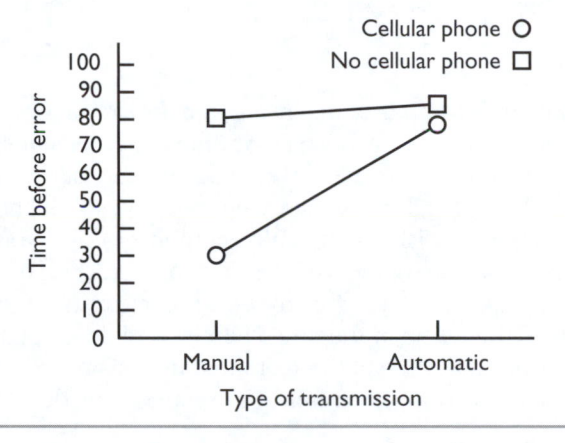

OTHER TYPES OF TWO-FACTOR DESIGNS

Our examples in this chapter have involved a two-factor design with two between-groups variables (positive or negative feedback on a math or reading test in one example, male or female participants in happy or sad moods in the other example). But this isn't the limit of two-factor designs; they can be designed with all within-subjects factors or as a **mixed design** (sometimes called a **split-plot design**), where one factor is a between-groups factor and one is a within-subjects factor.

As an example of a within-subjects design with two factors, consider a study of the effect of cognitive processes and time of day on performance. The participants each take two tests: a logic test and a reading test. They take one test in the early morning and one in the late evening. After conducting the study, the researcher has data for four conditions: morning/logic, morning/reading, evening/logic, and evening/reading. There are two levels for each independent variable; provided the data meet the necessary assumptions, a within-subjects ANOVA can be conducted. This analysis (whose details need not concern us here) provides the researcher with information about the main effects for time of test and type of test and about the interaction between time and type of test, just as the between-groups ANOVA does, although there are differences in the formulas for the two types of ANOVA.

Concept Question 7.2

On the basis of the following hypothetical means generated by a study of the effect of time and type of test on performance, create graphs of the cell means and the marginal means.

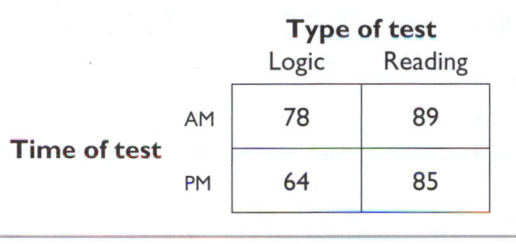

| | | **Type of test** | |
		Logic	Reading
Time of test	AM	78	89
	PM	64	85

Split-plot designs earned their name from agricultural research, where plots of land and types of seeds were tested simultaneously by planting more than one type of seed in numerous plots. In psychological research, split-plot designs involve testing participants in two or more independent groups (as in a between-groups design), but testing them more than once (as in a within-subjects design). In other words, the study includes a within-subjects factor and a between-groups factor. Suppose another study has been designed to investigate the effects of time and type of test on performance. As in the previous case, each participant takes both a logic test and a reading test. In this study, however, each participant is tested *either* in the morning or in the evening, but not both. Type of test is a within-subjects factor, because each participant is tested under both conditions, but time of test is a between-groups factor because each person is tested under only one level of this factor.

The ANOVA that might be calculated with the data from this study would yield the same type of information as the between-groups and within-subjects ANOVAs: the main effects for test type and time of test and the interaction between the two.

Although between-groups, within-subjects, and split-plot designs yield the same information, the decision to use one or another is not arbitrary. The design that best fits the situation and allows the researcher to control as many potential confounds as possible should be chosen. A practical consideration in designing studies is the number of participants that will be needed to carry out the project. A between-groups design with four groups and ten scores in each condition will require 40 participants. The same study run as a split-plot design will require 20 participants. As a within-subjects design, it will require only 10 participants.

The number of participants needed, while important from a practical standpoint, is not the only consideration. In one situation, a within-subjects design might be best; in another, the potential for carryover effects on one of the independent variables might call for a split-plot design; in yet another, a between-groups design might be needed to control all of the possible confounds; or because the study involves subject variables—such as gender—that are simply not amenable to a within-subjects design.

OTHER HIGHER-ORDER DESIGNS AND THEIR INTERACTIONS

In the last example, there were two independent variables: time of test and type of test. When used for a project involving two independent variables, analysis of variance is called a two-way ANOVA. It is also useful to describe the number of levels in each of the independent variables. In this case, there were two levels of time and two levels of test, thus, the design of the study could be referred to as a 2 × 2 design. When three types of tests are included, it is a 2 × 3 design. However, the analysis is still a two-way ANOVA because the number of independent variables is still two. Notice also that a 2 × 3 design involves six different experimental conditions. Multiplying the number of levels by the number of independent variables yields the number of different conditions.

It is also interesting to consider **higher-order designs**—for example, a project involving three independent variables. Let's expand our example to include time of test, type of test, and gender. Two levels of gender are involved, and then three levels of (types of) tests and three levels of time (morning, afternoon, and evening). This project would be described as a 2 × 3 × 3 design, because one independent variable has two levels and the others have three levels. (Can you determine the number of different conditions in this design? There are 18!) The researcher could use a three-way ANOVA to analyze the data, provided they meet the requirements for inferential statistics.

When a researcher designs a project involving three independent variables (A, B, and C), analysis of variance will supply information about three main effects, one for each variable. In addition, several interactions are analyzed: the interaction between A and B, the interaction between B and C, and the interaction between A and C. These are called two-way interactions, because they each involve two independent variables. An analysis of variance based on three independent variables also yields information about a three-way interaction, the interaction of A and B and

C, which is usually described as the $A \times B \times C$ interaction. It is somewhat more complicated to graph three-way interactions than two-way interactions since two graphs are required. And, as you can imagine, a four-way interaction that results from a four-way ANOVA can be very complex to illustrate and often difficult to comprehend. Practicality limits the number of factors that should be added to the analysis.

Imagine a situation where there are three independent variables—for example, time of test, type of test, and whether a person identifies his- or herself as a morning or evening person. A three-way ANOVA of this design ($2 \times 3 \times 2$ design) would yield three main effects (time of test, type of test, and type of person), three two-way interactions, (time × type of test, time × type of person, and type of person × type of test), as well as one three-way interaction (time × type of test × type of person). How would one go about graphing and interpreting a three-way interaction?

Unless a three-dimensional model of the interaction is to be created, graphing a three-way interaction will involve at least two graphs. A separate graph will be needed for each level of one of the independent variables. Which independent variable is divided between the graphs is up to the researcher. An example is presented in figure 7.5. In this interaction, it appears that there is a decrease in the performance of the morning people from morning to evening, and that this decrease is greater for the logic test than for the reading test. The evening people, on the other hand, show improvement from morning to evening, and the improvement is greatest for the logic test.

Factorial designs are quite appealing because of their flexibility; so much information can be gained in one investigation. But it's possible to have too much of a good thing; when there are too many factors, interpreting the results is very complicated. Four-way ANOVAs, for example,

Figure 7.5   A graph of a three-way interaction

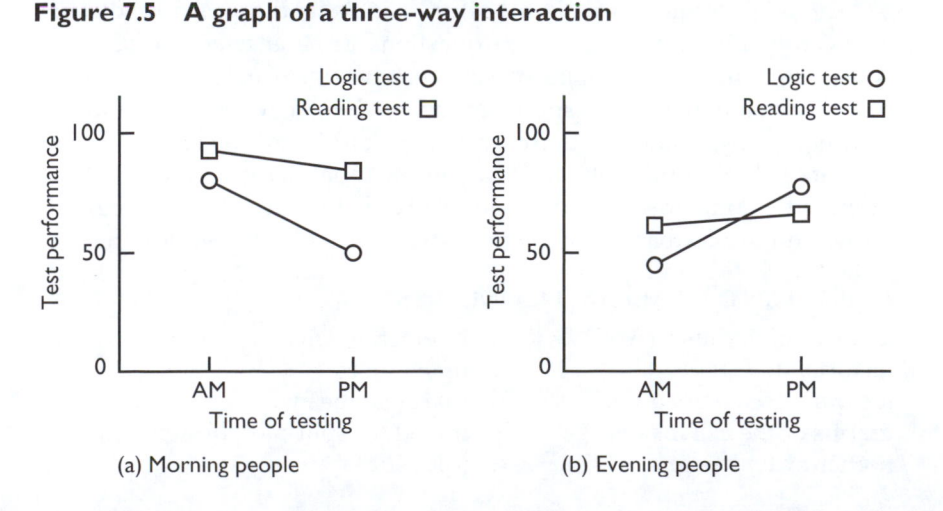

compare four independent variables and yield information about four main effects, six two-way interactions, four three-way interactions, and one four-way interaction. It can be difficult to decide whether adding a factor or including a variable is more trouble—in terms of difficulty of interpretation—than it is worth.

Summary

Factorial research designs involve two or more independent variables and allow the researcher to test several hypotheses simultaneously. Factorial designs can yield information about the main effects, which are the separate effects of each independent variable, and also about interactions among the independent variables.

Factorial designs are very flexible and can be used to design studies with many independent variables. In addition, they may involve between-groups or within-subjects variables or a combination of the two.

Because two-way and higher-order designs yield both main effects and interactions, the interpretation of the results needs special attention. Main effects identify general differences among the levels of a single independent variable. Interactions provide more specific information about how the effect of one variable reacts differently at different levels of the other variable. If there is a significant main effect for one variable and this variable is also involved in an interaction, the results for the main effect can be misleading. Care is required in interpreting the main effect when an interaction is also present. Is the main effect true across all levels of the independent variables, or is the main effect an overgeneralization that does not hold for all levels of the independent variables? When the independent variable is not involved in an interaction, or when the interaction does not contradict the main effect at any point, it is appropriate to emphasize the main effect.

Factorial designs provide a useful, flexible, and powerful tool; they allow numerous related research questions to be answered in a single study. Sometimes, though, if novice researchers get carried away and try to answer too many questions at once, they may end up with an unwieldy design and an uninterpretable multi-way interaction. When used in a thoughtful manner, however, factorial designs can save time, permit the comparison of the effects of several variables at once, and answer questions that would be unanswerable with simpler designs.

Important Terms and Concepts

analysis of variance (ANOVA)	interaction effect
factorial design	main effect
factors	marginal means
graphs of the cell means	mixed (or split-plot) design
higher-order designs	pilot study

EXERCISES

1. For each of the following, indicate which are the dependent and independent variables, the number of levels for each independent variable, and whether it is a within-subjects or between-groups variable.

    a. Researchers observed male and female children (4-, 5-, and 6-years-old) as they played with other children of the same age. For each child, the time spent in cooperative play with others was measured.

    b. Individuals with anorexia and bulimia take a cognitive distortions test upon entering a treatment program for eating disorders and again three weeks later.

    c. Participants' pulses are measured before a lifting task, directly after the lifting task, and 2 minutes later. Each participant performs three lifting tasks on three different days. The task involves lifting weights of 10, 15, or 20 pounds once every 2 seconds for 10 minutes.

    d. A researcher is investigating the effect of noise level and subject matter on reading speed. The participants in this study were measured three times—once reading poetry, once reading a novel, and once reading a history textbook. Half of the participants read in a noisy environment, and half read in a quiet environment.

    e. A researcher standing by the door of a grocery store stops half of the males and half of the females who enter alone and presents them with a free gift of a pen and small pad of paper; the other shoppers do not receive a gift. The researcher then notes how much money each shopper spends in the store.

2. Smokers and nonsmokers are asked to complete a test of attitudes towards smoking. Half of the participants complete the test after waiting in a room where they have been seated next to an ashtray full of cigarette butts.

    a. The accompanying table gives the means from that study. The smoking-attitudes test yields a score between 1 and 10; a higher score indicates a more favorable attitude. Graph the interaction between smoking and whether the ashtray is full.

Smokers		Nonsmokers	
With ashtrays	Without ashtrays	With ashtrays	Without ashtrays
8.25	5.25	2.00	4.75

    b. Graph the main effect for smoking and the main effect for ashtray fullness.

    c. On the basis of the information from the main effects and interaction, describe the results of this study.

3. A researcher interested in the effect of weather on mood hypothesized that overcast days yield more depressed moods than sunny days. Partic-

ipants were solicited from two sections of a college course (Introduction to Economics). Participants in one group were asked, on a sunny day, to rate their mood on a scale from 1 (depressed) to 10 (very happy). Participants in another group were asked, on an overcast day, to rate their mood. On both days the temperature was 68 degrees; the test days were three weeks apart. If the research yielded higher mood scores on the good weather days, can the researcher claim that good weather caused a good mood? What are some alternative explanations for the results? (You may want to review information from other chapters for ideas.)

4. A researcher tests three different cold viruses on two groups of people. One virus typically causes a runny nose; one typically causes a cough; and one typically causes congestion and a headache. One group of people has received mega doses of vitamins, and the other has received a placebo. After exposing the people to the viruses, the researcher waits several days, and then takes blood samples to determine how sick each person is. On the basis of this information, each person receives a score that indicates how infected he or she has become (the larger the number, the more infected). The researcher's hypothesis is that the vitamin treatment will be more effective than the placebo and that the vitamins will be most effective when the virus causes congestion or a runny nose. The means are as follows.

| | **Type of virus** | | |
	Runny nose	Cough	Congestion
Placebo	35	24	42
Vitamins	32	18	10

a. What would the ANOVA used to compare these means be described as?

b. Graph the means and interactions.

c. Based on your graphs, interpret the results of the study.

ANSWERS TO CONCEPT QUESTIONS AND ODD-NUMBERED EXERCISES

Note: There will often be more than one correct answer for each of these questions. Consult with your instructor about your own answers.

Concept Question 7.1

There appears to be a main effect for phone presence and an interaction between phone presence and type of transmission. The time elapsed before a driving error was committed was greater when no phone was present than when there was a phone. This difference was especially large when the simulator had a manual transmission.

Concept Question 7.2

The graph of the cell means is as follows:

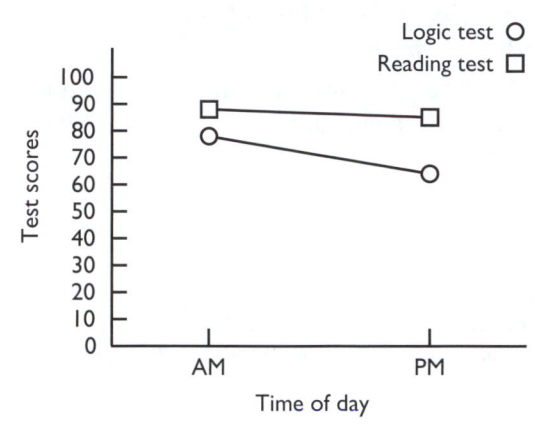

The graphs of the marginal means are as follows:

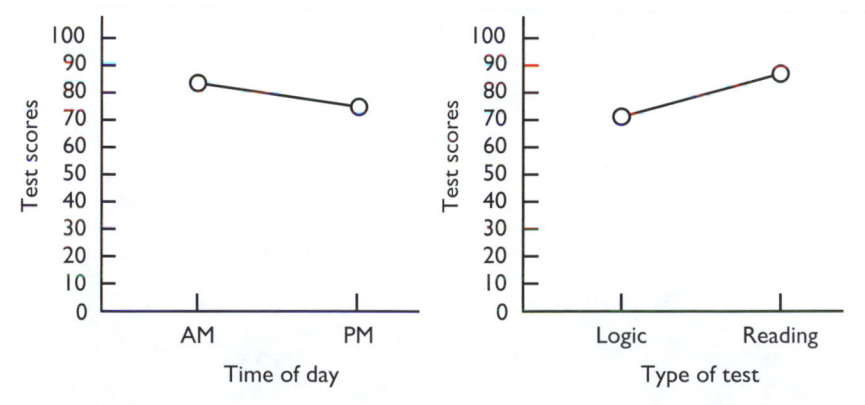

Exercises

1. a. The independent variables are age (three levels) and gender (two levels); both are between-group variables. The dependent variable is the duration of time spent in cooperative play.

   b. The eating disorder (two levels) is the independent variable and is a between-groups variable. Testing is also an independent variable (two levels) and is a within-subjects variable. The dependent variable is the score in the cognitive distortions test.

   c. The participants' pulse rates are the dependent variable. The independent variables are the lifting task (three levels) and the time of measurement (also three levels). Both of these variables are within-subjects variables. It would also be possible to include days as a between-groups variable (three levels). If the weights are counterbalanced across days, however, the day effect should not be significant.

   d. Noise level (two levels) and subject matter (three levels) are the independent variables. Noise level is a between-groups variable, and subject matter is a within-subjects variable. Reading speed is the dependent variable.

   e. Gift (two levels) and gender (two levels) are the independent variables; both are between-groups variables. The dependent variable is the amount of money spent.

3. This is a correlational study and not an experiment; consequently, the researcher cannot claim that the weather caused the mood change. Given that there were three weeks between measurements, the overcast day may have fallen closer to final exams, on the day of a test, or on the day exams were returned to the students. Alternatively, something that occurred during those three weeks may have caused moods to fall.

8

Using Natural Settings
Observational Studies and Field Experiments

OBSERVATIONAL RESEARCH DESIGNS

People watching can be a very enjoyable and entertaining pastime. But scientific observation of people or animals involves more forethought and planning than does casual observation. When conducted carefully and correctly, however, observational studies can provide a wealth of information that casual people watching would miss.

Uses of Observational Studies

Observational studies can be especially useful as a starting point for research on a new topic. Instead of simply jumping into a full-scale laboratory experiment, the researcher can save much time and effort by first making some careful observations. For example, a researcher may be interested in how children play and how interactions among children can be affected by the size of the group. Before delving into a complicated project where children of various ages are combined into groups of various sizes, the researcher needs some sense of what to look for. Our researcher may wish to first conduct some observational studies—perhaps to observe children at a playground or at a day care center. Do boys and girls play differently? What types of play occur? Is it aggressive or peaceful? Is it independent or cooperative? Does the type of play vary with age? Does the same child stay with one activity or switch rapidly from one type of play to another? By conducting an observational study first, a researcher can learn what type of behavior is common and what is unusual and thus better interpret the results of later laboratory research.

Observational research need not only be the starting place for a series of studies, it can also prove useful later in the process. Researchers who conduct most of their research in the laboratory can benefit by taking their studies to the field. By conducting observational studies later in the process, a researcher can learn whether the laboratory results also apply in the natural environment. If children's play behavior in the laboratory involves more cooperative play when there are more girls than boys in the group, does this also occur on the playground?

Observational studies, of course, can stand on their own merits. Often, observation is the only way a particular research question can be answered. For instance, an observational approach may be the best way to determine whether drivers are complying with a new speed limit.

TWO TYPES OF OBSERVATIONAL RESEARCH DESIGNS

Observational studies can be divided into categories—such as naturalistic observation and participant observation—that vary along a continuum of intervention. In naturalistic observation, there is no intervention; at the other end of the spectrum, in participant observation, the researcher is a part of the group of participants being observed.

Naturalistic Observation

In **naturalistic observation**, researchers unobtrusively observe behaviors in their natural setting; the investigator does nothing to interfere with the participants' behavior. Often, in fact, the participants do not realize they are being observed. The focus of this research tends to be relatively broad; a wide variety of behaviors is observed. For example, a researcher may observe the various behaviors of people at a botanical garden. The researcher might note that some people seem to wander about chatting and barely notice the plants around them, while others systematically examine each and every plant. Perhaps the researcher would find that more women than men visit the gardens and that more people enter in pairs than alone or in larger groups. Another researcher, however, may focus more on particular behaviors—for example, whether people tend to examine the plants while alone or with other people. An unobtrusive observational study focused on particular behaviors in a particular setting is often referred to as a systematic naturalistic observation.

Ideally, observations are made without the participants' knowledge, but it is not always possible (or ethical) to observe them without their awareness. When observations must be made overtly, the researcher may make some preliminary efforts to reduce the effect of his or her presence. In one such approach, **desensitization**, the researcher gradually moves closer to the participants until he or she can sit near or even among them; this technique is often used in animal studies. Animal researchers and those interested in human behavior also employ a technique called **habituation**, in which the researcher appears in the setting numerous times until his or her presence no longer appears to affect the participants' behavior.

Jane Goodall, the famous ethologist, studied chimpanzees in their natural settings in Africa. She used a combination of desensitization and habituation to study the animals. At first, the chimpanzees would flee at the first sight of her. After several weeks, she could sit about 60–80 yards from the chimps if she was very still and totally silent. The chimps had habituated to her at that distance. For the next five-month period, Goodall attempted desensitization. When she moved closer to the chimps, they tended to express hostility towards her; they would shake sticks and bark aggressively. One chimp even came up behind her and hit her on the head. After Goodall had observed the chimpanzees from a distance for more than six months, they came to realize that she was no threat and would let her get closer. Eventually, some of the chimps would allow her to touch and tickle them. However, she and her co-observer realized that this was a mistake, not only because fully grown male chimpanzees are large and powerful animals that could easily hurt a human, but also because the interaction of humans with chimps interferes with the collection of data on natural behavior (van Lawick-Goodall, 1971).

In your career, you will probably not be observing primates in Africa, but the same techniques—habituation and desensitization—can be used with humans and other animals. As a college student conducting research on the effect of gender-role stereotypes on children's comprehension of stories, I worked with a third-grade class. The teacher suggested that I come to the class several Friday afternoons in a row before attempting to collect any data, so that the children would get used to my presence in the classroom. She was suggesting that I use habituation.

Unfortunately, it is hard to be sure that the presence of an observer is not affecting behavior. The researcher should seek input on this question from other sources, whenever possible. For example, in a classroom, the observer might ask the teacher whether the students were behaving differently in the presence of the observer. In this way, the researcher avoids depending on his or her own judgment, which may be biased or simply uninformed.

Participant Observation

Naturalistic observation studies can provide very useful information about natural behaviors, but sometimes passively observing a situation is impossible or yields limited or biased information. In these cases, a researcher might decide to conduct a participant observation study.

In **participant observation**, the researcher is an active participant in the situation. The researcher can be a disguised participant or an undisguised participant. In **undisguised participant studies**, the other participants are aware that the researcher is observing their behavior. This is a common research method among anthropologists, who join and work with a society while also observing it.

In **disguised participant studies**, the other participants do not know that the researcher is observing their behavior. One of the most famous disguised participant studies in psychology was conducted by David Rosenhan (1973), who wished to investigate whether insanity is distinguishable from sanity. He chose to test this question by determining whether sane people who had been admitted to psychiatric hospitals would be detected.

In this study, eight sane individuals were admitted to 12 psychiatric hospitals. The pseudopatients told the admissions office that they had been hearing voices that said "empty," "hollow," and "thud." After being admitted to the psychiatric ward, each patient immediately ceased simulating any symptoms. The pseudopatients spent their time engaging others in conversation and taking notes on their observations. These notes were taken openly, since nobody seemed to care one way or the other.

The pseudopatients were discharged after an average of 19 days. (The range was 7–52 days.) At discharge, each was given the diagnosis of schizophrenia in remission. None of the pseudopatients were detected by the hospital staff, although about one-third of the other patients realized that the observer was not really ill.

Rosenhan's study provides some food for thought about the nature of mental illness and the effect of diagnoses and labels. In addition, it supplies some interesting information and insights into life on a psychiatric ward—information that probably could not have been gained without the disguised participant research design.

Research involving participant observation can be very interesting and often makes for fascinating reading; a potential pitfall, however, is that observations made by the participant observer can be subject to bias. George Kirkham (1975), a criminologist, served as an undisguised participant in his research on police work. He went through police academy training and became a uniformed police officer in a high-crime section of a medium-sized city. In his article, he describes how his attitude and personality changed during his time as a policeman.

> According to the accounts of my family, colleagues and friends, I began to increasingly display attitudinal and behavioral elements that were entirely foreign to my previous personality—punitiveness, pervasive cynicism and mistrust of others, chronic irritability and free-floating hostility, racism, a diffuse personal anxiety over the menace of crime and criminals that seemed at times to border on the obsessive. (Kirkham, 1975, p. 19)

In evaluating participant observation research, we need to be aware of the potential for personal biases to slip into descriptions and observations. Researchers who adopt a participant observation study need to be aware of the possibility of bias and to realize that they are not in a position to recognize bias in themselves. While not all bias can be avoided, a goodly amount can be eliminated by carefully defining the types of behaviors that will be observed and recorded before entering the observation setting.

Just as the observer can be affected by the situation, the other participants can be affected by the observer. The participation of an observer will have the greatest effect on the behavior of small groups. Kirkham's participation as a police officer probably had no significant effect on the police force as a whole, although he may have influenced those around him in unknown ways. Similarly, the presence of Rosenhan's pseudopatients probably did not alter the psychiatric wards, but it may have affected the behavior of the staff or other patients around them. Since some of the patients recognized that the pseudopatients were not ill, their presence clearly did not go totally unnoticed. The ethical ramifications of a participant observation study must be carefully considered before data collection begins. What if the real psychiatric patients had become very upset by the presence of Rosenhan's pseudopatients? Or what if the other police officers were negatively affected by Kirkham's joining the force? Should the studies have been continued in these circumstances?

Participant observation studies have their limitations, which may affect the accuracy and usefulness of the observations. However, careful planning and attention to potential flaws can reduce the scope for such problems. For example, by preplanning what observations to make and how to make them, observer bias can be minimized. When used carefully, participant observation can provide invaluable information that could not be gained in any other manner.

Concept Question 8.1

A researcher interested in the treatment of older people in our society asks your advice on observational methods. Together, you consider naturalistic observation, disguised participant observation, and undisguised participant observation. Describe how each of these types of observational studies might be carried out.

FIELD EXPERIMENTS

Field experiments are controlled studies that occur in a natural setting. In a field experiment, the researcher manipulates an independent variable and measures its effect on a dependent variable in an effort to find a causal relationship. For example, a researcher may wish to study altruistic behavior by observing whether participants will come to the aid of an individual who has dropped some books. Suppose the researcher wants to know if helping behavior will be affected by how the person is dressed. In this study, a confederate (a research assistant) dresses casually—faded blue jeans, a T-shirt, and sneakers—in one condition, and dresses up more—a suit and tie or a skirt, blouse, and heels—in the other condition. The mode of dress is the independent variable. The confederate then stumbles and drops a pile of books in the presence of the participant. The participant's behavior is then observed and recorded. The observations are the dependent measure. In this type of study, often the participant is unaware of any involvement in a research project. Obviously, informed consent cannot be gained in this case and, consequently, the ethical ramifications of such a project must be carefully considered before it is carried out.

Field experiments can provide greater external validity than what is obtained in laboratory research alone. A researcher may conduct a field experiment to see if laboratory results generalize to a natural setting. In terms of internal validity, the difficulties encountered in a field experiment are the same as those in a laboratory experiment. For instance, do any confounds—such as experimenter bias—suggest alternative explanations for the results? If two or more groups of participants are being compared, how were the groups formed? Can the researcher be confident that the groups are equivalent? As with any experiment, the field experiment must be internally valid if the results are to be useful and meaningful.

PROBLEMS AND PITFALLS OF OBSERVATIONAL STUDIES

With the exception of field experiments, most observational studies are correlational studies and, thus, do not allow us to establish causal relationships. Still, by ensuring that observational studies have strong internal validity, we can maximize the useful information that they provide. Internal validity is gained by avoiding potential confounds. In observational studies, the two primary sources of confounds are the influence of the observer on the participants and biased observations.

Influence of the Observer on Behavior

The presence of an observer can greatly affect the behavior of research participants, as Jane Goodall found out when studying chimpanzees. In the social sciences, the effect of the observer on the behavior of the subjects is called the **Hawthorne effect**. During the 1920s and 1930s, the Western Electric Company conducted a series of studies on workplace behavior (Jones, 1992). Worker productivity was observed as the researchers varied a number of factors—for example, the addition of small incentives for groups, increasing and decreasing rest times, changing the starting and stopping schedule, changing the workers' chairs, modifying the supply of raw materials, and changing the number of days of work per week. Some of these variables were studied because the researchers were truly interested in their effects, others were included because economic hard times called for them.

The researchers at the Hawthorne plant noted that the workers' productivity improved over the course of the study. The researchers hypothesized that the additional attention from the researchers and management was the cause of the workers' increased productivity. To the Hawthorne researchers, this finding was an interesting side note; to researchers in the social sciences, however, it was of great import and become known as the Hawthorne effect. Interestingly, a reanalysis of the raw data from the Hawthorne studies suggests that there may not have been any significant increase in productivity after all (Jones, 1992).

In research psychology, the effect of the observer on participants' behavior is a major concern. Observers must assume that their presence will affect behavior and then take steps to minimize that effect—for example, by making observations surreptitiously.

If a participant's behavior changes with the awareness that he or she is being studied, the resulting measurement is called a **reactive measure**. **Reactivity** is the change in participants' behavior due to their awareness of being observed. Reactivity can be a problem in observational research and can decrease a study's internal validity. As mentioned earlier, the effects of reactivity can be minimized by allowing the participant to become accustomed to the observer either through desensitization or through habituation. Unfortunately, there is no way to be sure that measurements of the dependent variable are no longer reactive. Only by unobtrusive observation—that is, making observations without the participants' knowledge—can the researcher be fairly confident that observation is not changing behavior. In some cases, this is relatively easy. For example, observations in a college classroom might be made in a notebook; observations at an intersection might be made from a parked vehicle. In other situations, making unobtrusive observations may require some creativity.

Reactivity in participant observation is always a concern since it is not possible to determine what effect the participant observer may be having on the behavior of others. Efforts can be made, however, to minimize such effects. In disguised participant observation, it is important to take notes or record data as unobtrusively as possible. In undisguised participant observation, it is possible that, with time, the participants will become accustomed to the observer and reactivity will be reduced.

Expectancy Effects

A second threat to the internal validity of observational research is bias in measurements of the dependent variable. Psychological researchers recognize that a person's conscious or unconscious preferences can affect his or her perception of a situation—this is called **observer bias**. Researchers, therefore, design their studies carefully, so that any bias they may have cannot affect the results.

A simple way to avoid observer bias is to train research assistants to make the observations for a study, without mentioning the expected results. Unless the goal of the investigation is intuitively obvious, these observers are likely to have no expectations about the results; if they do, these expectations are unlikely to be systematic and thus, with more than one observer, may cancel each other out. Luckily, research suggests that errors in recording data due to experimenters' expectations occur in less than 1% of the data (Rosenthal, 1978) and that experimenter bias may have so little effect that it is not worth considering as a replicable phenomenon (Barber & Silver, 1968). Moreover, if a research finding is considered important, it will be investigated repeatedly by other researchers. Any experimenter bias is likely to become evident when other researchers have difficulty replicating the result (Kantowitz, Roediger, & Elmes, 1991, p. 425).

Biases Resulting from the Use of Nonhuman Observers

One way to avoid observer bias is to make the observations on audiotape or videotape. The advantage of a human observer, however, is flexibility. Humans can see, hear, smell, taste, and feel; machines typically perform only a subset of these behaviors. An audiotape recorder can only record sounds, such data do not reflect what can be perceived visually by a human observer. If some information from the tape is potentially ambiguous, bias in interpretation may ensue. In a study of language use, for example, the researcher may have difficulty in establishing whether a participant's pun was intentional without such nonverbal cues as smiling and winking. A video camera records both auditory and visual information, but it does not have the peripheral vision of a human. If the video camera is left unattended, it will simply record whatever is in front of it. Actions outside of the camera's view that might help explain some of the visible behaviors will not be available when the data is being coded. On the other hand, employing a human camera operator reintroduces human biases in data collection.

Even when information is obtained on videotape or audiotape, it still must be interpreted and coded by a human. Thus, although the use of mechanical observers may reduce observer bias, it cannot eliminate it, either in data collection or in data interpretation.

The researcher's awareness of the risks of reactivity and observer bias is essential to the internal validity of an observational study. A researcher who is aware of these problems can take steps to minimize their effects and thus optimize the interpretation of the results. Observational investigations can provide much useful and important information if researchers are careful to take advantage of the benefits of such studies and to minimize the threats to their internal validity.

Concept Question 8.2

Do males ask and answer questions more often in class than do females? A researcher wishes to observe student behavior in order to address this question. The researcher operationally defines "asking and answering questions" so that the behaviors can be categorized easily. The researcher suspects that males do speak up more often in class, but is concerned that this bias might affect data collection. What advice would you give this person? What method of data collection would you suggest—human observers or nonhuman means? How could the researcher avoid observer bias (human or nonhuman)? Would the data collection involve a reactive measure? How could reactivity be minimized or avoided?

Choosing the Type of Observational Design

Choosing a type of observational design for a particular study is often a question of balancing advantages and limitations. Naturalistic observations have the advantage of good **ecological validity**, which means that the results can be readily generalized to real life. Ecological validity is greater for field experiments than for laboratory experiments, but is greatest for naturalistic observations. On the other hand, field experiments allow the researcher more control over the environment than do naturalistic observations. Participant observation studies offer an insider's view of a situation, but at the risk of biased observations and of influencing the situation being observed.

A researcher must weigh carefully the advantages and disadvantages of each technique along with practical considerations—such as the time, money, and assistance available—as well as the ethical ramifications of the research. With these factors in mind, the researcher designs a project that maximizes advantages and minimizes flaws.

Data Collection

In designing an observational study, the researcher will also have to decide what behaviors will be observed and how these behaviors will be recorded. In other words, the researcher must decide what variable to measure and how to measure it. In any type of scientific research, a primary concern is to ensure that the dependent measure is reliable and valid.

Reliability

As discussed in chapter 3, **reliability** is the consistency with which a measurement technique yields the same results. To determine if an observation technique is reliable, a researcher would calculate the interobserver reliability.

Interobserver reliability is the degree to which a measurement procedure yields consistent results when used by different observers. For example, suppose that two observers watch children play and categorize the play activity as independent play, parallel play (when two or more children engage in the same activity—such as coloring—but with little interaction), cooperative play (when two or more children engage in an activity in which they must cooperate, such as a board game), or rough-and-tumble play. They watch the same child for 5 minutes and categorize the play activity every 30 seconds. Each observer makes 10 observations, but not all of their observations are in agreement—they disagree on one occasion where one observer interprets play activity as parallel and the other interprets it as cooperative. To determine how reliable their measurements of play activity are, they can calculate their interobserver reliability. There are several mathematical formulas available for this purpose, but an initial estimate of interobserver reliability can be obtained from a relatively simple formula:

$$\frac{\text{Number of agreements}}{\text{Number of opportunities for agreement}} \times 100$$

For our example, the interobserver reliability would be as follows:

$$\frac{9}{10} \times 100 = 90\% \text{ agreement}$$

The reliability of the measure increases as the agreement approaches 100%. When using this formula for interobserver reliability, researchers usually regard agreement over 90% as quite good, but this figure could be lower (or even higher) for any particular research project.

TECHNIQUES FOR DATA COLLECTION

The research question determines what will be observed and how it will be observed. For example, what factors you measure and how you observe people in an airport will be very different if you are looking for security risks than if you are looking for a pocket to pick. Thus, it is impossible to describe the single best way to make observations. Let's look at several techniques that have been used in observational research, along with their pitfalls and advantages.

Narrative Records

Narrative records are running records of behavior in a given situation. They can be very complete or rather sketchy. Narrative records can be created by audiotaping or videotaping a situation or by writing notes by hand. Later these notes can be organized, and various hypotheses can be tested.

Narrative records can differ substantially in terms of observer interpretation and subjectivity. Especially with handwritten notes, the researcher must decide at an early stage how much the observer should infer about a situation. When watching people in a cafeteria, should the observer note that "a young couple distanced themselves from others and enjoyed a private conversation," or should he or she take a more objective approach: "A male and female, each apparently of traditional college age, sat at a table no closer than two tables from anyone else. At this table, the two individuals talked with each other." The amount of subjectivity allowed in a record may be determined in part by the purpose of the data collection. A narrative record that is to serve as a source of research hypotheses may be more useful with subjective information, but more objectivity may be best in a record that is to serve as a faithful reflection of behaviors so that specific hypotheses may be tested.

Operational definitions—definitions of variables in terms of how they will be measured (chapter 3)—are of less use in narrative records than in other types of research. The reason for this is that research in which narrative records are used as a means of data collection is often broadly focused, and specific behaviors are not of primary interest. Of course, clear writing still mandates that all terms be defined; a researcher would not want to use a term such as "interaction" without specifying whether an interaction occurred between people, animals, inanimate objects, or some combination of the three and, if between people, whether it was verbal or nonverbal. Operational definitions are of more importance as the research becomes focused on a few specific behaviors. It is central to define those behaviors carefully and precisely, so that other researchers and consumers of research can understand what is being observed and evaluate the conclusions drawn from the observations.

From a practical point of view, the researcher who decides to use narrative records must determine a way to make notes in an unobtrusive manner. It may be possible to desensitize or habituate the subjects to the presence of the observer and to the observer's notetaking, but this takes a considerable amount of time. To avoid disrupting the setting, the observer may have to make cryptic notes on scraps of paper or perhaps even leave the setting on occasion to make notes in private. For the sake of accuracy, notes must be made as soon as possible after the observations are made; as time passes, notes are more likely to be contaminated by the observer's biases and memory distortions.

Narrative records provide lots of information, but organizing that information can sometimes be quite cumbersome. Suppose that a person has an audiotape and field notes of a verbal interaction between a child and a researcher. The researcher may be interested in the types of questions a child asks. To use the information that has been collected, the audiotape must first be transcribed for a written record. Then the transcription must be coded; that is, each question must be categorized as one of the several types the researcher has recognized—for example, questions about feelings, questions about people, questions about things, questions about words, and others. This coding is performed by more than one person so that the reliability of the coding system can be assessed. For example, do the coders agree as to which questions are about people and which are about feelings, or do they confuse these categories? The researcher's field notes could also be coded according to some system that the researcher has established. Such coding serves to reduce the amount of information available to a more manageable level;

this is referred to as a **data reduction** procedure. Data reduction can be time-consuming, but it makes testing hypotheses and drawing conclusions from the observations considerably easier.

Narrative records do not always need to be coded; full narrative records in their original form can be an excellent source of information when a researcher is first investigating a possible area of inquiry. For example, a researcher with a hypothesis about the behavior of fans at sporting events may wish to observe several different sporting events and create a narrative record of behavior. This narrative record may allow the researcher to refine the hypothesis, as well as to develop operational definitions for a project with a more specific focus.

Checklists

In observational studies with a focus on a limited number of specific behaviors, operational definitions can be developed. Characteristics of the situation and of the participants in the study will also probably be important. To record these specific types of information, a **checklist** can be used to guide observations; a checklist can also save time by allowing the record-making procedure to be efficiently organized.

In general, two types of checklists can be designed—they are often combined on the same sheet of paper. A **static checklist** is used to record characteristics that will not change during the course of the observations; these might include characteristics about the setting, such as where the observations are being made, what the weather is like (if relevant), and perhaps how many people are present. The static checklist also includes characteristics of the participants, such as gender and age. Other characteristics may also be important for certain types of study. For instance, observations in a nursing home might include information about the participants' state of health, or observations of driving behavior may include the make and color of the vehicle.

An **action checklist** is used to record the presence or absence of specific behaviors and characteristics over time. An action checklist could be used to record the types of play behavior a child demonstrates on the playground over a period of time, or to record what a small group of people do in a library. Table 8.1 presents an example of an action checklist with data about driving behavior at a three-way intersection.

Table 8.1   Driving Behavior at a Three-Way Intersection

Vehicle	Stopped	Slowed	Ran
1. Auto		*	
2. Auto		*	
3. Auto		*	
4. Bus	*		
5. Auto		*	
6. Auto		*	
7. Auto		*	
8. Auto	*		
9. Truck	*		
10. Auto	*		

Depending on how an action checklist is organized, it can provide information simply about the frequency of different categories of behavior or, when combined with time information, it can provide information about the order of behaviors and their duration.

For either type of checklist, each characteristic or category of behavior must have its own operational definition. For example, the operational definition of a vehicle slowing at an intersection might be that the tire rotation decreases as the vehicle approaches the intersection and reaches a minimum at or near the crosswalk, after which rotation increases. An operational definition of stopping at the intersection might be that the tires cease rotating within a half-vehicle length of the crosswalk. It is a good idea to make some practice observations with the operational definitions. Even when it seems that the definitions are clear and the observations are straightforward, surprises may cause ambiguity in the operational definitions. To accommodate those surprises, an additional miscellaneous category is often included in the checklist.

The disadvantage of checklists is that they focus on a relatively small subset of behaviors or characteristics and ignore all others; data collection by means of narrative records is free of this disadvantage. On the other hand, in comparison with narrative records, checklists have the advantage that the data do not need to be reduced by coding; they are already organized and can thus be more easily summarized.

Concept Question 8.3

Suppose that a researcher wishes to observe the frequency of three behaviors in the classroom: visiting, working alone, and watching the teacher. The researcher will be observing this classroom for an hour, and will note the behavior of a specific child once every 2 minutes. Other information about the child must also be recorded: gender, age, and seating position in the classroom. Design the checklist for this study and describe its properties. Would it be an action checklist, a static checklist, or a combination of both?

TYPES OF DATA COLLECTED

Many different types of questions can be answered by data from observational studies. Information about the existence of various characteristics of the participants and situations can be obtained and organized to establish what characteristics tend to occur together. These characteristics could be recorded on a static checklist or gleaned from narrative records.

Observations of behaviors supply even more information. Simply recording whether a behavior occurs provides information about the frequency of its occurrence. An observer may watch a classroom and simply note if students talk to other students at inappropriate times. The results would allow the researcher to estimate how often this behavior occurs on a given day.

How often a behavior occurs may not be all that the researcher needs to know. The researcher may also need information related to time, such as the duration of the behavior or at what intervals it tends to occur. For example, an observer who watches a classroom for whole days could record not only whether a behavior occurs, but at what time it occurs. Later analysis of the data may suggest a pattern to the behavior; for example, the students may be more apt to talk inappropriately before lunch, but less apt to do so directly after recess. Information about the duration of behaviors may supply additional important insights into a research area. Information about frequency, duration, and timing—for several participants or for one participant—can be gained from narrative records, if they are complete enough, or can be recorded directly on appropriately designed checklists.

Sometimes, it is more useful to rate characteristics and behaviors than simply to note their existence. Consider the example of drivers at an intersection. Instead of noting whether vehicles stopped at, slowed for, or ran the stop sign, observers could rate each driver on how fast the vehicle was going on a scale from 1 (vehicle stops) to 5 (vehicle runs sign without slowing). Or, as a different example, observers may rate each member of a couple on attractiveness to test the hypothesis that couples are composed of people of relatively comparable levels of attractiveness.

Ratings have the advantage of providing a more continuous, and less categorical, description of behavior or characteristics than do checklists. A disadvantage of ratings, however, is that because subjective judgments are required, it is more difficult to obtain agreement between or among raters.

SAMPLING TECHNIQUES

A researcher who is interested in the types of food people choose in a college cafeteria cannot observe all cafeteria customers all of the time. Instead, only a sample of all of the customers can be observed. The goal is to choose a sample that is representative of the population. A sample that is unrepresentative of the population is called a **biased sample**. Two sampling techniques that increase the generalizability of observational research and decrease the probability of creating a biased sample are behavior sampling and situation sampling.

Behavior Sampling

If it is not possible to observe all of the patrons in a cafeteria, then a sample of the patrons—or more precisely, a sample of the patrons' behaviors—must be chosen for observation. During **behavior sampling**, a researcher observers subsets of a participant's behavior at different times and/or in different situations. There are various techniques for behavior sampling, such as time sampling and event sampling. In **time sampling**, the times at which observations will be made are chosen in an effort to obtain a representative sample of behaviors. Time sampling may be done randomly or systematically. Random time sampling means that each interval of time is equally likely to be chosen. Systematic time sampling occurs when time intervals for observation are chosen purposefully. Often, random and systematic time sampling are employed within the same study. For example, it may not be particularly useful to randomly choose hours to observe a college cafeteria that wouldn't be in use for much of the day. Thus, systematic time sampling could be used to choose particular hours during the morning, noon, and evening meal times. The observers may also decide (systematically) to make observations for 10 minutes at a time. Random time sampling could then be employed to determine which 10-minute intervals would be used. These intervals could be randomly chosen by means of a random-numbers table (as provided in appendix A) or by picking intervals from a hat.

Time sampling is appropriate when the behaviors of interest occur on a nearly continuous basis. When the behaviors occur less frequently, it may not be feasible to identify a particular observation period, since no behaviors may be occurring during that time period. In that case, **event sampling** may be useful. Event sampling is the random or systematic sampling of events that include the behavior of interest. A researcher interested in neighbors' reactions to a building fire may need to sample among fires at various points in a city. It would not be possible to use time sampling in this case, because a fire may not be occurring during the appointed time.

In systematic event sampling, events are chosen in a purposeful manner—as in attending every fifth fire announced on the police radio. In random event sampling, events are chosen in a manner so that each event is equally likely to be chosen, perhaps by using a random-numbers table to determine which fires to attend. A risk of systematic event sampling is that observations may be made only when it is convenient for the researcher, which can lead to an unrepresentative sample of events.

Situation Sampling

In **situation sampling**, observations are made in different settings and circumstances. This technique can greatly enhance the generalizability of an observational study. A researcher interested in how children play together on a playground might make observations at a number of playgrounds in different neighborhoods. This would increase the likelihood that the observed play behavior is representative of all children's play behavior and not just the play behavior of a specific neighborhood.

Concept Question 8.4

A researcher is interested in the factors that affect whether an individual will pick up litter or let it lie. The researcher wishes to place some litter (a paper cup from a fast food restaurant) on the ground, to see if passers-by will pick it up and dispose of it. This person asks for your assistance in designing the study. How could this researcher use time sampling? Could the researcher use event sampling? If so, how? If not, why not? How could situation sampling be incorporated into this design? Would the sampling techniques be employed randomly or systematically?

SUMMARY

Observational studies have great potential for helping researchers to clarify their hypotheses before carrying out more complicated projects, for determining how well the results from laboratory studies can be generalized, and for investigating topics that can only be studied by observation.

Observational studies can be subdivided into a number of types: naturalistic observation, disguised and undisguised participant observation, and field experiments. Each of these approaches has particular advantages and disadvantages. The best approach to use depends on the specific situation at hand.

Observational data are only of use if they are both reliable and valid. The reliability of the data is often assessed by calculating the interobserver reliability between two independent observers.

How the data are collected is also important. Researchers may create a narrative record or an active and/or static checklist. Regardless of the particular method of data recording, the researcher must operationally define the behaviors to be observed before data collection begins.

The researcher must also determine when and where to collect the data. Behavior sampling involves determining what sample of behavior will be observed. In time sampling, specific observation times are determined either randomly or systematically. Event sampling might be used when the behavior is relatively uncommon and not likely to occur at any specific time. In situation sampling, observations are made in different settings and circumstances to increase the generalizability of the results.

As with all research, observational studies are only as good as the planning that goes into them to avoid confounds that can plague certain designs. For observational studies, a major concern is reactivity, in which the behavior observed is affected by the presence of the observer. Another potential confound is observer bias, in which the expectations of the observer affect the data collection. Nonhuman observers can also provide biased data because equipment can only record limited types of data.

While observational studies have both limitations and advantages, they can be a great source of information about behavior in natural settings.

IMPORTANT TERMS AND CONCEPTS

action checklist
behavior sampling
biased sample
checklist
data reduction
desensitization
disguised participant
  studies
ecological validity
event sampling
field experiments
habituation
Hawthorne effect

interobserver reliability
narrative records
naturalistic observation
observer bias
participant observation
reactive measure
reactivity
reliability
situation sampling
static checklist
time sampling
undisguised participant
  studies

EXERCISES

1. Shopping malls have been described as the new town meeting places. A colleague of yours wants to study the people and types of activities at shopping malls and comes to you for advice on how to begin.

   a. What would you suggest that this person do first?

   b. What types of information should be collected? How should the information be collected?

   c. After some initial observations, your colleague wishes to investigate whether people shop at the mall alone or whether they shop in groups. What terms need to be operationalized? What definitions might you suggest?

   d. What type of observational study would you suggest to study the question of shopping alone or in groups?

   e. How would data collection be done? Would you use a static checklist? An action checklist? If so, what would it look like?

   f. Would your design allow for an assessment of the reliability of the measurements? If so, how would you assess interobserver reliability?

2. Do males and females carry their books differently? Design and conduct an observational study to address this question.

   a. What is your operational definition for "carrying books"? What are the different ways books can be carried and how have you defined them for reliable observations?

   b. Design your checklist. Is it an action or static checklist, or both?

   c. Plan your data collection. Will you use behavior sampling? Situation sampling? Event sampling? Will your sampling be done randomly or systematically? Will you make observations for a specific period of time or until you have gathered a certain amount of data?

d. Will you be able to assess interobserver reliability? If so, how? Assess your interobserver reliability, if possible.

3. Two observers collect data on the behavior of people who come out of their homes when an emergency vehicle is in the neighborhood. The observers note whether the individuals approach the vehicle, stand alone, or stand with other neighbors. They make observations of 350 individuals, but disagree 28 times in their observations. On the basis of this information, what is their interobserver reliability?

ANSWERS TO CONCEPT QUESTIONS AND ODD-NUMBERED EXERCISES

Note: There will often be more than one correct answer for each of these questions. Consult with your instructor about your own answers.

Concept Question 8.1

A naturalistic observation study might involve unobtrusively watching how older people are treated in stores, on buses, and in other public places. In a disguised participant study, you might dress as an older person and observe how you are treated by others. In an undisguised participant study, you might join a group of senior citizens on an outing and observe how they are treated.

Concept Question 8.2

The researcher should probably ask a trained observer to make the observations, so that the researcher's biases do not affect data collection. An alternative is to use a video camera, but the presence of the camera might affect the students' behavior; also, after the data have been collected, they will need to be scored by observers, who might still introduce biases. I would put trained observers in classrooms, preferably at the beginning of the semester when the students will not know who is and isn't a student.

Concept Question 8.3

Gender_____ Age_____ Position in classroom_____		
Two-minute segments Visiting	Working	Watching teacher
1		
2		
3		
4		
—		
30		

The first line would be a static checklist; the rest would be an active checklist.

Concept Question 8.4

Suppose the researcher wishes to conduct this study on a college campus. Time sampling might be used to determine when the study would be conducted. First, systematic time sampling would permit the choice of time periods when pedestrians are around. Next, random time sampling might be used within these chosen time periods to pinpoint when, exactly, data would be collected. Event sampling would not be helpful in this study, unless the researcher wished to address particular situations, such as the behavior of a crowd leaving a ball game or theater. Situation sampling could be used by varying the locations at which the study was conducted.

Exercises

1. a. My recommendation is that this person should go to the mall and write a narrative record of behaviors that he or she observes.

   b. In the narrative record, the researcher might note how many people are around; the size of the groups they are in; the numbers of males and females; and the relative ages of the people. The researcher might also observe whether people are actually purchasing things or are meeting others or perhaps exercising.

   c. The researcher needs to operationalize "shopping," "shopping alone," and "shopping in groups." "Shopping" might be defined as walking into a store and looking at merchandise. "Shopping alone" could be defined as the situation in which a person enters the store without anyone else and leaves without anyone else. "Shopping in groups" might be defined as the situation in which two or more people enter and leave stores together.

   d. I'd recommend a naturalistic observation.

   e. I'd use an action checklist much like this:

Alone	Two	Three	Four	Five or more
1.				
2.				
3.				
4.				

   f. If two or more observers watch the same area independently of each other, then interobserver reliability can be assessed.

3. Using the approach described in the chapter, the interobserver reliability is

$$\frac{350 - 28}{350} \times 100 = 92\%$$

9

Mail Surveys, Telephone Surveys, and Personal Interviews

How often have you completed a survey or answered questions for a researcher? Perhaps you responded to a telephone poll during an election year. Or maybe you answered questions posed by a market researcher at a shopping mall. You may have participated in survey research as a college student. If you haven't yet, sooner or later you are likely to have the opportunity to serve as a respondent in survey research.

In survey research, participants are asked to respond to a series of questions about a topic. The topic might be very specific—for example, where and why you purchased that brand of orange juice—or very broad—for example, your general philosophy of life. The purpose of the survey might be to provide answers to an applied research question or to advance basic research. Survey research is an especially appealing approach to data collection because it seems so simple: just write a series of questions to address your specific research problem and then find the appropriate sample of people to answer your questions. Yet survey research must be done as carefully and conscientiously as any other type of scientific research if the results are to be useful and interpretable.

Many researchers speak interchangeably of surveys and questionnaires, as we will do throughout this chapter. Some, however, make a distinction between the two, in terms of the types of research questions that surveys and questionnaires ultimately intend to answer. Survey researchers may be more apt to look for distinctions among subgroups of respondents. For instance, during a political campaign, a surveyor might be interested in how those who would vote for a certain candidate differ from those who would not vote for the candidate. Questionnaire researchers, however, may be more interested in relationships between variables—for example, the possibility of a relationship between weight gain and the amount of time spent watching television. However, this distinction between surveys and questionnaires is not clear and distinct; survey researchers can look for relationships, and questionnaire researchers often detect differences among subgroups of respondents.

Surveys can be presented to potential respondents in a number of ways—for example, by mail, in person, or over the phone. The primary advantages and disadvantages of mail surveys, telephone surveys, and surveys conducted in person will be presented in this chapter, along with a discussion of practical concerns in survey design.

SURVEYS: HOW AND WHY TO USE THEM

Surveys can be conducted orally and in person, can be read over the telephone, or can be self-administered by the respondent in written form. They may call for in-depth answers to questions or simply the choice of an option. The topics addressed may be as innocuous as opinions about a new ice cream product or as sensitive as personal sexual behaviors or past dishonest activities. Regardless of the topic or the format of a survey, however, the primary purpose is to gather reliable and valid information. Thus, it is important to design and conduct the study so as to maximize truthful responses. The factors that affect whether a respondent will reply honestly vary for different types of surveys. In addition, particular types of surveys are better suited for gaining particular types of information. For example, a researcher is likely to obtain more information on sensitive topics by conducting a mail survey than by posing the same questions during a personal interview. Because of the wide variety of types of surveys, types of questions, and types of information a researcher can expect to obtain, surveys are an important research tool.

Mail Surveys

Mail surveys are written, self-administered questionnaires. As such, it is especially important that the survey be self-explanatory and that all questions be clearly worded. Ideally, the survey should also be interesting, so that the recipient will be willing to respond.

Mail surveys are popular because they have several advantages over other methods of gathering data. Chief among these advantages is that they can reach a large number and a wide variety of potential respondents. Because mail surveys can be distributed widely, there is less chance for sampling bias. **Sampling bias** occurs when a sample overrepresents some subset of the population and underrepresents other subsets, so that the sample is not representative of the population as a whole. For instance, people of color may be underrepresented in a sample of a city's population, or more males than females may be selected for a sample that should have equal numbers of each gender. Mail surveys can be sent to neighborhoods where individual interviews might not be safe to conduct and can reach remote areas that would be impractical for interviewers to travel to. Moreover, whereas an interviewer who works during particular times of the day may miss certain respondents, every intended respondent will eventually receive a survey in the mail, regardless of whether he or she works at home, at an office, during the day, or during the night. In all these ways, mail surveys reduce the likelihood of sampling bias.

Another advantage of the mail survey over the personal interview is that the self-administered questionnaire eliminates interviewer bias. **Interviewer bias** occurs when an interviewer's behaviors, questions, or recording procedures result in data that are consistent with the interviewer's personal beliefs and do not provide an accurate reflection of the participants' beliefs. Interviewers must be carefully trained to ask questions and record answers in an objective manner. Yet bias can still be a problem when interviewers have expectations about the results of a survey or when their own personal opinions are made apparent, even subtly, to the respondent. For example, Paul Erdos described this incident of unintentional interviewer bias:

> In one town where 6 interviewers administered a questionnaire to 400 people, 20 respondents stated that they liked a certain soap because ". . . it has a fragrance like lilacs." All 20 interviews were made by the same interviewer. A check showed that she hadn't been cheating. She just happened to like lilacs and had introduced this particular question with a little aside about the lilacs then in bloom. (Erdos, 1983, p. 8)

Mail surveys have the advantage over personal interviews when it comes to interviewer bias because with a mail survey no interviewer is present.

Another benefit of mail surveys is that, because the respondents complete the survey according to their own schedules, the replies are likely to be more complete. For example, Erdos (1983, pp. 8–9) reported a comparison between a mail survey and a telephone survey that both asked whether the respondents listened to the radio, watched television, read the newspaper, or read magazines. In addition, both surveys asked for the programs, newspapers, and magazines the respondents listened to, watched, or read. The mail and telephone surveys gave similar results on the number of individuals who listened to, watched, or read the various forms of media, but the mail survey resulted in more specific information about the programs, newspapers, and magazines involved.

Finally, mail surveys are more likely to provide valid responses than telephone surveys and personal interviews for collecting sensitive information. A respondent can more readily believe that his or her responses are anonymous when no interviewer is recording the information. Some thought, though, must be given to the wording of questions requesting sensitive information. Specific recommendations on question writing will be given later in the chapter.

Disadvantages of Mail Surveys

A number of disadvantages of mail surveys must also be recognized. One example is that mail survey distribution is not perfect. Obviously, individuals who do not have mailing addresses cannot be included in the sample, and individuals who cannot read or write will not be able to reply to a survey. A primary concern with mail surveys is the percentage of the sample that is willing to respond.

The extent to which people who receive a survey actually complete and return it is called the **response rate**. For mail surveys, the response rate is determined by dividing the actual number of responses by the potential number of responses, which is calculated by subtracting from the total number of requests those requests that were made to ineligible people (for example, a survey for students given to a faculty member) and those surveys that were undeliverable by the postal service. Multiplying this ratio by 100 yields a percentage. Thus, a formula for response rate is as follows:

$$\frac{\text{Number of responses}}{\text{Number in sample} - \left(\text{Ineligible and undeliverable requests}\right)} \times 100$$

Typically, if a mail survey is sent out only once, the researcher can expect approximately 30% of the surveys to be completed. To increase the response rate, a researcher may send out a second or even a third mailing of the survey to those who have not responded. A risk of multiple mailings, however, is that those who receive multiple copies may be less likely to believe that their responses will be anonymous, since the researcher is obviously keeping track of who has and has not completed the survey. To address this problem, the researcher might provide respondents with a postcard for record-keeping purposes and ask them to mail it at the same time as their completed survey to remove them from subsequent re-mailings of the survey. An explanation of this procedure might reassure respondents that their responses are truly anonymous.

The response rate for mail surveys is considerably lower than for other types of surveys and this is a major disadvantage of mail surveys. A poor response rate can invalidate all the effort put into selecting a representative sample of the population. The 30% of a carefully selected sample that responds to a survey could very well be a subset of participants with specific characteristics. Thus, the respondents may not represent the population, even though the original sample did. Only if the respondents were distributed randomly throughout the sample could the researcher be confident that they maintained the original characteristics of the sample.

As a rule, it is impossible to determine how or why a particular subsample responded to the survey. The best way to reduce the possibility of a biased sample of respondents is to increase the response rate. A suggested minimum percentage of responses is 50%, unless there is some other form of verification that the nonrespondents and the respondents are similar (Erdos, 1983, p. 144).

The researcher must make efforts to increase the likelihood of a response. As we have seen, multiple mailings somewhat increase the likelihood. Personal touches, such as a hand-addressed envelope and a personally signed cover letter, are also effective. First-class postage may also increase the likelihood of a response but is significantly more expensive than bulk-mail rates. The response rate also increases if the recipients have advance notice that the survey is coming. Another approach is to supply an incentive. Respondents might be offered a chance in a raffle or a free gift. Alternatively, the researcher might provide an incentive to all recipients, with the hope that it will motivate more of them to respond. For example, sometimes surveyors send a few quarters with their questionnaires and invite respondents to have a cup of coffee on them while completing the survey.

It almost goes without saying that the researcher should provide the respondent with a self-addressed postage-paid envelope. Finally, the appearance of a mail survey will have a considerable impact on the response rate; all efforts should be made to create a survey that is neat, well-organized, and easy to read.

Because they are self-administered, mail surveys must be self-explanatory. No interviewer is on hand to explain what is meant by a question or to provide additional information. This may limit the amount of information that can be obtained with a mail survey; by asking follow-up questions, a personal or telephone interviewer might obtain more complete information. Mail surveys will be of little use with the very old, the very young, or those simply uninterested in the topic. When choosing the type of survey design appropriate for a study, the researcher needs to consider whether the information needed is likely to be provided by a mail survey or is better solicited by an interviewer of some sort.

Group-Administered Surveys

Surveys that are given to a group of respondents—in a classroom, for example—share many characteristics with mail surveys. They are essentially self-administered; the researcher typically cannot clarify questions for individuals without weakening the validity of the study. Therefore, the survey needs to be self-explanatory. Also, like a mail survey, it needs to be enticing and interesting so that people feel inclined to respond.

Because group-administered surveys are usually given in a setting where it is easy for recipients to complete them, most people will comply; correspondingly, the response rate is much stronger than for mail surveys.

Telephone Surveys

When mail surveys or group-administered surveys are inappropriate, the researcher might consider **telephone surveys**. Surveys conducted over the telephone have several advantages over mail surveys and personal interviews. For instance, a telephone interviewer can ask for clarifications of an answer or ask follow-up questions for additional information; this is not possible in mail surveys.

Telephone surveys also benefit from a higher response rate than do mail surveys. It is not unusual to obtain response rates of 59–70% (Groves & Kahn, 1979, p. 63), whereas the comparable figure for a single mailing of a mail survey is 30%. People are just more likely to throw out a mail survey than to hang up on a telephone interviewer.

One reason that the response rate is higher for telephone surveys than for mail surveys may be that the interviewer is able to establish a rapport with the respondent. If the interviewer is effectively supervised, any practices that are likely to reduce response rates can be changed in a timely fashion.

As compared with personal interviews, telephone interviews are inexpensive; the interviewer need not travel and can complete more interviews in a given amount of time than can a face-to-face interviewer. The relative cost effectiveness of telephone surveys and mail surveys is less clear, however.

The cost of a mail survey depends on the costs of printing and postage, while telephone survey costs depend on phone rates. For mail surveys, the cost differs little with distance, but distance can increase the cost of a telephone call. Similarly, the length of a questionnaire will have minimal effect on postage costs but will increase the cost of a telephone call. A small sample is likely to make a mail survey more expensive per survey than would a larger sample. However, in the telephone survey the price per call is unaffected by sample size; if it costs $1.50 per call to give 100 people a survey, it will still cost $1.50 per call to give 1,000 people the same survey. Therefore, in the case of a short survey meant for a small sample, telephone interviews may be more cost effective; in the case of longer surveys for a larger sample, a mailing may be less expensive.

Disadvantages of Telephone Surveys

An important pitfall of telephone surveys is that a sampling bias can occur when all members of the population do not have telephones or when some people have telephones with unlisted numbers. The effect of unlisted phone numbers can be reduced by using random-digit dialing, but this increases the chance of calling telephones that are irrelevant to the survey—for example, calling businesses in a survey of residences. As more and more people use answering machines and caller ID to screen their calls, the samples obtained in telephone surveys are likely to become steadily less representative. Sampling bias is of little concern, however, when the population of interest is made up of businesses, few of which are likely to screen their calls or to have unlisted phone numbers or no phone at all.

A more serious concern in telephone surveys is interviewer bias. Training before interviewing and supervision during the interviews can minimize this risk, but researchers must recognize that whenever two humans interact interviewer biases may affect the responses and records.

Personal Interviews

A third type of survey involves **personal interviews** with respondents. This type of survey might be conducted on the street, in a shopping mall, in the respondent's home, or anywhere else that two people can talk.

The personal interview has several advantages over the telephone survey and, in particular, over the mail survey. In telephone and mail surveys, a directory—a telephone directory or a city directory of residents, for example—is often used for sampling purposes. These directories, however, are almost never up to date, even when they are first published, because some people will have moved since the data were collected (Dillman, 1978, pp. 41–43). Personal interviews can avoid any bias hidden in a directory (such as changes in the neighborhood when people move or the absence from the telephone directory of those with unlisted numbers) because the researcher can approach those who actually live at a particular address.

Another disadvantage of mail and telephone surveys is that the researcher cannot be sure of the identity of the individual who responds to the survey. Especially with mail surveys, the researcher has no way of knowing whether only one person responded or the response was a collaborative effort. Did the head of the household respond, or did a bored

child complete the survey? On the telephone, the interviewer cannot easily determine with whom he or she is speaking or whether there is someone who would be better suited to respond to the survey. For example, is
the person on the telephone the manager of a business, the assistant manager, or a low-level employee? In a personal interview, the interviewer
can actually see the respondent and can much more easily establish what
that person's role is in the family or business.

Personal interviews typically yield a high response rate—often
between 80 and 90% (Dillman, 1978, p. 51; Erdos, 1983, p. 141). Also, as
compared with mail surveys and telephone surveys, the researcher has a
greater ability to determine the characteristics of nonrespondents (refus-
als) in personal interviews because the people are visible to the would-be
interviewer. Moreover, the nonrespondent typically must verbally refuse
to participate and may provide a specific reason—for example, being in a
hurry or being late for an appointment. Even without speaking with the
nonrespondent, the researcher may be able to identify certain characteristics—such as gender, approximate age, and perhaps even socioeconomic and marital status—by looking at the individual or the individual's setting (Dillman, 1978, pp. 52–53). This information (although
susceptible to observer bias) can help the researcher determine whether
the nonrespondents shared any characteristics different from those of the
sample of respondents.

People who are willing to be interviewed for a survey will often
devote a considerable amount of time to the interview. Therefore, the personal interview is often the method of choice when the survey is long and
the questions tend toward the tedious (Dillman, 1978, pp. 54, 59–69).

The interviewer has the opportunity in a personal interview, as in a
telephone interview, to clarify any questions that the respondent might
have and to obtain complete answers to open-ended questions. By means
of follow-up questions, the interviewer can encourage further clarification
of an incomplete answer; this opportunity is unavailable in a mail survey.

Disadvantages of Personal Interviews

One disadvantage of the personal interview, especially in comparison
with a mail survey, is that it may be more difficult to assure potential
respondents that their responses will be anonymous when the interviewer is right there in the room with them (Erdos, 1983, p. 9).

Respondents in personal interviews may also be more likely to give
socially desirable responses to questions. Socially desirable responses
reflect what is deemed appropriate by society, but are not necessarily suggestive of the respondent's practices or beliefs. For example, a respondent
may say that he or she reads the newspaper every day when the person
actually reads the newspaper once a week—and then only the sports and
the comics. The likelihood of receiving socially desirable responses
increases as the questions become more threatening or more sensitive—

that is, when the respondent feels the answer is more likely to affect the interviewer's impression or opinion of the respondent (Hochstim, 1967). Relatedly, participants may provide the responses that they think the interviewer would want to hear; for example, if the interviewer is a woman, the respondent might tend to answer questions about women's rights and roles in a supportive manner. The major problem with socially desirable responses or responses chosen to satisfy interviewer expectations is that they have little or no validity and thus are of little worth.

Another pitfall is that the respondent may sometimes need to consult with others in order to obtain the most accurate information for a survey. In a business setting, for instance, an employee may need to ask a manager about their average profit each month; in a family setting, one member of the household may need to consult with others about the number of hours spent watching television. In a personal interview, however, it is less likely that others will be available for consultation; an interview may need to be rescheduled with the more knowledgeable person. A mail survey, completed at the respondents' convenience, allows more opportunity for consultation.

Because the interviewer collects the information directly from the respondent and close supervision of individual interviewers is difficult and inefficient, the personal interview provides considerable opportunities for interviewer bias or outright subversion by the interviewer (Dillman, 1978, pp. 63–64). As with the telephone survey, subtle interviewer biases and expectations may be communicated to the respondent verbally. In personal interviews, nonverbal cues may also be used, such as a smile or a nod that may encourage one set of answers, or a frown or moment of silence that may discourage another. With the lack of supervision, in contrast to telephone surveys, there is also the risk that interviewers will simply lie about the interviews; they might not have conducted any interviews at all.

Assuming that the interviews are actually conducted, the researcher must take care that the responses do not include a sampling bias. If an interviewer conducts door-to-door interviews, in an attempt to gather information from a representative sample of a community, those who work at home, are unemployed, or are retired may be overrepresented in the responses. If interviews are conducted in a shopping mall, those who enjoy shopping and/or have money to spend may be overrepresented.

On a practical note, personal interviews tend to be more expensive and time-consuming than other types of surveys. For small samples, the time and cost may not be prohibitive; as the sample grows larger, however, the time allotted for the study or the number of interviewers needed for the study or both must be increased. Unfortunately, the monetary cost of a project sometimes determines which method is used, regardless of which method would supply the most valid and reliable results.

Concept Question 9.1

What types of survey would you recommend in the following situations? Give a brief summary of why you would use that particular type of survey.

a. A survey of sexual preferences, habits, and number of partners.

b. A long survey on the cleaners used by households.

c. A short survey of car-buying history in a large metropolitan area.

d. A nationwide survey of attitudes toward a recent presidential decision.

SURVEY CONSTRUCTION

Careful planning of the questions and their wording and order is required to develop a survey that will yield reliable and valid information. The type of survey—a telephone survey, personal interview, or self-administered survey—also plays a role in determining what questions are asked and in what order.

Layout of Questions

In a survey that the participants will see, such as a mail survey or a survey conducted in a large group, the appearance of the survey is especially important. It should look as if it would be easy and, ideally, interesting to complete. For a mail survey, length is important: Shorter surveys encourage a higher percentage of returns (Erdos, 1983, p. 39). As we saw earlier, respondents to personal interview surveys seem more tolerant of longer surveys.

Demographic questions are descriptive questions about the respondent's social statistics, such as gender, age, and income level. These questions are usually as important to the researcher as any other question on the survey, but the respondent sometimes finds them boring or too personal. For this reason, it is often recommended that demographic questions be placed at the end of the questionnaire, where they are more apt to be completed because the respondent has made something of a commitment to the survey by this point (Dillman, 1978; Sudman & Bradburn, 1982). However, this is not a hard and fast rule. In some cases, especially when a personal interview or telephone survey is being conducted, the demographic questions—or a subset of them—may serve as an icebreaker. The interviewer may use the demographic questions to establish a rapport with the respondent before getting to the more substantial questions.

All the questions on the survey should be ordered in a logical manner. To prevent respondents from having to answer irrelevant questions, filter questions might be used. A **filter question** instructs the respondent or interviewer which is the next question for different answers by the respondent. An example of a filter question is as follows:

Do you smoke cigarettes, cigars, and/or a pipe? _____ yes _____ no
(If you answered NO to this question, please skip to question 5.)

Funnel questions may also be used in a survey. **Funnel questions** are ordered from the most general to the most specific; they serve to introduce a topic and then slowly focus on more detailed aspects of it. A major function of funnel questions is to prevent earlier responses from biasing later responses (Sudman & Bradburn, 1982, pp. 219–220). An example of a set of funnel questions is as follows:

Indicate the extent to which you agree or disagree with statements 1–5.

1. Men and women should have equal rights under the law.
1	2	3	4	5	6	7
Disagree						Agree

2. A woman should earn as much as a man for comparable work.
1	2	3	4	5	6	7
Disagree						Agree

3. A woman with the physical ability and desire should be allowed to hold a physically demanding job.
1	2	3	4	5	6	7
Disagree						Agree

4. Ideally, a mother should stay home with her young child.
1	2	3	4	5	6	7
Disagree						Agree

5. I consider myself to be a feminist.
1	2	3	4	5	6	7
Disagree						Agree

Consider if the order of the questions were reversed. Whether the respondent considers himself or herself to be a feminist might very well influence how strongly he or she agrees or disagrees with each of the other items.

Wording of Questions

Writing the questions for a survey takes considerable thought and planning to ensure that the answers will be useful to the researcher. If the researcher takes insufficient care in wording the questions, they may be ambiguous and may be misunderstood by the respondents. A general rule of thumb is that if a question can be misunderstood, it will be. If a researcher finds herself saying "everyone knows what we mean by that," then the question probably needs to be rewritten.

It may seem obvious, but in determining how to write questions, the researcher must decide what specific information is needed and then ask for that information. If you want to know the number of years a person has lived in an area, it is best to specifically ask for the number of years. Asking "How long have you lived in Centerville?" may elicit responses such as "Since I was a child," "I moved here after I got married," or "For many years." A better approach would be to simply ask, "How many years have you lived in Centerville?" or "How long have you lived in Centerville? _____ yrs" (Erdos, 1983, p. 66).

The questions that appear in surveys can be divided into two types: open-ended questions and closed questions. **Open-ended questions** provide room or time for the respondent to formulate his or her own response. **Closed questions** ask the respondent to choose from alternative potential answers.

Open-ended questions have the advantage of allowing the participant to provide complete information, including any explanatory information that may be necessary. On the other hand, open-ended questions are much more difficult to score for statistical analysis. Typically, some type of coding system must be designed, and two or more judges must code the responses. The reliability of the coding system can then be assessed by comparing the agreements among the judges, as for interobserver reliability (see chapter 8).

Closed questions do not require that the responses be coded. However, they limit the responses to a predetermined list of alternatives. Unless the researcher is very careful, alternatives that the respondents would have used may be omitted; for example, providing only yes or no as options ignores the subset of respondents who would prefer to indicate that they don't know. Another limitation is that the respondent does not have the opportunity to expand on or explain answers. Thus, closed questions may lead to less complete information than open-ended questions.

There are various ways to solicit information using closed questions. A researcher might ask simple yes/no/don't know questions, for instance. To find more subtle differences among subgroups of respondents than yes/no questions might allow, the researcher can use rating scales. For example, a researcher could ask the following question using a rating scale and potentially find differences between groups (such as Republicans and Democrats or men and women) that a yes/no answer would not divulge.

If the election were held today, would you vote for President Smilegood?
1   2   3   4   5   6   7
Definitely would not   Definitely would

It is important to provide meaningful anchor statements at the beginning and end of the rating scales, so that everyone understands what the numbers on the scale mean.

Closed questions must be written with care, so that a respondent has a single option that accurately reflects his or her answer. Consider the following question:

On average, how many hours per day do you watch television?
a. 0–1 hour
b. 1–2 hours
c. 2–3 hours
d. 3 hours or more

The respondent who watches an average of 2 hours of television per day has to choose between option (b) and option (c). When using closed questions, it is important to provide options that are mutually exclusive and exhaustive. Mutually exclusive options do not overlap. Exhaustive options cover the full range of possible answers so there are no gaps between categories and the full range of possible categories is provided. Another way to avoid problems with closed questions when quantitative information is requested is to provide a carefully worded open-ended question instead, such as:

On average, how many hours per day do you watch television? _____ hours.

Here the respondent is provided a labeled space to provide a number. A small space suggests a short response, such as a number. A larger space would allow for greater explanations, such as, "I watch only four hour-long shows per week." With the open-ended question there is still the risk of an uncodable response being provided, but it avoids forcing the respondent's answer into a preset mold that might not be appropriate.

As a question is read, the respondent is likely to begin formulating an answer immediately, even before the sentence ends. For this reason, it is important that any conditional information be placed at the beginning of the question. For instance:

Do you believe in the right to abortion if the woman's life is at risk?

The respondent may have already answered the first part of the question, "do you believe in the right to abortion," before ever getting to the conditional information about the risk to a woman's life. A preferable wording would be as follows:

If a woman's life is at risk, do you believe in her right to an abortion?

In this case, with the conditional information first, the reader is given all of the relevant information before the key question is asked. This same principle holds when the conditional information is a definition of a term or a description of a setting. It is important—and logical—to present the relevant information before asking the specific question.

The wording of a question must be chosen so as to be clear and unambiguous. Survey writers must avoid loaded questions, leading questions, and double-barreled questions. **Loaded questions** include terms that are emotionally laden and nonneutral. An example of a loaded question is: Do you believe that radical extremists have the right to burn our country's symbol of freedom, the flag? The terms "radical extremist" and "symbol of freedom" are loaded and suggest the writer's opinion of flag-burners. Loaded questions tend to produce biased responses that reflect what the questioner wants to hear but not necessarily what the respondents believe. Obviously, emotionally laden terms should be avoided. A better wording of the flag-burning question might be: Do you believe that people have the right to burn the American flag?

Leading questions present information within the question that leads the respondent to answer in a desired manner. An example is: Most people believe that recycling is an important way to help conserve our resources; do you agree? By suggesting what most people believe, the question encourages the respondent to agree. Introductory information should be limited to the absolute minimum required by the respondent in order to answer the question. For instance, depending on the population, it might be important to define recycling. A better, less leading wording might be as follows:

> Recycling is the re-use of goods that would otherwise be disposed of. Do you believe that recycling is an effective way to conserve U.S. resources?
> 1   2   3   4   5
> Very ineffective   Very effective

Both loaded and leading questions suggest to the respondent what the correct reply is, instead of soliciting an unbiased reply.

Even when individual questions are not leading, the order of a set of questions may be leading. For instance, suppose that a survey seeks opinions about people smoking cigarettes in public places. Consider this question:

> To what extent do you agree that cigarette smokers should be able to smoke in all public places?
> 1   2   3   4   5
> Strongly disagree   Strongly agree

Now consider this set of questions:

> To what extent do you agree with the following statements?
> All people have the right to be present in any public place.
> 1   2   3   4   5
> Strongly disagree   Strongly agree
> All people have the right to smoke cigarettes if they choose.
> 1   2   3   4   5
> Strongly disagree   Strongly agree
> Cigarette smokers should be able to smoke in all public places.
> 1   2   3   4   5
> Strongly disagree   Strongly agree

The first two questions, on their own, are not especially leading. As a context for the third, however, they might lead the respondent to agree with the statement that cigarette smokers should be able to smoke in public places.

A third type of wording problem in survey questions are double-barreled questions. Consider the following question: Do you find your job interesting and exciting? It is unclear to the respondent whether the researcher wants to know if his or her job is interesting or whether it is exciting or whether it is both interesting and exciting. **Double-barreled questions** ask more than one question at the same time. A test of whether a question is double-barreled is to attempt to imagine a person who could answer yes to part of the question and no to the other part. A person who had a job that was interesting but not very exciting would have difficulty answering the question posed above. If a question is double-barreled, it is usually best rewritten as two or more separate questions.

In writing questions for a survey, the goal is to write straightforward, unambiguous, and unbiased questions that will elicit usable, reliable, and valid information. With careful planning and attention to wording and layout, a survey can provide meaningful and interpretable information. Finally, it is important, especially for self-administered surveys, to have clear and thorough instructions for answering questions. Is the respondent to provide only one answer or to circle all the options that apply? Must all questions be answered or may some be skipped? If it would be helpful, examples of how to answer questions should be given.

Concept Question 9.2

What is wrong with the wording of the following question, and how might it be better worded?

How many individuals in the United States do you believe have AIDS or are HIV positive?

Survey Development

To maximize the probability that a survey will be useful, it is important not to skimp during the development stage. The first step is to determine exactly what information is needed and then to ask for that specific information. Researchers should not waste their time or their respondents' with irrelevant questions. After the questions are written, a common practice is to develop a first draft of the survey, but not to immediately use it to collect data. Instead, the researcher would carry out a pilot study, in which a small group of people is given the survey. This gives the researcher the opportunity to work out any bugs in the survey questions or the data gathering. Comments are solicited from the group.

Were the questions straightforward, or were some difficult to understand? How long did it take to complete the survey? Did the questions solicit the type of responses that were anticipated? Were there any unexpected responses because some questions were ambiguous? Did most of the respondents answer a particular question in the same manner? If so, perhaps that question is leading in some way.

After modifying the survey in light of the pilot study results, the researcher then takes the final version of the survey for a test run before putting it to work. After presenting it to a small sample of participants who complete it using the same procedures that the larger sample will use, the researcher can ascertain if the changes introduced are adequate and that no new problems have emerged. If the survey survives this final test, it is ready to be put to use.

SAMPLING TECHNIQUES

If the results of a survey are to be interpreted accurately, the sample of respondents must adequately represent the population under investigation. A **population** consists of all of the members of a given group, and a **sample** is a subset of that population. The sample is chosen from a **sampling frame**, which is a list of all of the members of a population. For example, the telephone directory is often used as a sampling frame for all of the residents in a particular geographical area. The sampling frame serves as the operational definition of the population. The **elements** or members of the sample are then chosen from the sampling frame. If you wanted to select a sample of students from your college, the student directory might serve as your sampling frame and the individual names chosen from the directory would be the elements of your sample.

The goal of sampling is to create a sample that is representative of the population. One way to obtain a representative sample is to select the sample randomly. **Random selection** means that all members of the population are equally likely to be chosen as part of the sample. This should not be confused with haphazardly or arbitrarily choosing elements for a sample. Haphazard or arbitrary selection is open to the subtle biases of the person doing the selecting. Random selection avoids these biases and results in a **random sample**, where the elements are randomly chosen from a sampling frame.

In **systematic sampling**, elements are not chosen randomly but, instead, are chosen according to some specific plan or strategy. For example, if every third person on a list of registered students is chosen to be a part of a sample, this is systematic sampling. One combination of random and systematic sampling would be to randomly select a starting point and then choose every kth person as a member of the sample—for example, every tenth person or every third person. This method is considerably less time-consuming than simple random sampling.

Sometimes a population is made up of members of different categories; for instance, a college may have only recently begun accepting male students and thus may consist of 80% female students and 20% male. A representative sample of a population consisting of members of distinct categories must also consist of members of those categories and in the same proportions as found in the population. In such cases, the researcher may not be willing to leave category membership up to chance, as in random or systematic sampling, but instead may choose to use stratified sampling.

Stratified sampling is intended to guarantee that the sample will be representative of the population on specific characteristics. The sampling frame is divided into subsamples or strata on the basis of specific important characteristics. Elements of the sample are then chosen from each strata. The elements may be chosen systematically or randomly. If they are chosen randomly, this technique is called **stratified random sampling**. A researcher using stratified random sampling to guarantee a representative sample of a population that is 80% female and 20% male would divide the sampling frame according to gender. The researcher would then randomly select 80% of the sample from the female strata and 20% of the sample from the male strata.

When the population is too large for simple random sampling or no sampling frame is available for the population, cluster sampling may be used. In **cluster sampling**, clusters of potential respondents that represent the population are identified, and then all of the people in those clusters are included in the sample. In other words, clusters of respondents are chosen (either randomly or systematically) as opposed to choosing individual respondents. At my college, two researchers wished to collect survey information about date rape. The college requires all students to take two English composition courses—a freshman composition course and a junior-level composition course. Because these two courses are required of all students and each class tends to be representative of the population of students, the researchers chose to solicit responses to their survey from the composition classes during one semester. The composition classes served as the representative clusters of the people from the population (Finley & Corty, 1993).

The use of random sampling—alone or as part of stratified or cluster sampling—is usually ideal, but not always feasible. Sometimes a researcher must use a different approach. In a **convenience sample** (also called a **haphazard** or **accidental sample**), participants are chosen from a readily available situation; examples include surveying a class or interviewing shoppers at a mall. Convenience sampling allows the researcher to collect data with relatively little bother, but there is a risk of creating a biased sample. For instance, suppose a researcher surveyed members of a 9:00 AM economics class on their political attitudes. The results might differ considerably from those of a 6:00 PM economics class, which may contain more students with full-time jobs. The researcher must consider the population he or she wants to represent and then identify a situation in which a sample is likely to represent that population.

Quota sampling is a combination of convenience sampling and stratified sampling. As with stratified sampling, a sample of participants is created by choosing differing numbers of participants from various subgroups of a population. Stratified sampling uses random or systematic sampling from the subgroups; in quota sampling, by contrast, convenient sources of subgroup members are identified and participants are sought from these sources. For instance, imagine a college that consists of 25% psychology majors, 10% English majors, 20% biology majors, 30% business majors, 5% history majors, 5% math majors, 3% art majors, and 2% philosophy majors. A researcher using quota sampling might identify courses taken predominantly by students in each major and solicit participants in the appropriate numbers from each of these classes.

Finally, sometimes a researcher needs to contact members of a hard-to-find population. A technique that can be used for this purpose is **snowball sampling**. In snowball sampling, research participants are asked to identify other potential participants. For instance, a researcher might be interested in surveying new mothers. The initial participants might be known personally or through acquaintances; these participants would then be asked for information about other potential participants. I was once involved in snowball sampling, as a participant. As a volunteer in a project on infants' language development, I was asked to provide other parents of infants with information about the study, so that they could also volunteer if they wanted.

Snowball sampling, quota sampling, and convenience sampling sometimes provide the only way a researcher can acquire a reasonable number of participants. However, these are **nonprobability sampling techniques**, which means that each member of the population is not equally likely to be selected and the outcome could easily be a biased sample of the population. The researcher should only use these techniques when necessary and should make every effort to minimize the potential bias.

Obtaining a representative sample is crucial to survey research, for the results of the research are only meaningful if they can be generalized to the population. Remember, however, that a representative sample will only result in representative responses if the response rate is 100%. Almost always, there will be fewer responses than individuals sampled, and so there is the possibility of distortion in the responses; that is, the responses may not be a totally accurate representation of the population's attitudes, beliefs, thoughts, or behaviors. This makes it all the more imperative to begin with a representative sample; then, by making efforts to maximize the response rate, the researcher can minimize distortion caused by a less than perfect response rate.

Concept Question 9.3

The student body of a college consists of 20% science majors, 75% social science majors, and 5% art majors. Which sampling technique would you recommend in order to select a representative sample of the college's population?

Now suppose that the population of interest is a city of 150,000 people, composed of 79% white, 12% African American, 6% Latino, 2.5% Asian, and 0.5% other. How would you suggest that a researcher sample this population?

SUMMARY

Survey research is very popular in psychology and other social sciences. But, as with any type of research, the results are only useful if the research is carried out carefully and correctly. An important step is to use the most appropriate type of survey. Mail surveys are self-administered. Because they can be administered widely, they are less susceptible to sampling bias than other types of surveys. Also, because they are self-administered, there is no opportunity for interviewer bias to contaminate the results. In addition, mail surveys are appropriate for collecting sensitive information that a person may be unwilling to tell an interviewer either in person or over the phone. The response rate to mail surveys is weak, unfortunately; often multiple mailings are required.

Telephone surveys bring a stronger response rate than do mail surveys. In addition, the interviewer can ask for clarification when a response is unclear. However, telephone surveys are more susceptible to both sampling bias and interviewer bias than are mail surveys.

Personal interviews have a very strong response rate, and respondents are often willing to commit a considerable amount of time to answering a personal interview survey. However, the respondents might also be more likely to give socially desirable responses than would respondents to the other types of surveys. Personal interviews are susceptible to interviewer bias, even when that bias is unintentional and nonverbal. Also, personal interviews can be quite expensive and time-consuming.

Regardless of the type of survey used, the results will be of little use if the sample of respondents is biased. Random selection is often ideal, but systematic sampling might also be useful. When subgroups of the population need to be represented carefully, stratified sampling may be the most appropriate alternative. Cluster sampling might be used when the population is large, but representative clusters of members must be available. Convenience sampling, quota sampling, and snowball sampling are nonprobability sampling techniques that can be used when other techniques cannot; they may lead to a biased sample, however.

No less important than the sample is the actual survey. Great care is required in survey development. Careful wording is essential; special effort must be made to avoid loaded, leading, and double-barreled questions. A pilot study can be helpful in developing a successful survey. As with all research, thoughtful planning is essential to the collection of useful data.

IMPORTANT TERMS AND CONCEPTS

closed questions
cluster sampling
convenience (or haphazard or accidental) sample
demographic questions
double-barreled questions
elements
filter question
funnel questions
interviewer bias
leading questions
loaded questions
mail surveys
nonprobability sampling techniques
open-ended questions

personal interviews
population
quota sampling
random sample
random selection
response rate
sample
sampling bias
sampling frame
snowball sampling
socially desirable responses
stratified random sampling
stratified sampling
systematic sampling
telephone surveys

EXERCISES

1. A survey is conducted by asking every third person entering the building to participate. What type of sampling is being used? Would this procedure yield a random sample?

2. A colleague wishes to conduct a survey on residents' attitudes towards the creation of a nuclear waste dump in their state. The researcher would like to get responses from 3,000 individuals such that the sample is representative of the state's population. There is one city in which 25% of the state's population lives; another 10% live in the suburbs of that city. Three other cities of roughly equal size account for 35% of the state's population. The remaining 30% of the population live in rural areas. The researcher has access to all of the city and town directories in the state, as well as all of the phone books.

    a. How could the researcher sample this population? In other words, how could the researcher use random sampling, stratified sampling, systematic sampling, cluster sampling, or some combination of these techniques?

b. The questions on this survey will include some demographic questions and about ten questions related to the topic. Given the topic and length of the survey, what are the advantages and disadvantages of a mail survey, a phone survey, and a personal interview? Which would you suggest to the researcher?

3. You are creating a survey to address people's attitudes toward those with AIDS. Rewrite the following questions so that the wording and choices are more appropriate for a survey.

AIDS is a plague affecting millions of Americans either directly or by afflicting loved ones. To what extent do you think AIDS research money should be devoted to counseling those with AIDS and their loved ones?

How many people who have AIDS do you know?
a. <1
b. 1–10
c. 10–20
d. >20

Do you have unsafe sex or worry about contracting the AIDS virus?
Yes _____ No _____ Sometimes _____

4. Develop a six-item survey on a topic of interest to you. Pay special attention to the wording and organization of your questions. How will this survey be administered? How will you sample your population?

5. The results of a survey indicate that two variables are related to each other: As the amount of money that the respondents spend each week on nonessentials increases, their life satisfaction scores decrease.

a. Is this a positive or a negative correlation?

b. The researcher interprets these results to indicate the following: if people spent less money on nonessentials, they would be more satisfied with their lives. What other interpretations are possible?

ANSWERS TO CONCEPT QUESTIONS AND ODD-NUMBERED EXERCISES

Note: There will often be more than one correct answer for each of these questions. Consult with your instructor about your own answers.

Concept Question 9.1
a. A mail survey, because the topic is sensitive.
b. A personal interview, because the topic is not inherently interesting and the survey is long.
c. A telephone survey or mail survey to cover the whole area; a telephone survey might be more economical.
d. A telephone survey or mail survey; a mail survey might be more economical.

Concept Question 9.2

This question is double-barreled; having AIDS or being HIV positive are not mutually exclusive. If the researcher is interested in the more inclusive category of HIV positive individuals, a single question will suffice:

How many individuals in the United States do you believe are HIV positive?

If the researcher wants the respondent to provide two numbers, two questions should be asked:

How many individuals in the United States do you believe are HIV positive?

How many individuals in the United States do you believe have AIDS?

Concept Question 9.3

I would recommend stratified random sampling of the college population and would choose the appropriate percentage of potential respondents from each major. For the city population, I might recommend cluster sampling. The researcher might identify organizations that represent each of these subgroups, such as civic organizations and church groups (assuming that this would not bias the survey responses). The researcher might then select clusters, either randomly or systematically, to represent each subgroup in the appropriate proportion.

Exercises

1. This is systematic sampling, and not random sampling. This procedure might yield a representative sample, but not a random sample. To yield a random sample, every person must be equally likely to be chosen, which is not the case for the procedure described in this question.

3. Here are possible answers. Your versions might be even better.

Should research money for AIDS be used to counsel those with the syndrome?
Yes _____ No _____

Should research money for AIDS be used to counsel family and friends of those with the syndrome?
Yes _____ No _____

How many people who have AIDS do you know?
a. 0
b. 1–10
c. 11–20
d. more than 20

Do you have unsafe sex?
Yes _____ No _____ Sometimes _____

Do you worry about contracting the AIDS virus?
1   2   3   4   5
Never   Always

5. a. This is a negative correlation (see chapter 4).

   b. Another possibility is that people who are unsatisfied with their lives tend to spend money on nonessentials. Alternatively, it may be that some third variable—such as the amount of depression experienced by the respondent—is causing both the spending on nonessentials and the life satisfaction scores, but the spending doesn't actually cause lower life satisfaction.

10

Quasi-Experimental Designs

If every research investigation were a true experiment, causal explanations could be drawn from the conclusions of every project. Alas, the reality is that we do not always have the freedom to conduct a true experiment because we cannot always create equivalent groups for comparison.

There are many situations in which a researcher is studying a variable that cannot be manipulated—such as age, gender, or whether a person has arthritis—but the researcher adds considerable control to the testing environment. As a **quasi-experimental design**, these cases resemble true experiments, because an independent variable is manipulated, but they do not involve random assignment of the participants to conditions. In quasi-experimental designs, special efforts are made to acknowledge threats to the study's internal validity and limit their effects, so that the results may be interpreted meaningfully, if not always causally.

Quasi-experimental designs were first described by Campbell and Stanley in a chapter of the *Handbook of Research on Teaching* (Gage, 1963). Their chapter was then published as a short but classic book, *Experimental and Quasi-Experimental Designs for Research* (Campbell & Stanley, 1963), and later reworked and expanded by Cook and Campbell (1979). Much of what follows is a summary of the ideas of Campbell and Stanley and of Cook and Campbell.

175

TYPES OF QUASI-EXPERIMENTAL DESIGNS

Quasi-experimental designs are conducted when true experiments cannot be carried out—for example, in applied settings where, for ethical or practical reasons, participants cannot be randomly assigned to experimental conditions. Because random assignment cannot be used, the researcher can make multiple observations, compare the experimental group with a specially chosen control group, or do some combination of both.

Let's consider quasi-experimental research more closely. Imagine that a researcher is interested in the effectiveness of a prenatal care program aimed at reducing the infant mortality rate within a state. One approach to this problem might be to utilize a **preexperimental design**. In a preexperimental design, data are collected in such a manner that several alternative explanations for the results are present; thus, it is difficult—if not impossible—to draw conclusions from the data. The researcher might simply compare the infant mortality rate prior to the introduction of the program with the infant mortality rate after the program has begun. The results of this data collection would be difficult to interpret; no matter what the results were alternative explanations would abound. A reduction in infant mortality could have occurred as a result of many factors, such as the mothers' increased awareness of good health during pregnancy, or an increase in the number of free clinics available to them. The rate itself could have been due to a flu epidemic during the year in which the pretest data were collected and not to the new program specifically. Likewise, an increase in infant mortality during the study could be attributed to any number of causes. Perhaps an increase in drug abuse among the mothers counteracted any benefits of the program, or an unusually harsh winter or a flu epidemic resulted in greater infant mortality. As a rule, comparing one group's scores before and after an event does not provide data that can be interpreted in any reasonable manner. Accordingly, Campbell and Stanley (1963) refer to this as a preexperimental design.[1]

To try to overcome some of the shortfalls of the preexperimental design in the example given above, we might add a second group, which can be compared with the group participating in the prenatal care program. If the comparison groups are equivalent before the experiment, the design is a true experiment, if not, it is a quasi-experiment. Designing a true experiment is not feasible in the present situation. A true experiment would require the participants to be randomly assigned to each condition, but ethical considerations prevent a researcher from randomly

---

[1] In some specific situations, a preexperimental design yields results for which the only reasonable interpretation is causal. For instance, if I have not been ill but I get violently sick soon after eating a tuna sandwich, I conclude that the tuna sandwich made me sick. Similarly, if all the participants taking an experimental drug in a study suddenly exhibit the same symptoms, the odds are that the experimental drug caused the illness.

assigning pregnant women to conditions with prenatal care or no prenatal care. Thus, something between a true experimental design and a preexperimental design must be developed.

Nonequivalent-Control-Group Designs

One type of quasi-experimental design involves comparing the experimental group with a comparable, but not necessarily equivalent, control group. In adopting a **nonequivalent-control-group design** for the prenatal care study, the researcher might attempt to identify a group of pregnant women who are comparable to those in the state instituting the prenatal program. For example, if Illinois is the state establishing the program, women in Indiana might serve as a comparable, albeit nonequivalent, control group. To create truly equivalent groups, participants would need to be randomly assigned to Indiana or Illinois and it's highly unlikely that many pregnant women would volunteer for that study.

A researcher might make the mistake of simply comparing these two groups after the prenatal program is established. Comparing two nonequivalent groups once, however, is not much better than comparing one group with itself. Alternative explanations for the results prevent the study from providing useful information. Any difference between the infant mortality rates of Indiana and Illinois could be due to the new program or due to an initial difference in the states' mortality rates. In this design, there is no way to know. Therefore, a single comparison of two nonequivalent groups must again be regarded as a preexperimental design.

A better alternative is to take **pretest and posttest measures** from the nonequivalent groups. In other words, the infant mortality rates of Illinois and Indiana should be measured prior to the establishment of the program and then again after the program is underway. This is sometimes called a **pretest-posttest design with nonequivalent groups**. The pretest measures can be used to assess the equivalency of the two comparison groups, and the posttest measures can then be used to assess the relative effect of the prenatal program. For instance, suppose that, at pretest, the infant mortality rate is slightly higher for the Illinois group than for the Indiana group but, at posttest, the infant mortality rate for the Illinois group has decreased, while that of the Indiana group has stayed constant. This would suggest that the prenatal program did have an effect—that is, that there is a relationship between the introduction of the program and the decrease in infant mortality. Figure 10.1 presents two possible outcomes of a nonequivalent-control-group design.

Time-Series Designs

When there is no appropriate nonequivalent control group, another type of quasi-experimental design can be used. In the **time-series design**, the researcher makes multiple observations of a single group. Assume that there is no state with which infant mortality rates can be compared.

Figure 10.1   Two possible outcomes of a nonequivalent-control-group design

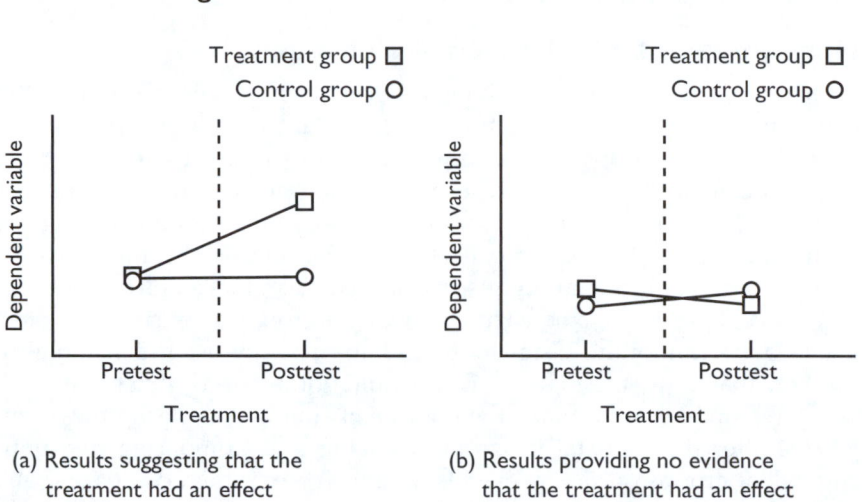

(a) Results suggesting that the
    treatment had an effect

(b) Results providing no evidence
    that the treatment had an effect

An alternative approach is to make observations of the infant mortality rate a number of times before and after the introduction of the program. Recall the preexperimental design in which the researcher made observations once before the program and once after it had begun. We noted that the number of alternative explanations for the results was rather large. However, we can correct this problem by making more observations. Then, should we find that infant mortality decreases over time after the program has begun (but hadn't already begun to decrease before the program started), we can have greater confidence that the program was effective. In other words, although there may be numerous factors that could provide alternative explanations for the difference between any two observations, it is unlikely that these factors will also affect all of the other pairs of observations. Figure 10.2 presents two possible outcomes for the prenatal care research project.

Another possible quasi-experimental design is a combination of the time-series design and the pretest-posttest design with nonequivalent groups. In the **multiple time-series design**, the researcher makes multiple observations of two nonequivalent groups. In the prenatal care example, the researcher would make multiple observations of the infant mortality rate before and after the introduction of the prenatal program in Illinois. Additionally, the researcher would make the same observations in Indiana, where the program was not initiated. Two possible outcomes of a multiple time-series design are presented in figure 10.3.

Quasi-experimental designs are used to make the best of a less-than-perfect research environment. In the social sciences, we cannot always use

Figure 10.2 Two possible outcomes of a time-series design

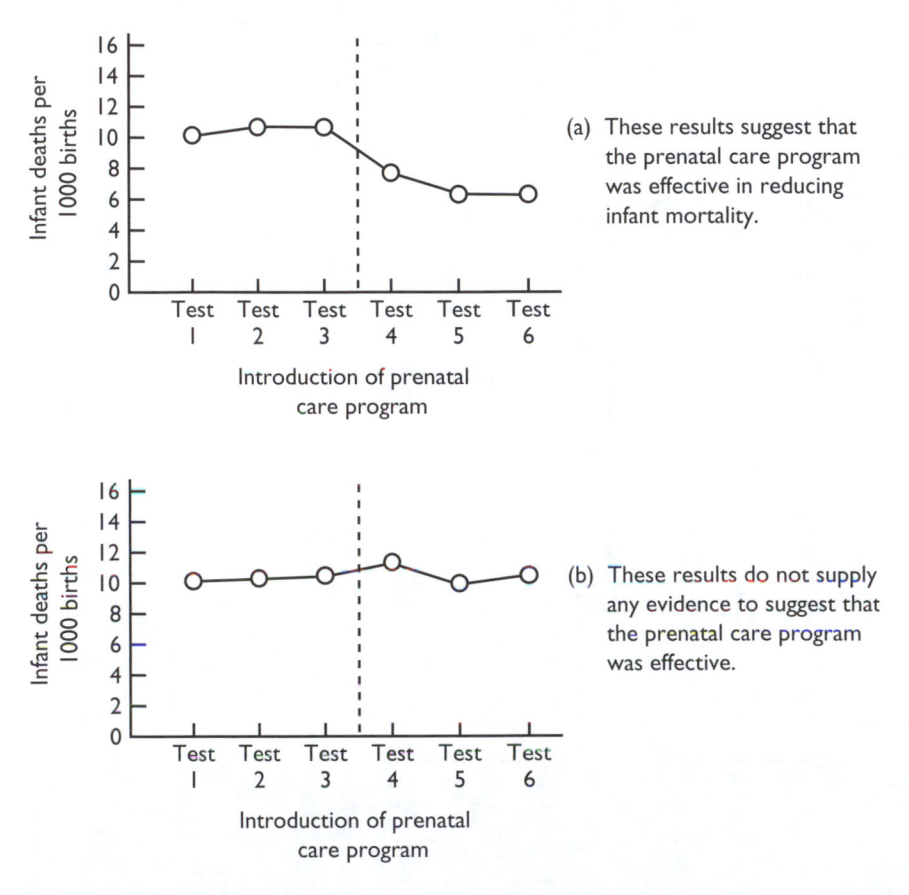

(a) These results suggest that the prenatal care program was effective in reducing infant mortality.

(b) These results do not supply any evidence to suggest that the prenatal care program was effective.

a true experimental design to test our hypotheses. Instead, we must patch together designs that decrease the influence of major extraneous variables; the results that we obtain are interpretable but not ideal. A summary of the three quasi-experimental designs we have considered here is presented in table 10.1. In the next section, we will discuss some of the most important extraneous variables that can affect quasi-experimental designs.

Concept Question 10.1

A former high school English teacher of yours asks for your assistance in designing a study to determine whether a teaching system involving a series of weekly quizzes or a system with less frequent testing leads to better learning by the students. Describe possible time-series, nonequivalent-control-group, and multiple time-series designs that the teacher could use.

Figure 10.3 Two possible outcomes of a multiple time-series design

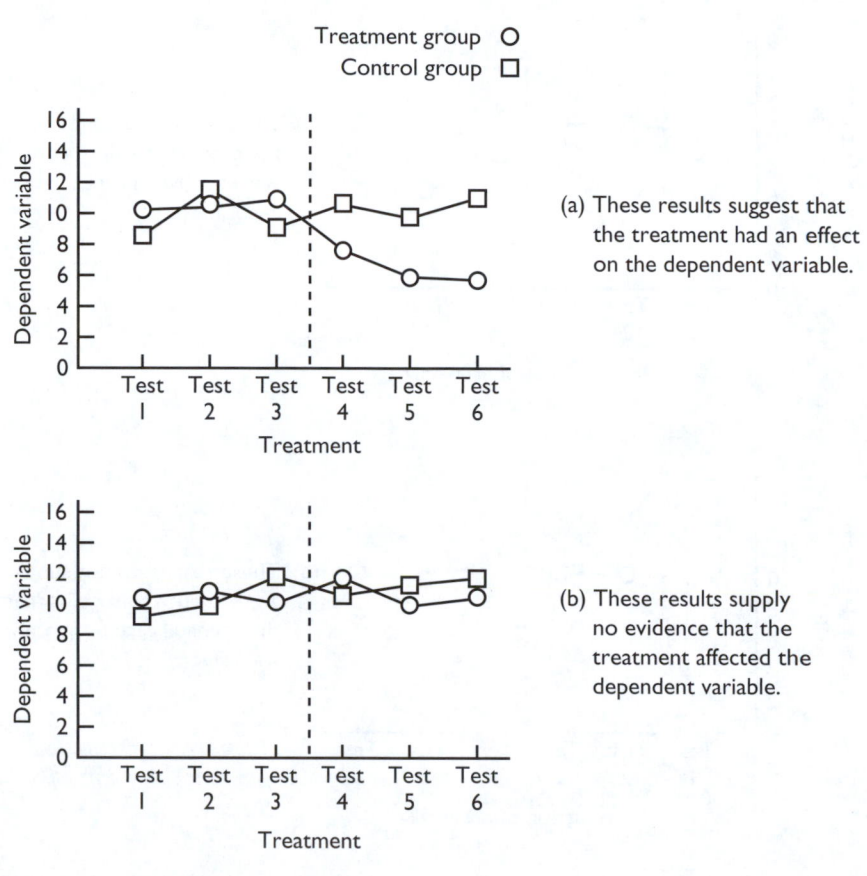

Treatment group ○
Control group □

(a) These results suggest that the treatment had an effect on the dependent variable.

(b) These results supply no evidence that the treatment affected the dependent variable.

Table 10.1   A Summary of Three Quasi-Experimental Designs

Type of quasi-experimental design	Characteristics
Nonequivalent-control-group design	Compares two comparable but not randomly assigned groups of participants before and after treatment
Time-series design	Observes one group several times before and several times after treatment
Multiple time-series design	Observes two nonequivalent groups several times before and several times after treatment

THREATS TO INTERNAL VALIDITY
OF QUASI-EXPERIMENTAL DESIGNS

When determining the adequacy of a research design, the experimenter needs to foresee criticisms and alternative explanations for the results. These alternative explanations and rival hypotheses arise from the limited internal validity of a study. In quasi-experimental designs, where a group is being compared to a nonequivalent control group or one group is being observed a number of times, it is important to foresee the numerous pitfalls that await the interpretations of the results. Only when such threats to the internal validity of a quasi-experimental design are foreseen and controlled can the researcher cautiously make some causal statements about the results.

Because participants are tested two or more times in quasi-experimental designs, the same threats to the internal validity of within-subjects designs (discussed in chapter 6) are also a concern for quasi-experimental designs. History, maturation, testing, and instrumentation effects are all possible causes of concern when designing a quasi-experimental study, but all can be assessed and accounted for quite successfully by including a control group in the study. As the similarity of the control and experimental groups increases, the researcher is able to feel more confident that the history, maturation, testing, and instrumentation effects can be assessed.

As we have seen, researchers must be aware of statistical regression toward the mean, which occurs when participants are chosen because of their extreme scores on a dependent variable or a variable correlated with the dependent variable. Regardless of the intervention, extreme scores are likely to move toward the mean upon retesting. Regression toward the mean can be prevented in quasi-experiments by not choosing participants on the basis of extreme scores, or it can be compensated for by choosing a control group with equally extreme scores. If the change in the experimental group is different from the change in the control group, this is evidence that the change was the result of something more than regression towards the mean.

Subject mortality (or **subject attrition**) is the loss of participants' data either because the participants withdrew from the study or because a decision was made to drop their data on the basis of some criterion. Subject mortality becomes a threat to the internal validity of a study when the dropout rate is very high (in which case the remaining participants may share some characteristic that distinguishes them from the other members of the initial samples) or when the dropout rate varies between comparison groups. Given that the comparison groups were not equivalent in the first place, but merely as comparable as could be reasonably contrived, quasi-experimental designs simply cannot tolerate the additional level of nonequivalency due to differences in participants' dropout rates from these groups.

When there are differences between the comparison groups within a study, a **selection bias** has occurred. Because the control group in a quasi-experimental design will always be a nonequivalent control group, a selection bias can be counted on. For example, suppose a researcher is studying the effects of sleep apnea treatment on memory performance. Very likely, the researcher will not have access to enough sleep apnea patients to assign some to a no-treatment control group. (Creating such a group would also raise ethical concerns.) A common technique in these cases is to ask each participant in the experimental group to recruit a friend or family member of approximately the same age for the control group (e.g., Hurd, 1989). Clearly, there is a selection bias here; the control group does not suffer from sleep apnea. Given no better alternative, the researcher must keep this in mind while interpreting the results of the study.

An **interaction of selection with other threats to internal validity** can occur when extraneous variables affect one group, but not the other. For example, an interaction of selection with history might occur when an event unrelated to the study affects the performance of one group of participants but not the other (or not to the same extent). Suppose that a researcher investigating anxiety levels in children uses a classroom of children in a separate school district as a control group. If a thunderstorm strikes one school district but not the other, different levels of anxiety between the groups may be due to the storm and not necessarily to any intervention by the researcher.

Selection can also interact with other extraneous variables, such as maturation, instrumentation, or regression toward the mean. These interactions can wreak havoc with the interpretations of the results, causing changes in behavior that are either consistent with or counter to the expected results. The researcher can never be sure if the results are due to the change in the independent variable or to an interaction of selection with some extraneous variable.

Use of a quasi-experimental design is not ideal. In research on applied topics or in applied settings, however, a quasi-experimental design will often be as close to a true experimental design as a researcher can reach. By carefully considering potential pitfalls and confounds, the researcher can choose a quasi-experimental design that makes the best of a less-than-perfect situation to provide useful and interesting results. Table 10.2 summarizes the research designs that might be used to control for particular threats to internal validity.

Concept Question 10.2

To familiarize yourself with threats to internal validity, convene a small group of students and take turns inventing research projects in which there are one or more flaws. Once the inventor is finished, the other people in the group will evaluate each project and identify the threats to its internal validity. For example, a researcher wishes to investigate the effect of quizzes on course performance. In an introductory psychology course there are no quizzes during the first half of the term, but during the second half (after the midterm exam) there are quizzes at the start of each class period. At the end of the semester the students take a final exam on the material presented during the last half of the course. The students perform better on the final exam than on the midterm. What might be responsible for this change in performance other than the quizzes?

Table 10.2   A Summary of Threats to Internal Validity and Designs that May Control for Them

Threat to internal validity	Quasi-experimental design that may control it
History effects	Time-series design, multiple time-series design
Maturation effects	Nonequivalent-control-group design, multiple time-series design
Testing effects	Nonequivalent-control-group design, multiple time-series design
Subject mortality	No control; researcher must watch for this confound
Selection bias	Time-series design
Interaction of selection with other threats to internal validity	Time-series design

SUMMARY

Quasi-experimental designs are quite common in research literature because so much of psychological research is applied research, where true experimental designs cannot be conducted. In addition, the results of applied research tend to be immediately applicable to everyday situations, consequently the results of quasi-experimental designs are often publicized by the media. Therefore, the accurate interpretation of results is very important.

In some quasi-experimental designs, one group is compared with a nonequivalent control group. Because participants are not randomly assigned to these conditions, we cannot be very optimistic that the groups are equivalent. Since they are nonequivalent at the outset, any differences between the groups on a dependent measure may be the result of the independent variable or of some other unknown difference between the groups. The researcher must be mindful of the initial difference between the groups when conclusions are drawn. In some cases, the control group may be quite comparable to the experimental group, and selection bias will not present a particular threat to the internal validity of the study. In others, the bias may be strong and impossible to avoid and must be taken into account in the interpretation of the results.

In other quasi-experimental designs, one group of participants is tested numerous times. The primary criticism of this design is that we have no evidence that the experimental group is behaving any differently than a control group would have done. However, with an increase in the number of testing situations and a greater change in scores between pre-treatment testing and posttreatment testing, we may be more confident in concluding that the treatment did affect the dependent measure.

In all designs, whether experimental, quasi-experimental, or preexperimental, the researcher must take care to identify possible confounds and to construct alternative explanations for the results. Preexperimental designs are replete with threats to their internal validity; the best a consumer of those studies can do is to try and determine whether the evidence for an effect is strong enough to be worthy of further study. Confounds to watch for are history effects, maturation effects, testing effects, instrumentation effects, subject mortality, selection bias, and the interaction of selection bias with other threats to internal validity. The results of carefully constructed quasi-experimental studies can provide as much useful information as those experimental studies that are done well and may be interpreted with nearly as much confidence.

IMPORTANT TERMS AND CONCEPTS

interaction of selection with
   other threats to internal validity
multiple time-series design
nonequivalent-control-group design
preexperimental design
pretest and posttest measures

pretest-posttest design with
   nonequivalent groups
quasi-experimental design
selection bias
subject mortality
   (or subject attrition)
time-series design

EXERCISES

1. You hear on the news about a research project that addressed the effectiveness of a children's in-school health program. The researchers compared the number of absences during the school year prior to the introduction of the program with the number of absences during the school year after the program was introduced.

   a. Would you categorize this as a true experimental, preexperimental, or quasi-experimental design?

   b. Suppose that absences were fewer after the health program was established. What conclusions could the researchers come to, if any? What alternative hypotheses, if any, may explain the results?

c. Which threat or threats to internal validity are most likely in this study?

d. How would you improve the study?

2. In the psychology department of Smarter U, statistics is taught in two ways. One course is a standard lecture and discussion course; the other is self-paced/self-taught, involving a series of assignments and tests. You wish to compare these two course formats. Because you have begun this project in the middle of the semester, your only option this term is to present each class with the same exam at the end of the course and to compare those scores.

a. Is this a true experimental, quasi-experimental, or preexperimental design?

b. What conclusions, if any, would you be able to draw from the results? Present any alternative explanations and identify any threats to internal validity.

c. You will also have access to these two courses next semester. How will you design your investigation to control for some or all of the threats to the internal validity of the first approach?

3. One irritating side effect of allergies is general fatigue. An allergist asks for your assistance in assessing whether desensitization treatment results in a decrease in fatigue. Desensitization involves injections on a biweekly or monthly schedule over the course of one or more years. The results are usually cumulative, that is, the patient shows increasing improvement over time.

a. A preexperimental design in which one group is tested twice could be used to investigate this question. Describe such a design and provide some alternative explanations for any results it produces.

b. Describe a one-group time-series design and explain in what ways it would be superior to the preexperimental design.

c. Describe a multiple time-series design and explain its advantages over the other two designs.

4. A shop owner wants to assess the effectiveness of a shoplifting-prevention system that employs undercover floor-watchers. The shop owner estimates the amount of inventory (in dollars) lost to shoplifters during the month prior to the use of floor-watchers, and compares that with the amount of inventory shoplifted under the new system.

a. What type of design is being used?

b. What potential confounds are there, if any?

c. What conclusions would you draw from this study?

5. A major corporation moves its headquarters and factory from a small city. Approximately 10% of the city's population worked for this corporation. You wish to assess the effect of this corporation's move on housing sales and prices.

a. You wish to use a multiple time-series design to assess the effect of the move on housing prices. You have access to the median housing prices calculated at six-month intervals for the last two years for this city and a city of comparable size and comparable median income. You will have access to this information in the future also. How would you design this study?

b. You have access to information about the number of housing sales for the last two years, calculated every month, in this city (but not the comparable city). You will continue to have access to this information for the next two years. What kind of study would you design now?

ANSWERS TO CONCEPT QUESTIONS AND ODD-NUMBERED EXERCISES

Note: There will often be more than one correct answer for each of these questions. Consult with your instructor about your own answers.

Concept Question 10.1

In the time-series design, the teacher uses monthly exams for three months, then weekly quizzes for three months (but with monthly exams at the end of each month), thereby having multiple observations before and after the introduction of the change in the independent variable (the use of weekly quizzes). The teacher can compare the scores on the monthly exams. In the nonequivalent-control-group design, the teacher could teach two classes (the same course, but different students in each class). One group would receive monthly exams and one would receive weekly quizzes and monthly exams. The teacher can compare the two groups on their monthly exam scores. In the multiple time-series design, the teacher proceeds as in the nonequivalent-control-group design, except that the two groups will be compared on monthly exams for three months before the experimental group begins taking weekly quizzes (and monthly exams). The two groups will then be compared on the monthly exams.

Concept Question 10.2

A preexperimental design has been described: one group tested twice. The change in performance from midterm to final could be caused by the quizzes, but it could also be caused by maturation, a history effect (such as a sudden downturn in the economy that made the class suddenly feel that they needed to do well in college), subject mortality (the poorer students may have dropped the course), or some combination of these.

Exercises

1. a. This is a preexperimental design; there is only a pretest and a posttest without a control group.

    b. No conclusions could be drawn; it might be that the program worked or it might be that there were fewer illnesses in general after the program was installed.

   c. A history effect, possibly a maturation effect.

   d. I would consider a nonequivalent-control-group design, in which this school's absentee record was compared with that of a similar school in the area.

3. a. The doctor could ask people to rate their general fatigue before they begin the treatment and then ask them again a month or two later. Possible confounds are history (there may be fewer allergy-causing pollens in the air at the second testing) and placebo effects (people think the injections should be working), as well as demand characteristics (the patients think the doctor wants them to say they feel better).

   b. In a time-series design, the patients could be asked to rate their general fatigue once a week for several weeks before the treatment begins and then continue to rate their fatigue weekly for several months. This design would control for potential history effects (caused by changes in pollen levels), but would still be susceptible to the placebo effect and demand characteristics (although probably less and less so over time).

   c. A multiple time-series design would be similar to the time-series design, but would also include a control group of patients who receive injections of a placebo. This design would control for history effects and also assess the presence of the placebo effect and/or demand characteristics (although it could not tell those two apart).

5. a. I would compare housing prices at six-month intervals for the two years before the company moved and for the following two years for both of the cities (a multiple time-series design).

   b. I would use a time-series design, on the basis of the data from the previous and subsequent two years for one city.

Single-Subject Designs

Most research in psychology can be called **nomothetic** research—research that is conducted on groups and attempts to identify general laws and principles of behavior. But sometimes a research question deals not with what the average person does in a situation, but with how a particular person acts or reacts. Research that focuses on the behavior of an individual adopts an **idiographic** approach. Generally, idiographic approaches attempt to identify patterns of behavior within a single individual. Like research on groups, studies of an individual's behavior need to be planned carefully, with an eye towards objectivity and interpretability. In this chapter, we will focus on the single-subject research design—how it is conducted, its advantages, and its disadvantages.

It is important to distinguish between single-subject designs and case studies. **Case studies** are descriptions of an individual and that person's experiences, but they do not involve the systematic manipulation of an independent variable. Case studies may be very objective or very subjective; they may utilize a number of methodological techniques—naturalistic observation, surveys, interviews, or other approaches. Case studies, however, do not typically involve the use of experimental designs, as do

189

single-subject designs. Like case studies, **single-subject designs** focus on one individual (or, at most, a few), but bring with them the rigors and objectivity of the scientific method, in an effort to determine the effect of an independent variable on some dependent variable.

The single-subject design has been used in both basic research and applied settings. It is one of the oldest approaches to research in the field of psychology. Wilhelm Wundt, the man most often credited with establishing the first psychological laboratory, studied consciousness through a method known as introspection, in which the responses of a single participant to a number of stimuli were studied. In 1860, before Wundt's lab was established, Gustav Fechner published research in psychophysics (the study of our experience of physical stimuli) that involved repeatedly testing one participant (or a very few). For example, a blindfolded participant might be touched with two dull points separated by given intervals. The intervals varied randomly and the participant reported whether he or she felt one or two points. On the basis of his results with single participants, Fechner was able to determine at what distance two distinct points become noticeable to the participant 50% of the time—the *just noticeable difference*, or JND. Fechner was also one of the first behavioral scientists to use statistics in the interpretation of his results. He noticed that the same participant's JND would vary from session to session. By applying functions related to the normal curve, he was able to demonstrate that the JNDs varied normally around a mean (Hersen & Barlow, 1976).

Ivan Pavlov's (1928) work on classical conditioning was based primarily on the behavior of one dog and then was established more firmly by replicating the results with other dogs. Another famous researcher, Hermann Ebbinghaus, also utilized the single-subject design. Ebbinghaus (1913) investigated learning and forgetting by having his participant memorize and recall long lists of nonsense syllables. His work yielded the now famous forgetting curve, which indicates that most forgetting occurs soon after learning. Ebbinghaus' single subject was himself.

The introduction of statistical methods by Karl Pearson, Francis Galton, Ronald Fisher, and others provided researchers with the tools to determine the probability that behavior occurred by chance. Also, Fisher's advances in the conceptualization of induction and inference allowed researchers to generalize their results beyond their sample. These statistical advances greatly enhanced the capabilities of group research, which became the standard. The ensuing domination of group comparison research in psychology was such that by the 1950s (except in psychophysics) it was practically impossible to publish research based on a single participant. However, at first B. F. Skinner conducted his extensive work on operant conditioning with a single organism and then replicated the results with a few more to demonstrate generalizability. To circumvent psychology's bias against single-subject designs, Skinner and his colleagues established the *Journal of the Experimental Analysis of Behavior*, which specialized in publishing research based on single participants.

For a number of reasons, the hold of group comparison designs on psychology has loosened during the last 40 years. This is especially true in applied research, where group comparison methods have a number of problems.

First, group comparison research prompts ethical concerns among clinicians who wish to assess the effectiveness of a treatment. A group comparison typically involves withholding treatment from a clinical control group, which clinicians are reluctant to do. These concerns are somewhat paradoxical. Withholding treatment is only unethical if the treatment is known to be effective, and if the treatment is known to be effective, it need not be tested. However, if it is not known to be effective, withholding the treatment is not unethical. Yet, many clinicians and others are very uncomfortable with the idea of withholding any treatment from someone who is suffering. Whether or not the argument is entirely logical, it carries considerable emotional weight (Hersen & Barlow, 1976).

Second, group comparisons in applied research pose practical problems related to identifying and soliciting the cooperation of a large enough sample (Hersen & Barlow, 1976). To conduct a group comparison study, a researcher who is interested in autism must identify and secure the participation of perhaps a minimum of 20 people with autism. Unless the researcher has access to an institution that serves this population, it may take years to collect the relevant data.

Finally, several applied researchers have criticized the practice of averaging across participants in group comparison studies (see, for example, Sidman, 1960). The argument is that averages hide any nonrandom variance caused by an uncontrolled factor and that, more often than not, the measurement they provide does not represent the behavior of any of the participants. An example may make these concerns clearer.

Imagine that a researcher is comparing two groups of individuals with phobias—a group that has received a new treatment and a no-treatment control group. The results suggest no significant differences between the groups, because the average performance of the experimental group after treatment was no better than the average performance of the control group. To put it another way, the variance between the two groups was not significantly greater than the variance within each group. We would infer from this that the treatment had no effect. However, a closer look at the performance of the individuals may provide us with a different picture.

It may be that no significant difference was observed because some of the participants in the treatment condition improved while others actually got worse. Why might this happen? Although phobia was a shared characteristic of the participants, they still differed on innumerable other qualities. Some of the participants may have been coerced into therapy with no real motivation to change; some may have more deeply ingrained or more severe phobias than others; some may have additional mental disorders that control their behaviors more than the phobias do; and so on. Using group comparison, these individual differences will not be addressed, the effectiveness of the therapy will be judged on the basis of an average across a rather diverse population. Group data describe the average participant, even when no one in the group scored an average score or exhibited an average behavior.

An advantage of the single-subject design over a group design is that it can determine the effectiveness of a treatment for a specific individual, and replications of that study on similar people can help determine how well the treatment may be generalized. Single-subject designs in applied research are not typically designed to identify general laws and principles of behavior or to identify a treatment that will be effective with a broad range of clients. Clearly, the results of one single-subject study cannot be used to make inferences about an entire population since a single participant is not a representative sample of a population. However, if replicated numerous times with the same results single-subject designs are certainly capable of revealing general patterns of behavior, as they did in Skinner's and Ebbinghaus' work.

TYPES OF SINGLE-SUBJECT DESIGNS

Baseline Measures

The primary logic behind a single-subject design is to compare behavior after an intervention with a baseline measurement of that behavior. A **baseline** is a measurement of the dependent variable taken prior to the manipulation of the independent variable. Typically, a baseline measurement is taken at the beginning of the study; in some designs, additional baseline measures are taken during the study. Also, baseline measures may be taken on several different behaviors. When behavior during treatment is compared with baseline measures taken when no treatment is conducted, the researcher can often ascertain whether the treatment is having any effect.

To detect a difference between baseline and intervention measurements, the researcher must first establish a stable baseline—that is, a baseline measurement with relatively little variability. Imagine that a researcher is trying to develop a technique to improve a speaker's verbal presentation. If the researcher were to measure the number of times that a person uses filler phrases and sounds (such as "uh" and "you know") during a series of 15-minute conversations, several different types of baseline might be obtained. Ideally, as in the top half of figure 11.1, the baseline would be stable, with little variability across the testing sessions. Then, if the intervention causes a change in the number of filler sounds, the difference will be readily apparent, as in figure 11.2. (Note that this figure is only a portion of the experimental graph; single-subject designs usually include more than two phases.)

Figure 11.1 Graphs representing a stable baseline and a variable baseline

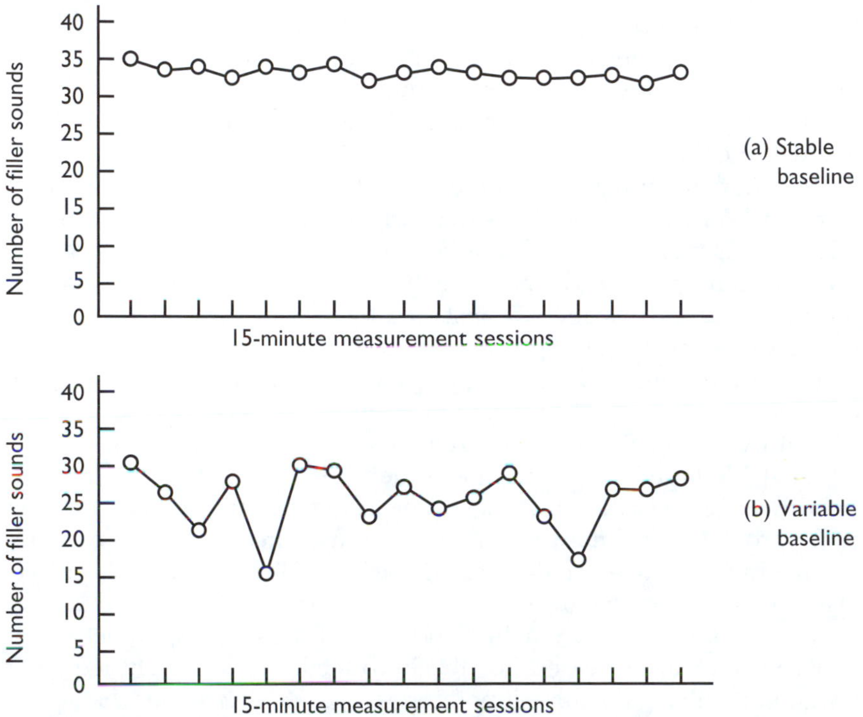

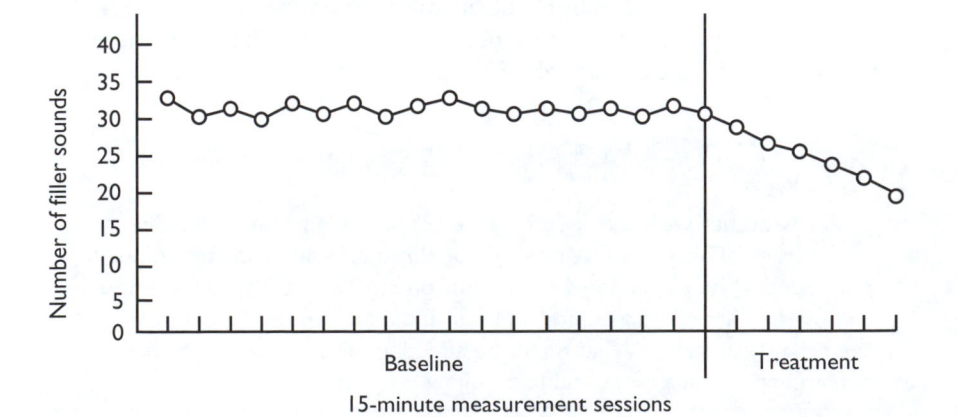

Figure 11.2 The beginning of a graph of baseline and treatment scores in which the treatment appears to have had an effect

Another possibility is that there is a great deal of variability among the data in the baseline, as in the bottom half of figure 11.1, because the participant uses a large number of filler sounds in some testing sessions but very few in others. In that case, it will be difficult to ascertain whether a treatment is having an effect. To address this problem, the researcher might continue taking baseline measurements until there is some stability in the baseline. This sounds easy enough, but it postpones intervention and prolongs the study and, of course, there is no guarantee that the baseline will ever be stable.

A different approach is to determine the source of the variability and control it. For example, perhaps the number of times the participant uses filler sounds varies because his or her level of anxiety varies from conversation to conversation. The baseline can be made more stable by holding the anxiety level constant—for instance, by making measurements when the person is speaking to a group of 5–10 people, but not when the person is speaking to smaller or larger groups. Controlling the variability of the baseline by controlling the source of the variance, however, is easier in the laboratory setting of basic research than in applied research.

A stable baseline not only has little variability, but it also does not steadily increase or decrease. Increasing or decreasing baselines are especially problematic if the trend is in the same direction as the expected change in behavior after the independent variable is manipulated. For instance, if the baseline measurement of a participant's weight decreases over a number of measurements and the researcher expects the participant's weight to decrease after the introduction of a weight-reduction program it will be difficult—if not impossible—to determine whether the weight-loss program had an effect. On the other hand, if the trend is in the direction opposite of the expected effect of the independent variable, there is less concern. For a participant with anorexia, weight measures may decrease steadily across the baseline. A successful treatment will show, at best, a reversal of that trend. Less extremely, the participant's weight might not increase but instead might stabilize. In either case, the researcher would still have evidence that the manipulation of the independent variable, the treatment, affected the participant's behavior.

Concept Question 11.1

A researcher wishes to decrease her child's video-game habit. She keeps track of his game playing time for three days and finds that on day one (Sunday) he played for 4 hours, but on day two he played for 1 hour and on day three he played for an hour and a half. So far, the baseline seems fairly unstable. What might be affecting this and how might the researcher obtain a more stable baseline?

Single-Subject Time-Series Designs

Time-series designs for nomothetic research were presented in chapter 10 in the discussion of quasi-experimental designs. In this class of research designs, several measurements are made before and after the introduction of the independent variable. Many single-subject designs are variations on the time-series design.

One of the most common single-subject designs is the **withdrawal design**. In this design, a series of baseline measurements is compared to measurements taken after the introduction of the intervention. The intervention is then withdrawn, and measurements are continued. Intervention is then reintroduced and further measurements are made. This pattern of intervention and withdrawal might be repeated several times so that the researcher can be certain that the behavior change is produced by the intervention and not by some other uncontrolled variable. The phases of the study in which the intervention is not presented are referred to as A phases, and those in which intervention is introduced are called B phases. Thus, a research design that involves baseline (A), followed by the intervention (B), followed by withdrawal (A), and then again the intervention (B) is referred to as an **ABAB design**.

Suppose that an elementary teacher has a difficult student who talks too much to the other students in class. The school psychologist suggests an intervention to reduce this behavior, and adopts a withdrawal design to test whether the intervention worked or if the student's behavior changed on its own. The teacher is told to first observe and document the child's behavior—in other words, to obtain baseline measures. The teacher notes for one week how often the child distracts the other students each day: this is the A phase. The intervention is then begun. As a reward, the child is given a sticker for every hour he behaves well. The teacher adopts this technique for a week (the B phase). At the end of the week, the teacher is pleased; the intervention appears to be working. But children mature quickly, and perhaps this child is simply learning not to distract others. To test whether the effect is caused by maturation or by the sticker intervention, the intervention is withdrawn. During the next week, the teacher does not give the student stickers for good behavior (the second A phase). The behavior begins to increase and approach baseline levels, which suggests that the intervention was the cause of the behavior change. The purpose of the whole project is to reduce the child's inappropriate behavior, so the intervention is reintroduced (the second B phase) and again the talking with others behavior decreases, as we see in figure 11.3.

There are many ways to vary the ABAB design. For example, additional withdrawal and intervention phases can be introduced to strengthen the results. Another possibility is to introduce a second intervention, which we will call C. In an ABAC design, for instance, B is intro-

Figure 11.3 The results of an ABAB withdrawal design in which good classroom behavior is reinforced during treatment

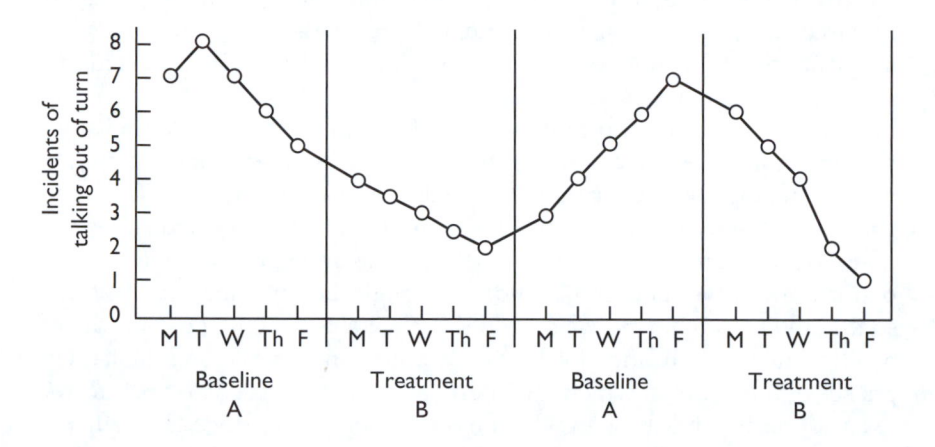

duced after baseline, then B is withdrawn to return to baseline (A), and finally the second intervention C is introduced.

A variation of the withdrawal design allows a researcher to test for possible placebo effects. A **placebo effect** occurs when the behavior being studied changes after the introduction of an intervention, even though the intervention is known to be ineffectual. For example, if a patient reports relief from headaches after taking a certain pill and that pill is made of an inert (ineffective) substance, the headache relief is due to a placebo effect. Placebo effects reflect a real change in behavior due to expectations, but not due to a particular treatment.

An ABCB design can be used to assess the effect of an intervention as compared with a placebo condition. After baseline, the B intervention is introduced and is then replaced by the noneffectual C intervention (the placebo condition), and finally the B intervention is reintroduced. If the effect of the B intervention on the behavior is primarily due to a placebo effect, there will be little change between the B phase and the C phase. However, if the change associated with the B intervention is not a placebo effect the behavior in the C phase should approximate baseline behavior.

Reversal Design

ABAB designs are described as withdrawal designs because the researcher studies what happens when the intervention is withdrawn from the situation. A different approach is to examine what happens when the intervention is replaced. In a **reversal design**, a new and opposite intervention is introduced. Suppose that two siblings play aggressively with each other, and the parents wish to increase cooperative play. A reversal design can assess the effectiveness of an intervention that increases cooperative play. It can also assess whether that same intervention might increase the unwanted behavior.

Imagine that the parents talk to a consultant, who suggests that the children play aggressively because they receive parental attention—albeit negative—when the play is aggressive. The parents are presented with a reversal design that will test this hypothesis and will also assess the effectiveness of an intervention to increase cooperative play between the siblings.

The first phase consists of measuring a baseline of cooperative play; one possibility is to measure the number of minutes of cooperative play during an hour of play each day for four days. During the next phase, the intervention is introduced; let's assume that the intervention involves ignoring aggressive play and offering adult attention during cooperative play.

In a withdrawal design, the intervention would be withdrawn during the third phase, and the behavior would be expected to revert to baseline levels. In the reversal design, however, the intervention is not simply withdrawn but is replaced with an opposite intervention; thus, in the third phase of this assessment, the parents attend to aggressive play (by disciplining the children) and ignore cooperative play. If attention is a mediating factor that can increase either aggressive or cooperative play, cooperative play should increase during the second phase of the study and decrease during the third phase. Since the goal is to increase cooperative play, a final reversal is needed, to leave the children and parents in the condition in which cooperative play is receiving attention. A graph representing the hypothetical results of this investigation is presented in figure 11.4.

Reversal designs are not as common as withdrawal designs in applied research—for instance, in behavior modification—because situations calling for a true reversal of treatment are rather uncommon (Kra-

Figure 11.4 The results of a reversal design in which the effect of attention on cooperative and aggressive play is assessed

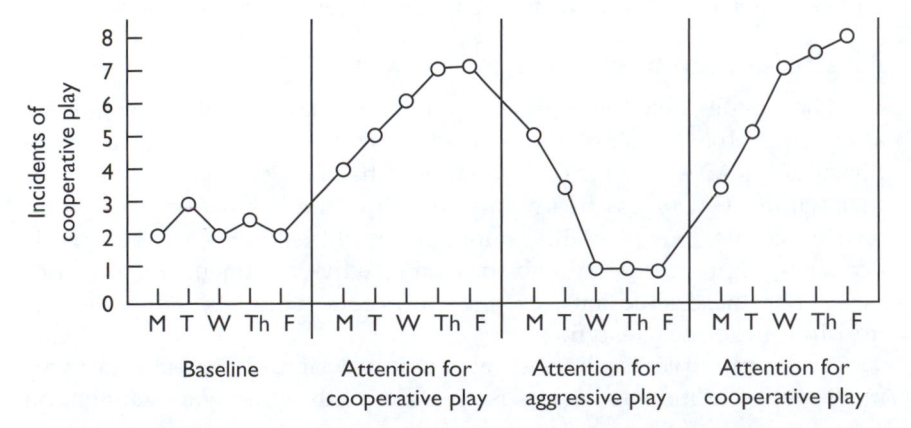

tochwill, 1978). In basic laboratory research, however, they can be very useful in assessing the causes and reversibility of changes in behavior.

Alternating-Treatments Design

A useful technique in either applied or basic research is a single-subject technique for assessing and comparing the effectiveness of two or more treatments called the **alternating-treatments design** (or the **between-series design**). The alternating-treatments design is a variation of the ABAB design; the difference is that the alternating-treatments design does not require a baseline (although a baseline may be included), and two (or more) treatments are presented to the participant instead of only one. In this design, the order of the two treatments may be random or systematic, with one treatment being presented for a given time period followed by the other.

Let's consider an example of an alternating-treatments design. Suppose a researcher wants to assess the relative effectiveness of two techniques for decreasing nail-biting behavior. One technique will be to put hot pepper on the participant's nails; another will be to ask the participant to sit on his or her hands for two minutes upon becoming aware of the behavior. The researcher will then observe the number of times that the participant's fingernails are put up to his or her mouth. (The researcher wouldn't want to measure duration, because the duration of nail biting is likely to be rather short after hot pepper has been applied to the nails.) Each day the participant opens an envelope that reveals which technique is to be used that day. If the techniques are assigned randomly, one technique may be used for many days in a row or only one day at a time. The data for the two techniques are graphed together. A hypothetical set of data is presented in figure 11.5. According to this graph, both techniques resulted in decreased nail biting, but the hand-sitting technique appears to have been more effective. Sessions of sitting on one's hands seems to show a general trend toward decreases in nail biting, while the pepper, also showing decline, is somewhat more variable.

Multiple-Baselines Design

The single-subject designs considered so far are all based on the assumption that, at least in the short term (for example, over a single phase of an ABAB design), the treatment has no permanent effects and that withdrawal of the treatment will allow the behaviors to revert to baseline levels. However, this is not true of all treatments; moreover, it is not always appropriate to withdraw an effective treatment, even temporarily. For these situations, another technique might be adopted—the **multiple-baselines design**.

In the multiple-baselines single-subject design, the effect of a treatment on two or more behaviors is assessed, or the effect of a treatment on

Figure 11.5   Hypothetical results of an alternating-treatments design

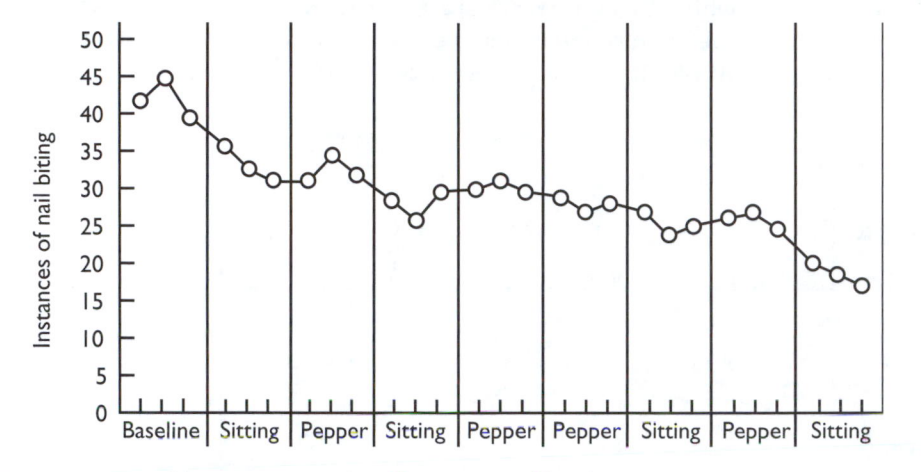

Measurement sessions for pepper and hand-sitting treatments

a behavior is assessed across two or more situations. Let's first consider assessment across two or more situations.

Suppose that a person wishes to stop smoking. The person adopts an approach that focuses on smoking in different situations—for instance, at home in the morning, at work, and at home in the evening. A reinforcement program might be developed in which the person is given ten points for every hour without a cigarette. At the end of the week, the person is rewarded with money to spend (at a certain rate per point) or with the right to purchase some item provided enough cigarette points have been accumulated.

Initially, baseline measures are taken for the three settings. Intervention is then introduced to one of the settings—say, at home in the morning—and baseline measuring is continued for the other settings. After a predetermined number of recording sessions, the intervention is also added to the second setting at work, while baseline measurements continue in the evening setting. Finally, intervention is added to the third setting. Figure 11.6 presents a graph of these hypothetical data.

The multiple-baselines approach would be a more appropriate way to assess the cigarette reduction intervention than a withdrawal or reversal design, since the researcher doesn't want to re-instill smoking at baseline levels once it has been reduced.

The other way in which the multiple-baselines design might be used is to measure the effect of the intervention on different behaviors. For this example, imagine a parent who wishes to reduce a number of annoying behaviors that a child exhibits—for example, whining, bickering with siblings, and talking back to the parent. The parent might install a point sys-

Figure 11.6 Hypothetical results of a multiple-baselines design in which three settings are compared. The unit of measurement on the vertical axes is the number of cigarettes smoked; six measurements were taken per phase

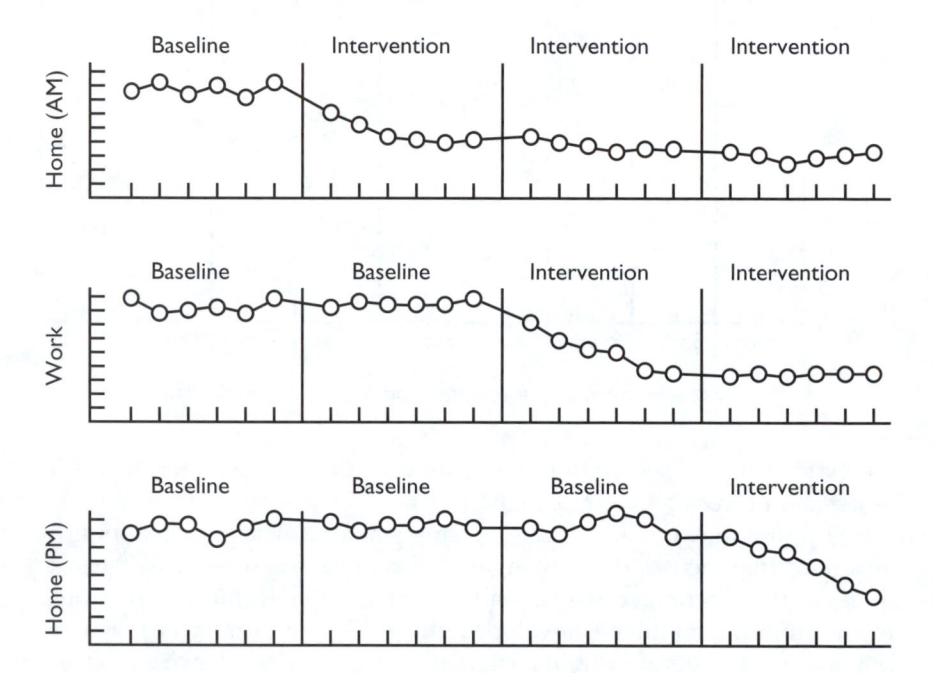

tem, in which the child earns a certain number of points for every day or half-day period that goes by without an incident and can trade those points in for television privileges.

To use the multiple-baselines design, baseline measures of each target behavior are made, and then the intervention is introduced for one of the behaviors. The parent might treat the whining behavior first by reinforcing time periods without whining; baseline measurements continue for the other two behaviors. After a predetermined number of recording sessions, this treatment is then introduced for the second behavior of bickering with siblings. Now both bickering and whining are being treated, and baseline will still be measured for talking back. Finally, talking back is added to the treatment regime. Sample data for this example are presented in figure 11.7.

Changing-Criterion Design

Like the multiple-baselines design, the **changing-criterion design** avoids withdrawing treatment. It is used to assess an intervention when the criterion for that intervention is routinely changed. For example,

Figure 11.7 Sample data for a multiple-baselines design in which three behaviors are treated. The unit of measurement on the vertical axes is the number of periods without the behavior; six measurements were taken per phase

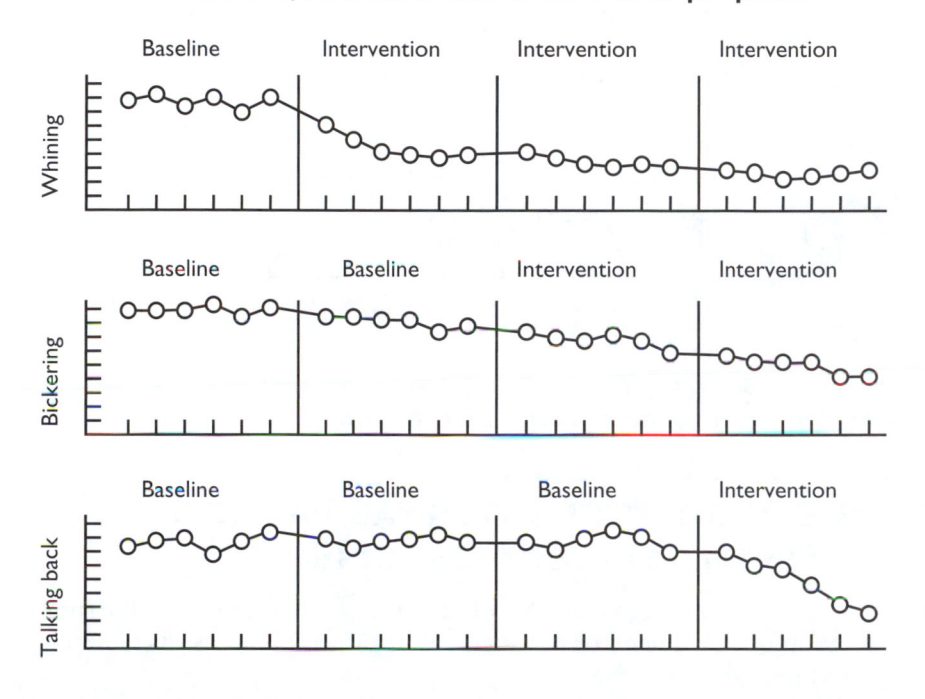

imagine that a person wishes to begin an exercise program. A changing-criterion design could be installed to assess the effectiveness of the intervention; in this design, if the treatment is effective, the criterion for the behavior is increased as time progresses. The person might agree to give himself or herself a $2 bonus in pocket money for every day he or she meets the initial target of 10 minutes of exercise. After this criterion has been met for some preset duration—let's say two weeks—the criterion is increased; now the individual must exercise for 15 minutes per day to earn the $2. Again, once the criterion has been met for two weeks, it can be increased again, perhaps to 20 minutes a day. This is repeated until the criterion reaches the ultimate goal for the behavior—say, 60 minutes per day. The data that might be generated by this changing-criterion design are illustrated in figure 11.8.

Single-subject designs are useful in basic and applied research. Not all research situations are alike, however; careful choice of the appropriate design is essential. Even then, modifications may be necessary if the study is to yield interpretable results. Often the most challenging part of a researcher's task is to foresee problems and alternative explanations for

**Figure 11.8 Possible results for the first portion of a changing-
criterion design**

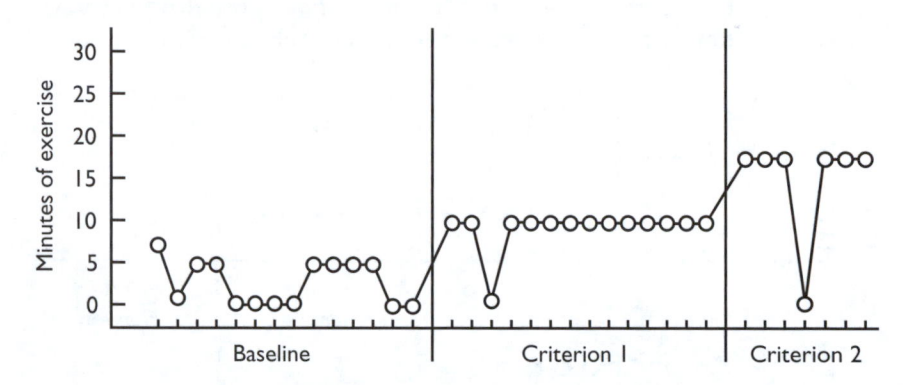

the results, so that serious confounds can be avoided. Let's look at some
common threats to the internal validity of a single-subject design.

THREATS TO THE INTERNAL VALIDITY
OF SINGLE-SUBJECT DESIGNS

Many of the same threats to internal validity that can affect the interpretation of nomothetic research can also influence the results of single-
subject designs.

Which particular confounds are likely to affect a particular study
depends greatly on the specifics of the project. If data are being collected
over a significant period of time, the researcher might watch for history
or maturation effects. Instrumentation, testing, fatigue, and practice
effects can also have detrimental effects in certain situations.

Human participants bring their own biases to the research. This **subject bias** and the familiar demand characteristics are a genuine threat to
result interpretation. Adults, in particular, are most likely going to be
aware that they are involved in the assessment of an intervention; ethical
considerations probably demand it. In an applied setting, the adult may
have instigated the intervention by requesting assistance in changing
some behavior. The participant, then, fully expects that his or her behavior will change. The challenge for the researcher is to design the study in
such a way that behavior changes caused by demand characteristics and
subject bias can be distinguished from behavior changes caused specifically by the intervention. An ABCB design testing for a placebo effect
may be a possible solution here. Another option might be a multiple-
baselines design in which the intervention is applied systematically to
two or more behaviors or in two or more settings. If the baseline mea-

sures of the untreated behaviors or settings show a change comparable to the treated situation, subject bias and demand characteristics may be playing a role.

Finally, the role of the experimenter must be considered when the results of a single-subject design are being interpreted. Experimenters can affect the results of their studies purposely, of course, but more commonly the effect is not purposeful at all. Therefore, it is essential that recording measures be as objective as possible. Ideally, they should be conducted mechanically or by others unfamiliar with the design of the study so that the results will be relatively free of experimenter bias.

Every single-subject design includes some risk from one or more of these threats to its internal validity, but not every situation is equally susceptible. The researcher cannot use a formula to decide which design to use in which situation; instead, he or she must carefully consider the setting, the participant, the behavior being studied, the time involved, and other factors in an effort to anticipate potential confounds. For many researchers, designing a solid investigation that is devoid of confounds is an enjoyable challenge.

SUMMARY

Single-subject designs are often used in applied research. In clinical research, they are typically employed to assess the effectiveness of an intervention. Single-subject designs are also prevalent in basic laboratory research, especially where testing of participants is labor intensive or where the focus is idiographic as opposed to nomothetic.

There are several types of single-subject designs; some are more effective than others in controlling particular threats to internal validity. A critical review of a single-subject investigation should include a determination of whether the design chosen adequately controls the most likely threats to internal validity. For example, are history effects a possible explanation for the observed results, or could the results be a function of a placebo effect? Ideally, the researcher foresees the major threats to internal validity when designing an investigation; in practice, some sneak by or don't appear until late in the investigation.

In most single-subject designs, baseline measures are compared with measures taken during the intervention stage. Ideally, the baseline is consistent and stable over time, so that differences between baseline and intervention measures are readily apparent. Stable baselines don't always happen on their own, unfortunately, especially in applied research.

Idiographic research differs in fundamental ways from group approaches. It acknowledges individual differences and does not attempt to average across these differences, in contrast to nomothetic research. In single-subject designs, the focus is typically on determining the effectiveness of an intervention for a given participant, rather than on how well those results will generalize to the population. However, the results—especially those of basic laboratory research—often generalize very well. The contributions of single-subject designs to knowledge in psychology should not be underestimated; as one of the oldest approaches to data collection it has provided the foundation for much of our present-day research.

IMPORTANT TERMS AND CONCEPTS

ABAB design	multiple-baselines design
alternating-treatments design	nomothetic
(or between-series design)	placebo effect
baseline	reversal design
case studies	single-subject designs
changing-criterion design	subject bias
idiographic	withdrawal design

EXERCISES

1. A friend wishes to stop smoking. Realizing that he wouldn't want to chew gum at the same time that he smoked a cigarette, you consider a gum-chewing intervention.

   a. Develop the outline for a study using a withdrawal design. Determine for how long and in what manner the baseline would be measured, and specify the duration of measurements during each other phase of the study.

   b. Graph hypothetical data to represent the results you would expect.

2. Another person, impressed by your success with your smoking friend, asks you to help her stop smoking and drinking coffee.

   a. Develop the outline for an assessment study using a multiple-baselines design. Determine for how long and in what manner behaviors would be measured during each phase of the study.

   b. Graph hypothetical data representing the results you would expect.

3. A year later, your friend asks for help in kicking an annoying gum-chewing habit. You suggest a changing-criterion design.

   a. Develop the outline for an assessment study using a changing-criterion design. Determine the criteria and intervention for this particular study.

   b. Graph hypothetical data representing the results you would expect.

4. A relative insists that caffeine makes her drowsy.

   a. Use an ABCB design to assess this claim using coffee in the B phases and decaffeinated coffee as the placebo. Determine the manner of measurement and the duration of each phase of the study.

   b. Graph hypothetical data suggesting a placebo effect.

c. Graph hypothetical data suggesting that caffeine truly does cause this person to become drowsy.

5. To ask for a special treat, your cat meows loudly. The meow is annoying, and you suspect you have unwittingly been reinforcing it by feeding the cat in response to every meow. You choose a reversal design to test whether reinforcing another behavior will change the signal for a special treat to something less offensive—say, rubbing against your leg.

   a. Create a reversal design to test the effectiveness of the treats as a reinforcer. Determine the duration and manner of measuring behaviors during each phase of the study.

   b. Graph hypothetical results of your study.

6. One article you have read suggests that a hot bath before going to bed will lead to a good night's sleep; another article recommends a glass of warm milk.

   a. Design an alternating-treatments study to assess the effectiveness of these two approaches. Determine what measurements you will make, how long each phase of the study will last, and whether you will alternate treatments randomly or systematically.

   b. Graph hypothetical data representing the results you would expect.

ANSWERS TO CONCEPT QUESTION AND ODD-NUMBERED EXERCISES

Note: There will often be more than one correct answer for each of these questions. Consult with your instructor about your own answers.

Concept Question 11.1

The unstable baseline might be attributable to measuring on both weekends and weekdays. Perhaps the child is busier on weekdays and thus has less time to play video games. One possibility for establishing a stable baseline is to use weekdays only (and then perhaps only undertaking a "treatment" for video-game playing on weekends). Another possibility is to measure the baseline differently. For instance, the researcher might measure the proportion of free time used for video-game playing instead of the time spent on the games. For example, if a person has 12 hours of free time and spends 4 hours playing video games, then they have spent one-third of their free time on that particular activity. This measurement might be more stable than recording the hours or minutes of playing time if the amount of free time varies considerably from day to day.

Exercises

1. a. You ask your friend to keep track of the number of cigarettes he smokes each day for one week. This is baseline. For the following week he is told to chew a piece of gum whenever he feels the urge to smoke, keeping track of the number of cigarettes he smokes for that

week. Then he is told to stop chewing gum for a week and to keep track of the number of cigarettes he smokes. Finally, he is told to chew gum in place of cigarettes again and to keep track of the number of cigarettes he smokes for another week.

b. The graph of the effect of the gum-chewing intervention on smoking might be as follows:

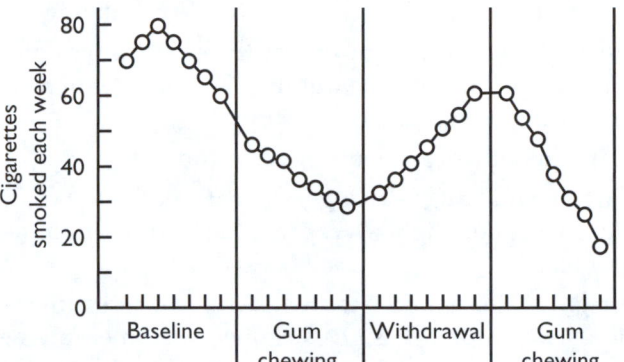

3. a. Your friend says he likes to drink a can of diet soda every day; this will be his reward as he cuts back his gum chewing. First, you ask him to track the number of sticks of gum he chews each day for a week. Next, you tell him to cut that number in half. So if he was chewing 30 sticks a day, he needs to cut back to 15 sticks a day. Each day he does so, he can have a can of soda (paid for by the money he saves on gum). He does this for a week. The next week, he must cut back his gum chewing by another 50% in exchange for the daily soda. The following week, he must cut his gum chewing in half again to earn the soda. Finally, he must stop chewing gum altogether to earn the soda each day.

b. The graph of the effect of the soda reward on gum chewing, in a changing-criterion design, might be as follows:

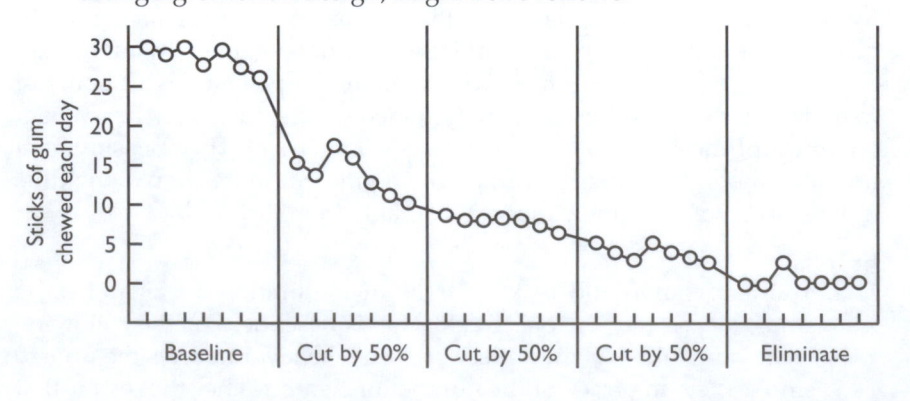

5. a. You record the number of times your cat meows for a treat each day for a week; this is baseline. The next week, you do not give a treat when the cat meows, but when the cat rubs your leg you do; you continue to note how often the cat meows for a treat. The third week, you again give treats when the cat meows; you still record the number of times the cat meows. Finally, during the fourth week, you return to giving treats for rubbing your leg only and continue to note how often the cat meows for a treat.

    b. The graph of the effect of treats on leg rubbing, in a reversal design, might look as follows:

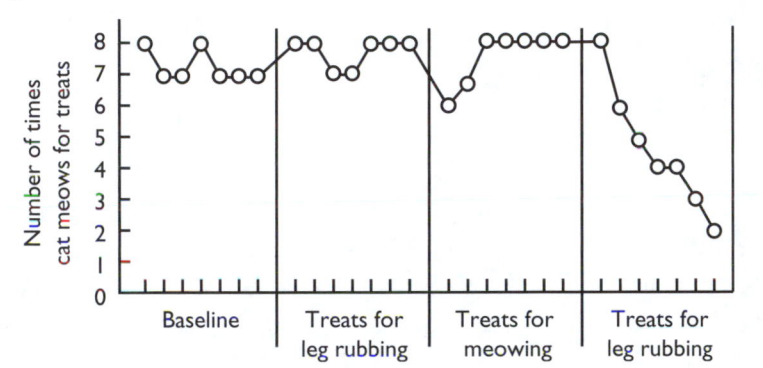

Physical Traces
and Archival Data
Two Nonreactive
Measurement Techniques

A fire inspector walks through what remains of a burned house. By observing whether windows are broken or melted, the inspector can determine where the fire was hottest; the manner in which the fire spread can be assessed by noticing the evidence of burning on the floor; and by noting which rooms were more heavily damaged by smoke than by fire, the room that contained the fire's origin can be determined (Webb, Campbell, Schwartz, Sechrest, & Grove, 1981). Fire inspectors, police detectives, and private investigators are often depicted as inferring behavior on the basis of physical evidence left at the scene. Researchers can do the same.

Researchers can infer much about people's behavior by inspecting the physical evidence left as a result of that behavior. Which animals at the zoo receive the most attention? Perhaps the wear on the railings around the enclosure can provide the answer. Which automatic teller machines receive the most use in town? A quick count of receipts left behind may be indicative. When physical evidence is assessed in the absence of the individuals whose behavior produced it, the researcher is using a **physical trace measure**.

Physical trace measures are **nonreactive** measures, because the act of acquiring the measures has no effect on the behavior; the behavior has already occurred. Physical trace studies are not the only way to acquire nonreactive measures, however. Useful information can also be obtained from **archival data**, which are records, written and otherwise. In **archival data studies**, such records are assessed to make inferences about behaviors, attitudes, beliefs, and so on. In this chapter, we will discuss both physical trace and archival data studies—their advantages and shortcomings, the types of data that they provide, and the ethical concerns posed by such investigations.

PHYSICAL TRACES

Physical trace studies involve the study of physical evidence left by individuals' behavior. This evidence is typically assigned to one of two categories: traces or products. **Traces** are evidence left as a by-product of behavior, while **products** are purposely created by individuals. It's not difficult to imagine anthropologists and sociologists using the evidence from products to draw inferences about a society. Many psychologists study products also; more often, however, they focus on traces, the by-products of behavior.

Traces

Traces can be further categorized as accretion measures or erosion measures. **Accretion measures** are based on the accumulation of evidence as a result of some behavior. For example, litter might indicate where people congregate; the appearance of dirt on particular spots of a door frame might indicate the relative age (as related to height) of people entering a room; and trash in waste cans might indicate liquor usage. **Erosion measures** are based on the wearing away of material as a result of some behavior. For example, the wear of carpets or lawns might indicate the usual route of traffic; wear on shoes might be used to determine the balance of a person's gait; and the frequency with which certain light bulbs must be replaced might indicate which rooms are used most often.

Accretion and erosion measures of physical traces can be further categorized as either natural or controlled measures. **Natural trace measures** occur without researcher intervention. For example, the wear of a carpet in a home occurs without the need for the researcher to install any particular carpet. However, should a researcher purposely install a carpet that wears easily in order to determine the areas with the most traffic, the measure would be a controlled trace measure. **Controlled trace measures** involve researcher intervention.

Concept Question 12.1

Would you categorize the following as an accretion or erosion measure?

a. Evidence of explosives on a bombing suspect's clothes.

b. Whether or not the binding of a textbook has been broken as an indication of whether it has been opened or not.

c. The amount of litter left after a festival.

d. The number of beer cans in the garbage from selected homes.

e. The amount of newspaper recycled by those participating in a curbside recycling program.

f. Wear in the pockets of men's jeans as an indication of where they carry their wallets.

Products

Products differ from traces in that they are the purposeful creations of individuals. Psychologists and other social science researchers may infer behavior and attitudes from these products as well as from trace information. For instance, the number of computer files on a person's computer might provide an estimate of his or her computer literacy; the number of articles published by college professors might provide an estimate of their scholarly productivity. Like traces, products may be categorized as accretion measures or erosion measures and as natural or controlled trace measures.

The major advantage of physical trace measures is that they have no bearing on the behavior that is being studied. This nonreactivity is very appealing. But that appeal is limited by various concerns that face researchers using this method.

Concerns with Physical Trace Studies

An important concern about physical trace measures—whether they are traces or products, accretion or erosion measures, controlled or natural—is the validity of the trace as an indicator of the focus behavior. For example, at one college, administrators viewed posters attacking people of color as a reflection of the beliefs of one or more people. Instead, it turned out that the posters had been distributed by a person of color who was trying to instigate a discussion ("Black Student," 1993). A researcher who evaluated community beliefs based on the content of the posters could come away with an overestimate of the racist attitudes on campus.

Also, not all traces are equally durable. A good-quality tile floor is likely to show less wear than a poor-quality carpet. To suggest that more people walk on the carpet because it is more worn than the tile would be risking a Type I error. Similarly, particular subgroups of a population may be more or less likely to exhibit a specific behavior and thus less likely to provide the corresponding trace than another subgroup. A researcher might estimate attendance at a glassed-in exhibit by the number of nose and fingerprints on the glass. Children, however, are probably more likely to leave prints (nose or finger) than are adults; if the question is whether more children or adults visit the exhibit, the data may be misleading.

The validity of physical trace measures is directly related to two concepts: the selective survival and selective deposit of the physical traces.

Selective survival refers to the notion that some trace or product evidence may not endure over time. Archeologists are faced with the extreme effects of time. Researchers of Mexican cultures have found an abundance of clay sealing stamps used in writing, but no stamps of other materials. Despite the temptation to assume that all the stamps were made of clay, it could also be that those made of materials such as bone or wood have disintegrated, while those made of metals may have been melted down and then re-used in another product (Webb et al., 1981).

Selective deposit refers to the circumstance in which not all traces are equally representative. It is a mistake to overgeneralize from a particular trace to all situations or all participants. As we mentioned above, not all surfaces show wear equally; not all people behave the same.

Because physical trace evidence is assessed after the behavior has occurred, it is not possible to infer much about the actors. A smudge on the glass surrounding an exhibit indicates that something rubbed against the glass, but whether it was a child's nose or the finger of a passerby is not easily knowable. These challenges to the validity of physical trace measures are of great concern. For this reason, physical trace measures are often combined with other research approaches, such as direct observation. If the findings of a physical trace measure study are backed by the results of direct observation or other research, the data from these diverse studies lend validity to each other.

Ethical Considerations

Depending on the physical trace being assessed, some ethical considerations may need to be assessed before carrying out the study. This is primarily a concern when the physical traces might identify the perpetrator of the behavior.

Researchers have sometimes sorted through people's garbage to find evidence supporting various hypotheses. Several court decisions have stated that once an item is in the garbage it is no longer the original owners' property; they have given up their claims to it, and thus it is public property. Legally, this may free the researcher to conduct the research, but the potential for ethical dilemmas still exists. The risk to the people who produced the garbage is that sensitive, personal information may become available to the researcher; the most dramatic example would be information that implicates them in a crime. Researchers should consider their policies regarding such information before they begin a garbage study (Webb et al., 1981).

There may also be threats to the welfare of researchers who conduct certain types of physical trace studies. One researcher who has conducted extensive garbage studies in Tucson asks the research assistants to sign consent forms, to receive tetanus shots, and to wear lab coats, gloves, and masks for their protection (Webb et al., 1981). Other research may not threaten the researchers' health, but may cause potential harm to their reputations. Students often suggest that checking car locks would provide an indication of how safe a neighborhood is perceived to be. However, researchers who are checking car locks might find themselves mistaken for someone with less pure motives.

To sum up, those who have left the physical traces typically are not aware that their traces might be evaluated. The evidence collected may be damaging, embarrassing, or incriminating, or the data collection itself may put the researcher and research assistants at some risk. Before data collection begins, the ethical ramifications of every study need to be considered carefully and weighed against the potential value of the results.

ARCHIVAL DATA INVESTIGATIONS

Another versatile type of nonreactive study is the archival data study, which involves the use of written or other types of records (such as videotapes, audiotapes, DVDs, and others) to investigate behavior. A very rough categorization of archives is to group them as continuous records or discontinuous records. **Continuous** (or **running**) **records** are maintained and added to on a routine basis. Income tax reports, the sales records for a shop, the U.S. census, and a diary are just some examples of continuous records. **Discontinuous records** are produced less continuously, or only once. Books, newspaper articles, letters to the editor, and photos of a vacation are all examples of discontinuous records.

Archival data sources can also be categorized as either records or documents. **Records** can be defined as written statements presented to provide an account or attest to an event. Thus, records are produced for the consumption of another. **Documents** are written or filmed materials that are not records and aren't created in response to some task or request by the investigator (Webb et al., 1981). Thus, documents are considered more personal than are records. They were produced for personal gratification and not to provide a public account of something. Records are created under the assumption that someone, someday, will read the material.

This book is a record; my journal is a document. While it is important to be aware of the distinction between archives meant for public and private consumption, both records and documents will be referred to as records in this chapter.

Glance through a newspaper, a magazine, or a library. The wealth of archival sources is awe-inspiring. And the questions that can be addressed are infinite. Do women in Peoria, Illinois marry earlier or later than women in Portland, Maine? How do *Time* and *Newsweek* differ in their presentation of a news event? Is there an increase in fires in a city after a major fire receives extensive news coverage? Do yearbooks include more pictures of females than of males? Are more babies born in one season than in the others? Is the full moon related to crime and other deviant behavior? In psychology and other social sciences, archival data studies have been used to investigate, for example, how crime victims are presented in the print and electronic media (Chermak, 1993), what the general public learns about schizophrenia from the popular press (Wahl, Borostovik, & Rieppi, 1995), the presentation of African Americans, Latinos, and Asian Americans in magazine advertising (Taylor, Lee, & Stern, 1995), and the content of horoscopes (Svenson & White, 1995). The questions are endless. They can range from the silly to the sophisticated, from the simple to the complicated, but somewhere in our information-laden world the information is sitting in an archive waiting to be tapped.

When researchers gather data from archives, they generally need to reduce the amount of information before them to a more useable amount. There are various ways in which a researcher might undertake this task, which is often called **data reduction**. A coding technique might be used, for instance, to evaluate how formally or informally men and women are presented in photographs in a newspaper. When written records are being evaluated, the data reduction technique is called content analysis. In **content analysis**, the researcher develops a coding system that is used to record data regarding the content of records. A researcher might wish to evaluate children's literature regarding the amount of violence depicted in stories for different age groups. The researcher would develop a coding system that would be applied to each item in the sample of literature so that the data regarding the violence depicted could be analyzed.

Concerns with Archival Data Studies

Because archives are prepared by people other than the researcher, and because those people do not know if research will ever be conducted, the review and recording of archival data are nonreactive. The collection of the data has no bearing on the information presented in it. However, this does not mean the information is a valid representation of the behavior being studied. Archival data suffer from two of the same problems as physical trace data—selective deposit and selective survival.

Why do people commit suicide? An archival approach to this question might be to assess the content of suicide notes. An immediate concern, however, is that less than 25% of those committing suicide leave notes, according to past research (Webb et al., 1981). Thus, the notes may not be representative of the feelings of all suicide victims. Similarly, an assessment of college professors' lecture notes may not be an accurate measure of class preparedness, because some professors pride themselves on not working from notes.

Selective deposit of archival data occurs when the records that are maintained are not representative of the relevant population. Some additional inquiries may be required to determine whether selective deposit is a concern. For example, a review of letters to the editor in local newspapers may seem to be an excellent source of information for a researcher to obtain a feel for attitudes in a particular area toward political questions, community concerns, racism, and other issues. However, not all editorial boards have the same policies. Some boards strive for a balance of perspectives, regardless of the balance of letters received; others will only publish one letter per author per month; still others will publish all letters. Editing policies may also vary. Letters to the editor may be edited as a matter of policy, or simply because of the amount of space available.

What information appears in the newspaper is also affected by the policies of institutions other than the newspaper itself. A hospital in my city will give the local newspaper all of the names of newborns and their parents, unless the parent is a single mother. However, that information is given to the newspaper only upon the request of the mother. So the birth announcements in the newspaper will probably not be an accurate reflection of the births in that hospital.

Just because information becomes part of an archive, it does not mean that it will remain part of that archive forever. Archival researchers must contend with selective survival. When data are missing from a running record, the researcher needs to ask why. Was there a fire? Was there a flood? Were documents shredded? Why are these particular data points missing? Do the missing data reflect random destruction or a bias of some type? For example, genealogical or historical research may be hampered because some families destroyed the military records of family members who served as mercenaries during the Civil War, a role that some saw as less than honorable. A study of love letters collected from a sample of individuals may overrepresent present relationships and/or positive relationships; letters from former lovers who are no longer fondly remembered may have been destroyed in a fit of pique, or letters from earlier sweethearts may have been discarded to protect the feelings of the current partner.

Archival information—even that presented for public consumption—is not always wholly accurate. Biases can occur in the most reputable archival record sources, and documents prepared for private use are sure to reflect the personal beliefs of the creator. Of course, the inherent biases themselves can provide subject matter for research.

Etaugh (1980) reviewed the seven most popular women's magazines in America published from 1956 to 1977. She identified nonfiction articles dealing with nonmaternal child care (that is, day care or babysitters). Child-care books published during that 20-year period were also reviewed. The content of these books and articles was coded for the attitudes expressed toward nonmaternal child care. Etaugh found that during the 1950s and 1960s, attitudes toward nonmaternal child care in the popular press were largely negative, but there was a shift toward more favorable attitudes in the 1970s. Etaugh postulates that this pattern reflects the time required for the results of scientific research to be assimilated by popular writers. Further evidence for this hypothesis comes from the finding that child-care books, which take longer than magazine articles to prepare and publish, exhibited more negative attitudes.

Interestingly, a sequel to Etaugh's research, in which articles published in women's magazines between 1977 and 1990 were coded in terms of their attitudes toward nonmaternal child care, found that there had been an increase in articles with mixed or negative attitudes since 1977 (Etaugh, Carlson, & Williams, 1992). Etaugh suspected that this trend reflected the attitude of the scientific community, which also expressed conflicting opinions regarding nonmaternal child care during this period.

As long as archives are the product of humans, they will be susceptible to biases. Biases in archival information may be deliberate, or they may be the result of error. Errors may be introduced into the archive by the producer of the record or document. A change in the record-keeping system used in the archive can result in errors if the researcher compares data recorded under the different systems without appropriate corrections. Error may result if definitions and criteria change during the course of record-keeping. Finally, the researcher may make errors when recording the information from the archive. A little error here and a little error there can add up to a lot of errors. An archival researcher must be mindful that the existence of an archive doesn't guarantee that it is an accurate representation of reality (Webb et al., 1981).

Ethical Considerations

When archival research is conducted using huge sets of anonymous records, issues of privacy and confidentiality are probably of little concern. However, ethical questions may arise for smaller sets of records or when cross-referencing sets of records.

In *Academe*, the monthly magazine of the American Association of University Professors, the average salaries of males, females, assistant professors, associate professors, full professors, and others are provided annually for colleges and universities across the United States. A quick perusal of this listing will reveal some blank spots. In some cases, the information was not available; in others, the omission is intended to protect the privacy of the few people within a particular category at a particular private college. If you are one of two female full professors at a college and you know your salary, it doesn't take too much mathematical finesse to calculate your colleague's salary from a published mean.

Researchers who cross-reference archives may find themselves in an ethical bind. They may learn information about people that they would never want known. Cross-referencing those who voted in Republican and Democratic primaries with a mailing list for an adult bookstore, for example, may provide interesting information about the relative numbers of Republicans and Democrats on this particular mailing list, but it may also violate the privacy of those individuals.

Typically, archival research is ethically innocuous, but there are exceptions. Each researcher must take into account the particulars of his or her project and consider any anonymity, confidentiality, privacy, or informed consent issues that might be relevant.

Although the archival researcher must be aware of several areas of concern, that does not mean that archival research should not be undertaken. Often the sources of information are sound, and the researcher can have confidence in its objectivity. Even when the validity of the data cannot be completely ascertained, archival research can be an important addition to a research program based on a multimethod approach. When archival data corroborates laboratory research, observational studies, surveys, or other research approaches, confidence in the veracity of those reports is strengthened.

SUMMARY

Physical trace and archival data studies have the major advantage of being nonreactive approaches to the study of behavior. The collection of these types of data has no bearing on the behaviors that preceded them. For this reason, information provided by such designs can be especially convincing.

Unfortunately, the advantage of nonreactivity is tempered by the disadvantage that the validity of physical trace and archival data is often unknown. Two primary sources of concern are selective deposit—a bias in the production of traces and archival records—and selective survival—a bias in the endurance of traces and records.

Researchers must also consider the ethical ramifications of their data collection and research. Because data collection is nonreactive, there is typically no opportunity for individuals to provide informed consent. Most often, those who produced the physical trace or whose behavior was recorded in the archive are unknown or even unknowable. In other cases, it may be possible to identify particular individuals and to make public information that they would not wish known. Researchers should remain conscious of privacy and anonymity concerns as they plan their research.

A researcher's interpretation of research data is as subject to personal bias and poor reasoning as anyone else's interpretation. Because physical trace and archival data studies are correlational studies, you should be especially watchful for insinuations of causal relationships.

Physical trace and archival data studies have their weaknesses; by themselves, they do not provide especially strong evidence in support of a hypothesis. However, in combination with other methods, physical trace and archival data studies can render research findings more credible and increase their external reliability. These approaches to research should not be lightly dismissed.

IMPORTANT TERMS AND CONCEPTS

accretion measures	erosion measures
archival data	natural trace measures
archival data studies	nonreactive
content analysis	physical trace measure
continuous (or running)	physical trace studies
records	products
controlled trace measures	records
data reduction	selective deposit
discontinuous records	selective survival
documents	traces

EXERCISES

1. What social science questions might you be able to explore on the basis of the following archival data sources?

    a. Obituaries in your city newspaper.

    b. Science-fiction stories from the present and from the 1920s.

    c. Cookbooks.

    d. Junk mail.

    e. TV listings.

    f. Computer software documentation.

2. What physical trace measures might you use to answer questions on the following topics?

    a. Political attitudes of college students.

    b. Attitudes toward poetry.

    c. Respect for private property.

    d. Compulsive tendencies among college professors.

    e. The relative importance of punctuality in various cultures.

    f. The nutrition and diet of a given population.

3. How would you determine whether photographs of women are as prevalent in your local newspapers as are photographs of men? How would you judge whether the photographs of women make them appear as professional as men? Design your own archival data study to address these questions. Determine the type of data you would collect, any coding scheme you might need, and the operational definitions for the codes. What is your hypothesis? Collect your data. Do your results support your hypothesis?

ANSWERS TO CONCEPT QUESTION AND ODD-NUMBERED EXERCISES

Note: There will often be more than one correct answer for each of these questions. Consult with your instructor about your own answers.

Concept Question 12.1

a. accretion

b. erosion

c. accretion

d. accretion

e. accretion

f. erosion

Exercises

1. a. The average age of those who die.

   b. Differences in the presentation of women today and in the 1920s.

   c. The amount of fat and calories in certain recipes.

   d. The percentage of items that asks for money and the percentage that tries to sell things.

   e. The percentage of situation comedies, dramas, news-related shows, and documentaries.

   f. The extent to which computer literacy is expected.

3. To carry out this project you would need to determine how far back in time you want to go and which sections of the paper you want to use. Perhaps you decide to use the past three months and focus only on pictures in the first section of the paper. You might have two or three people rate the pictures for how professional the subject looks. I won't bias your decision about your hypothesis by posing my own.

Basic Statistical Techniques

Statistics are the tools used by researchers to organize and interpret their data. In this appendix, several statistical techniques are discussed and demonstrated so that you may use them to better understand any data that you might collect and also to better understand the statistical techniques mentioned in research reports.

DESCRIPTIVE STATISTICS

As the name suggests, descriptive statistics are techniques used to describe a set of data. Two important characteristics of a data set are described with descriptive statistics: the average score and how spread out or clustered together the scores tend to be.

Averages

Perhaps the most commonly discussed characteristic of a data set is its average. However, three different averages can be calculated and each provides somewhat different information. These three averages are called the mode, the median, and the mean.

The **mode** is the score in a set of discrete data that occurs most frequently. Consider the following set of scores: 8, 10, 9, 4, 3, 8, 12, 10, 8, 7, 6, 8. The mode for this set of scores is 8, because that is the score that occurs most frequently.

Sometimes a set of data will have two scores that tie for most frequently occurring. Then the distribution is said to be **bimodal**. If three or more scores are tied for most frequently occurring, the distribution is said to be **multimodal**. The mode is a very straightforward measure that can be used with nominal, ordinal, interval, or ratio data.

The **median** is a measure of central tendency; it provides information about the distribution of the other scores, and it describes where the middle score is. In fact, the median is defined as the middle point in a set of scores, the point below which 50% of the scores fall. To determine the median of a distribution, the number of scores must be known. Also, the scores must be presented in rank-order from smallest to largest (or vice versa). The median of this distribution is the point below which half of the scores fall. Try to determine the median for the following test scores:

X
98
98
97
95
91
87
85
82
76
74
71
68
62
54

There are 14 scores in this set. The number of scores is usually denoted as N; thus, $N = 14$. The median will be the score marking the middle of this distribution:

$$\frac{N}{2} = \frac{14}{2} = 7$$

Thus, the top half of the distribution consists of seven scores, and the bottom half consists of seven scores. The seventh score from the top of this distribution is 85, and the next score is 82. Therefore, the median score is halfway between 85 and 82, or 83.5.

The median will always fall between two scores when the distribution consists of an even number of scores. When there is an odd number of scores, the median will fall on an existing score.

The median provides a measure of central tendency and some information about the rest of the data set. It can be used with ratio and interval data but not all ordinal data; it is inappropriate for use with nominal data.

Another measure of central tendency is called the **mean**. It is the arithmetic average of the scores in a distribution. The mean is calculated by adding up the scores in the distribution and dividing by the number of scores. The formula for the mean is as follows:

$$\mu = \frac{\Sigma X}{N} \quad \text{or} \quad \bar{X} = \frac{\Sigma X}{N}$$

where Σ is the symbol for summation; X stands for the scores; N is the number of scores; μ is the symbol for the population mean; $\overline{X}$ is the symbol for the sample mean.

If the scores do not represent an entire population but a sample from the population, the formula is the same, but the symbol for the sample mean, $\overline{X}$, appears on the left-hand side.

As a quick example of computing the mean, suppose we have the following set of test scores: 100, 74, 92, 83, 61. The sum of these five scores is 410. Thus, the mean test score is as follows:

$$\mu = \frac{\Sigma X}{N} = \frac{410}{5} = 82$$

If these scores were only a subset of a larger population of scores, the symbol for the mean would be $\overline{X}$. The mean can be used with interval and ratio data, but is not appropriate for use with data measured on either an ordinal or a nominal scale.

Measures of Dispersion

Another set of important descriptive statistics consists of measures of dispersion (also referred to as measures of variability or variation). Whereas measures of central tendency describe how and where the data tend to fall together, measures of dispersion describe the extent to which the data are spread out or clustered together. Although some measures of dispersion can be used with nominal and ordinal data, measures of dispersion are used primarily with interval or ratio data.

The most straightforward measure of dispersion is called the **range**. For a discrete data set, the range is the number of possible values of the scores; for data taken from a continuous distribution, the range is the interval of scores covered by the data set. The range is computed by subtracting the lowest score from the highest score and adding 1.

Range = Highest − Lowest + 1

We add 1 so that the range will include both the highest value and the lowest value. Let's revisit the test scores from the example for calculating the median.

X
98
98
97
95
91
87

85
82
76
74
71
68
62
54

The range for these scores would be as follows:

$$98 - 54 + 1 = 45$$

These data are spread across a range of 45 values, from 54 to 98.

The range tells us over how many scores the data are spread, but it does not give us any information about how the scores are distributed over the range. It is limited because it relies on only two scores from the entire distribution.

Another approach to measuring dispersion is to measure the distances that the scores fall from the mean score and then calculate the average distance (or mean distance) of each datum from the mean. This measure of dispersion is called the **average deviation (A.D.).**

In order to calculate the average deviation from the mean, we first must know the mean. Then we calculate the distance of each score from the mean; this is called the deviation score:

$$X - \mu$$

We will be summing the deviation scores to obtain the mean but, if we sum them as they are, they will sum to zero. Instead, we take the absolute value of each deviation score and sum those values:

$$\Sigma |X - \mu|$$

Lastly, we calculate the mean deviation score by dividing the sum of the absolute values of the deviation scores by the number of deviation scores. Thus, the formula for the average deviation is as follows:

$$\text{A.D.} = \frac{\Sigma |X - \mu|}{N}$$

Let's use our test score data again. I have also provided the deviation scores here.

X	$|X - \mu|$
98	16.714
98	16.714
97	15.714
95	13.714
91	9.714
87	5.714
85	3.714
82	0.714
76	5.286
74	7.286
71	10.286
68	13.286
62	19.286
54	27.286
Sums: 1138	165.428

$$\text{A.D.} = \frac{\Sigma |X - \mu|}{N} = \frac{165.428}{14} = 11.816$$

For our data, the scores fall an average of 11.816 points from the mean score of 81.286.

While the average deviation is quite straightforward and relatively easy to understand, it is not especially useful for other statistical procedures, primarily because it cannot be manipulated algebraically (because the absolute values do not perform the same operation on each member of the set) and so it is not used as often as are two other measures of dispersion: the variance and the standard deviation.

Variance and Standard Deviation

When calculating the average deviation, we used the absolute values of the deviations from the mean to make all of the numbers positive.

The absolute value eliminates the negative signs on deviation scores. Another technique for eliminating negative signs from a set of scores is to square each score. Thus, if we square each deviation score, these scores can then be summed to a number greater than zero. (The sum of the squared deviation scores is called the sum of squares for short and is often abbreviated SS.) The average of the squared deviation scores can be determined by dividing by N. This procedure results in a statistic called the population **variance**. The formula for the variance is as follows:

$$\sigma^2 = \frac{\Sigma (X - \mu)^2}{N}$$

This formula for the variance is called the deviation formula, because it involves calculating the deviation scores. When the number of scores in a data set is large, the deviation formula becomes unwieldy. For most purposes, researchers will use the raw-score formula (also called the computational formula) when calculating the variance or the standard deviation by hand. This formula is the result of an algebraic transformation of the deviation formula. The raw-score formula for the population variance looks like this:

$$\sigma^2 = \frac{\Sigma X^2 - \frac{(\Sigma X)^2}{N}}{N}$$

Let's use this formula to demonstrate the calculation of the variance. Here are the test scores once again, along with their squares:

X	X^2
98	9604
98	9604
97	9409
95	9025
91	8281
87	7569
85	7225
82	6724
76	5776
74	5476
71	5041
68	4624
62	3844
54	2916
Sums: 1138	95,118

Using our variance formula, we find the following:

$$\sigma^2 = \frac{\Sigma X^2 - \frac{(\Sigma X)^2}{N}}{N}$$

$$= \frac{95,118 - \frac{(1138)^2}{14}}{14}$$

$$= \frac{95,118 - 92,503.143}{14}$$

$$= \frac{2614.857}{14}$$

$$= 186.776$$

This number seems large compared to our original data, because it is based on squared deviation scores. To change the variance to the original unsquared units, we take the square root of the variance. This new measure is called the **standard deviation** and is denoted by σ when it represents the standard deviation for the entire population. For our data, the standard deviation would be as follows:

$$\sigma = \sqrt{\sigma^2}$$
$$= \sqrt{186.776}$$
$$= 13.666$$

The scores fall approximately 13.666 points from the mean.

The symbols and formulas for the variance and standard deviation given here are for the population variance and standard deviation. If the scores from a sample are being used to estimate the variance of a population, then the formulas and symbols look like this:

$$s^2 = \frac{\Sigma X^2 - \frac{(\Sigma X)^2}{N}}{N-1} \qquad s = \sqrt{s^2}$$

where s^2 is the sample variance; s is the sample standard deviation; N is the number of scores in the sample; and X is each individual score.

The formulas for the sample variance and sample standard deviation differ from the formulas for the population version of these statistics in two ways: The sample mean is substituted for the population mean; and the denominator for the sample statistics contains $N - 1$ and not just N. Dividing by $N - 1$ provides a better estimate of the population variance and standard deviation than does dividing by N alone, because it increases the values of the sample standard deviation and sample variance. This is especially important if the sample is small; in that case, dividing by N would underestimate the size of the population variance and standard deviation. For this reason, the sample standard deviation and sample variance are said to be unbiased estimators of the population standard deviation and variance.

CORRELATIONS

Correlations are statistical techniques used to determine the degree of relationship between two variables. When calculated, correlations yield a number—a correlation coefficient—that falls between +1.00 and −1.00. The closer the coefficient is to either +1.00 or −1.00, the stronger is the relationship. The plus and minus signs relay information about the *direction* of the relationship. When a correlation is positive, the two variables are changing in the same direction: as X increases, so does Y. When a correlation is negative, the two variables are changing in opposite directions: when X increases, Y decreases.

Let's consider an example. Assume that a researcher wants to know if there is a correlation between the number of semester hours of coursework completed and the number of hours a student reports studying for a midterm exam. Table A.1 presents the data for number of hours studied and number of semester hours completed.

Table A.1   Hours Spent Studying and Number of Semester Hours Completed for a Sample of 14 Students

Student	X Number of hours studying	Y Number of semester hours
1	14	24
2	6	60
3	4	125
4	28	30
5	9	14
6	9	31
7	12	33
8	18	55
9	8	93
10	5	45
11	10	56
12	18	13
13	16	87
14	10	112.5

Because both of these variables—number of semester hours and number of hours studying—are measured on either a ratio or interval scale, the appropriate correlation to compute is the **Pearson's product-moment correlation coefficient**, which is often referred to simply as **Pearson's r**. This coefficient—symbolized by the letter r—is the correlation coefficient most often used by behavioral scientists. The raw score formula for Pearson's r is as follows:

$$r_{xy} = \frac{N\Sigma XY - \Sigma X \Sigma Y}{\sqrt{\left[N\Sigma X^2 - (\Sigma X)^2\right]\left[N\Sigma Y^2 - (\Sigma Y)^2\right]}}$$

Table A.2 Hours Studying and Semester Hours Plus the Scores Squared and the Scores' Cross-Products

X	X^2	Y	Y^2	XY
14	196	24	576	336
6	36	60	3600	360
4	16	125	15,625	500
28	784	30	900	840
9	81	14	196	126
9	81	31	961	279
12	144	33	1089	396
18	324	55	3025	990
8	64	93	8649	744
5	25	45	2025	225
10	100	56	3136	560
18	324	13	169	234
16	256	87	7569	139
10	100	112.5	12,656.25	1125
167	2531	778.5	60,176.25	6854

In table A.2 the semester hours and hours studying data are presented again, along with columns for X^2, Y^2, and the cross-product of X and Y (the XY column). Using the raw score formula for these data, we calculate the Pearson's r as follows:

$$r_{xy} = \frac{N\Sigma XY - \Sigma X \Sigma Y}{\sqrt{\left[N\Sigma X^2 - (\Sigma X)^2\right]\left[N\Sigma Y^2 - (\Sigma Y)^2\right]}}$$

$$= \frac{14(6854) - 167(778.5)}{\sqrt{\left[14(2531) - 167^2\right]\left[14(60,176.25) - 778.5^2\right]}}$$

$$= \frac{95,956 - 130,009.5}{\sqrt{(35,434 - 27,889)(842,467.5 - 606,062.25)}}$$

$$= \frac{-34,053.5}{\sqrt{(7545)(236,405.25)}}$$

$$= \frac{-34,053.5}{\sqrt{1,783,677,611.25}}$$

$$= \frac{-34,053.5}{42,233.608} = -.8063$$

We have calculated an r_{xy} of –.8063. What does this tell us?

Our correlation coefficient is relatively close to –1.00. This would typically be interpreted as a strong negative correlation between X and Y. In other words, the more semester hours these students have under their belt, the fewer hours they spend studying. Whether a particular value of a correlation coefficient is interpreted as reflecting strong, moderate, or weak correlation will vary from topic to topic and project to project. In some situations, nothing lower than a correlation of .60 would be considered worthwhile; in others, .40 might be considered quite impressive.

The correlation coefficient can also indicate the amount of variation among the scores that is accounted for in the study. All of the students did not study exactly the same number of hours and did not complete exactly the same number of semester hours; that is, there is variation in the X scores and the Y scores. The variation in X (hours studying) is associated with the variation in Y (semester hours), but also with other undefined factors, such as the difficulty of the course, the general intelligence of the student, and the student's motivation to perform well. The more that the variation in X and the variation in Y are associated, the larger the absolute value of the correlation coefficient will be. If the correlation coefficient is squared, it represents the *proportion* of variance in Y associated with variance in X. Thus, $-.8063^2 = .6501$, which means that approximately 65% of the variance in hours studying is associated with semester hours completed, while 35% of the variance is associated with other factors.

Whether the amount of variation among the scores that is accounted for is regarded as considerable or modest, again, depends on the area of research. Pearson's correlation coefficient and r^2 supply descriptive information, but researchers must supply the interpretation.

Spearman's Rho

Pearson's product-moment coefficient is appropriate for use when X and Y are measured on a ratio or an interval scale. Other correlation coefficients may be used for other situations. **Spearman's rho** is a special case of Pearson's r that is appropriate for use with data that have been ranked. For example, suppose we are interested in the correlation between a person's ranked performance in a course and the number of hours he or she typically spends studying for an exam. These data are presented in table A.3; the data for hours spent studying have already been ranked, and columns for the difference between the ranks (d) and the difference squared (d^2) are also included.

The formula for Pearson's r can be used to calculate the Spearman's rho, but it is simpler to use the following formula:

$$\rho = 1 - \frac{6\Sigma d^2}{N(N^2 - 1)}$$

Using this formula and the information from table A.3, we can calculate Spearman's rho:

Table A.3   Ranked Performance in a Course and Hours Studying for an Exam: Data for Calculating Spearman's Rho

Class rank	Hours studying	Hours ranked	d	d^2
1	15	2	−1	1
2	18	1	1	1
3	10	6	−3	9
4	7	9	−5	25
5	12	4	1	1
6	13	3	3	9
7	11	5	2	4
8	8	8	0	0
9	9	7	2	4
10	6	10	0	0
11	4	12	−1	1
12	5	11	1	1
13	3	13	0	0
14	2	14	0	0
				56

$$\rho = 1 - \frac{6\Sigma d^2}{N(N^2 - 1)}$$

$$= 1 - \frac{6(56)}{14(14^2 - 1)}$$

$$= 1 - \frac{336}{14(195)}$$

$$= 1 - \frac{336}{2730}$$

$$= 1 - .1231$$

$$= .877$$

We interpret the Spearman's rho in the same manner as the Pearson's *r*. In this example, we have calculated a strong positive correlation of .877. This suggests that class rank and hours spent studying are related; specifically, that those with a higher class rank tend to spend more time studying. (The greatest number of hours was ranked first, the next greatest second, and so on.)

In the previous example of the Spearman's rho calculations, one variable was already rank-ordered and the other variable needed to be transformed to rank-ordered data. Ranking can be done from smallest to largest or largest to smallest, whichever makes the most sense to the researcher. A problem may arise, however, when there are tied ranks. Tied ranks occur when two or more observations for one variable are the same. Suppose we were to rank the following numbers from smallest to largest:

X: 5   8   7   6   9   4   6   3   2

The number 2 would receive a rank of 1, the number 3 a rank of 2, the number 4 a rank of 3, and the number 5 a rank of 4. The number 6 appears twice; these two observations would have received ranks of 5 and 6 if they weren't identical numbers. Instead, we will give these two observations the average of the ranks they would have received; that is, each 6 receives a rank of 5.5. The next higher observation is a 7; this number will receive a rank of 7, just as it would if the two previous numbers hadn't been tied. The next higher number then receives a rank of 8, and so on.

X:	5	8	7	6	9	4	6	3	2
Ranks:	4	8	7	5.5	9	3	5.5	2	1

When tied ranks occur, the Spearman's rho will never equal +1.00 or –1.00. If there is more than one pair of tied ranks within a data set, an alternative approach is to use the Pearson's r formula, which will yield a more accurate measure of the correlation (Howell, 2002).

INFERENTIAL STATISTICS

Inferential statistics are statistical techniques used to test hypotheses about a set of data in order to make inferences about the population from which the samples were drawn. Some inferential statistics, called parametric statistics, can be used only with interval and ratio data that meet certain assumptions—for instance, that the variance of groups being compared is equivalent and that the underlying populations of scores are normally distributed.

When the data are not appropriate for parametric statistical techniques, other types of statistical techniques—nonparametric techniques—can be used to test hypotheses. Nonparametric tests do not require interval or ratio data, and few assumptions about the underlying population of scores are made. However, these tests tend to be less powerful than parametric tests in the same situation, so with a given set of data, if the assumptions are met for inferential statistics they are tests typically conducted.

In this section, a number of inferential statistical techniques are described and demonstrated. The tests presented here are used to compare one sample to a population mean, to compare two separate sample means, or to compare the two means from pairs of scores. We will then consider two popular nonparametric tests—types of χ^2 (chi-squared) tests.

The z-Test

The z-test is used to compare the sample mean ($\overline{X}$) of a single sample to a known population mean (μ). For example, let's assume that IQ scores were collected from a random sample of 100 students at a summer program. We hypothesize that the students in the summer program have higher IQs than the general population. Our null and alternative hypotheses are as follows:

$$H_0 = \mu_{\text{summer school}} = \mu_{\text{general population}} \text{ or } H_0 = \mu_0 = \mu_1$$
$$H_1 = \mu_{\text{summer school}} > \mu_{\text{general population}} \text{ or } H_1 = \mu_0 > \mu_1$$

The population mean (μ) and the population standard deviation (σ) are known:

$$\mu = 100; \qquad \sigma = 15$$

To calculate the test statistic for the z-test, we also need to compute the standard error of the mean, which is an estimate of the normal amount of variance among the scores. This is calculated as follows:

$$\sigma_{\bar{x}} = \frac{\sigma}{\sqrt{N}}$$

The standard error of the mean based on samples of 100 subjects is as follows:

$$\sigma_{\bar{x}} = \frac{\sigma}{\sqrt{N}} = \frac{15}{\sqrt{100}} = \frac{15}{10} = 1.5$$

Suppose that, for this sample of 100 summer program students, $\bar{X} = 104$. To test our hypothesis that the sample of summer program students represents a population with a mean greater than the mean for the general population, we need to determine the likelihood that a sample mean as large as 104 would be randomly chosen from this sampling distribution if the null hypothesis were true. (A sampling distribution is a theoretical set of sample means chosen from a population.) In other words, with α at .05 (unless otherwise stated, α will always be .05 in this textbook), does a $\bar{X}$ of 104 fall in the top 5% of the sampling distribution? This area is called the region of rejection of the sampling distribution. Our next steps then are to determine what score marks off the region of rejection and to determine whether our $\bar{X}$ falls within that region.

Because our sampling distribution is a normal curve, we can use the standard normal-curve table to help us solve this problem. The normal curve (or normal distribution) is a bell-shaped, symmetric curve. From the standard normal-curve table, we find that the z-score that marks off the top 5% of the distribution is 1.645, which is called the z critical value (z_{cv}). The **z-score** denotes the distance measured in standard deviations from the mean. To determine if our sample mean is significantly greater than the population mean, we need to know if the sample mean lies more than 1.645 standard deviations above the population mean; that is, we need to determine the z-score for the sample mean.

The formula for calculating the test statistic for the z-test is as follows:

$$z = \frac{\overline{X} - \mu}{\sigma_{\overline{X}}}$$

Thus, for $\overline{X}$ = 104:

$$z = \frac{\overline{X} - \mu}{\sigma_{\overline{X}}}$$
$$= \frac{104 - 100}{1.5}$$
$$= \frac{4}{1.5}$$
$$= 2.6667$$

The z-score for our sample mean—2.6667—falls within the region of rejection; there is less than a 5% chance of randomly choosing a sample with a mean so great. Thus, we reject the null hypothesis (H_0) that the sample mean represents the general population mean, and support our alternative hypothesis that the sample mean represents a population of summer program students with a mean IQ greater than 100.

Let's consider the z-test for different alternative hypotheses. For example, in the problem just considered, the alternative hypothesis was as follows:

$$H_1 : \mu_0 > \mu_1$$

The z_{cv} was 1.645 and the region of rejection was in the right tail. Now suppose that the alternative hypothesis is in the opposite direction:

$$H_1 : \mu_0 < \mu_1$$

In this case, the region of rejection is in the left tail, because we expect the sample mean to be smaller than the population mean, and the z_{cv} will be –1.645. A rule of thumb for rejection of H_0 when H_1 is one-tailed is that H_0 is rejected when both z_{cv} and the calculated z (often called z-obtained, and symbolized z_{obt}) have the same sign (positive or negative) and $|z_{obt}| > |z_{cv}|$. When this is true, z_{obt} will fall within the region of rejection.

A third possibility is a two-tailed alternative hypothesis, in which a difference between the sample mean and population mean is predicted, but not the specific direction of that difference:

$$H_1 : \mu_0 \neq \mu_1$$

In the case of a two-tailed alternative hypothesis, the region of rejection is divided equally between the two tails of the sampling distribution, with 2.5% of the area in each. The z_{cv} now changes. From the standard normal-curve table, we find that the z-score that marks off the top (and bottom) 2.5% of the distribution is 1.96. Thus, $z_{cv} = \pm 1.96$. To reject H_0 when H_1 is two-tailed, $|z_{obt}| > |z_{cv}|$; when this is true, z_{obt} will fall within the region of rejection.

The z-test is appropriate for interval and ratio data, where a mean is a meaningful statistic. In addition, to calculate a z-score, both the population mean and population standard deviation must be known. When the sample size is small ($N < 30$) or the population standard deviation is not known, the researcher may need to conduct a single-sample t-test instead of the z-test.

The *t*-Distribution and the *t*-Test for Single Samples

The **t-distributions** (or **Student's t-distributions**) are a family of distributions that, like the normal distribution, are symmetric and bell-shaped. And, as z is used to indicate the number of standard deviations from the μ, t also indicates the number of standard deviations from the mean. However, in contrast to the normal distribution, there is a different t-distribution for each sample size. Thus, the critical value marking off the region of rejection changes with different sample sizes.

In appendix B there is a table of critical values for the t-distribution (table B.3), which supplies values of t_{cv} for one- and two-tailed alternative hypotheses over a broad range of α levels and sample sizes. However, there is no column giving the values of N (the sample size); instead, there is a column listing the values of df, which stands for **degrees of freedom**.

Assume you are given four numbers: 3, 6, 8, and 11. The mean of these numbers is 7. Now you are told that you can change the numbers as you wish, but you must keep the mean at 7. How many numbers can you change? You can change only three of the four numbers, because as soon as three numbers are changed the value of the fourth is determined by the restriction that the mean equal 7. Consequently, with four numbers and one restriction, only three numbers are free to vary—there are three degrees of freedom.

Most statistical tests involve setting one or more restrictions on the data set. In the case of the **single-sample t-test**, we will need to estimate the population standard deviation. It may not be obvious but, during the course of estimating the standard deviation, we have also estimated the population mean, and thus set a restriction on our set of numbers. For that reason, for the single-sample t-test, $df = N - 1$.

Let's consider an example using the single-sample t-test. The mean ACT score for those admitted to a certain university is 23. This is the population mean, but the population standard deviation is not known. A member of the psychology department thinks that those students who decide to be psychology majors may differ on their ACT scores from the population of students at the university in general. The null and alternative hypotheses are as follows:

$$H_0 : \mu_0 = \mu_1$$
$$H_1 : \mu_0 \neq \mu_1$$

The researcher obtains ACT scores for a sample of psychology majors. These data are provided in table A.4.

Table A.4   Hypothetical ACT Scores for a Sample of Psychology Majors

X
20
25
32
27
21
30
28
23
22

Sum: 228

$$\bar{X} = \frac{\Sigma X}{N} = \frac{228}{9} = 25.3333$$

The mean ACT score for the sample of psychology majors is 25.3333 points. This is our estimate of the mean ACT score for the population of psychology majors. We now must determine if this score is significantly different from the university mean of 23. Because we do not know, we will need to conduct a t-test instead of a z-test. The formula for t is as follows:

$$t = \frac{\bar{X} - \mu}{s_{\bar{X}}}$$

This is very similar to the formula for z:

$$z = \frac{\bar{X} - \mu}{\sigma_{\bar{X}}}$$

The only difference is the substitution of $s_{\bar{X}}$ for $\sigma_{\bar{X}}$. The symbol $s_{\bar{X}}$ represents the estimated standard error of the sampling distribution, where the sample standard deviation s is used as an estimate of σ. Thus, the formula for $s_{\bar{x}}$ is as follows:

$$s_{\bar{x}} = \frac{s}{\sqrt{N}}$$

As a reminder, the formula for s is as follows:

$$s = \sqrt{\frac{\Sigma X^2 - \dfrac{(\Sigma X)^2}{N}}{N-1}}$$

Table A.5   Squares and Sums of ACT Scores

X	X^2
20	400
25	625
32	1024
27	729
21	441
30	900
28	784
23	529
22	484
Sums: 228	5916

$$N = 9$$

The next step in conducting our t-test is to calculate s. On the basis of the data in table A.5, we proceed as follows:

$$s = \sqrt{\frac{\Sigma X^2 - \dfrac{(\Sigma X)^2}{N}}{N-1}} = \sqrt{\frac{5916 - \dfrac{228^2}{9}}{9-1}}$$

$$= \sqrt{\frac{5916 - \dfrac{51,984}{9}}{8}}$$

$$= \sqrt{\frac{5916 - 5776}{8}}$$

$$= \sqrt{\frac{140}{8}} = \sqrt{17.5} = 4.1833$$

The standard deviation for this sample is 4.1833. We now calculate the standard error of the sampling distribution by dividing the sample standard deviation s by $\sqrt{N}$:

$$s_{\bar{X}} = \frac{s}{\sqrt{N}}$$

$$= \frac{4.1833}{\sqrt{9}}$$

$$= \frac{4.1833}{3} = 1.3944$$

Now that $s_{\bar{X}}$ has been obtained, t may be calculated:

$$t = \frac{\bar{X} - \mu}{s_{\bar{X}}}$$

$$= \frac{25.3333 - 23}{1.3944}$$

$$= \frac{2.3333}{1.3944} = 1.6733$$

Our sample mean falls 1.6733 standard deviations above the population mean of 23. Our question now is whether that is within the region of rejection.

Because ours is a two-tailed alternative hypothesis, the region of rejection is divided evenly between the positive and negative tails of the sampling distribution. With α at .05, the region of rejection consists of the top and bottom 2.5% of the distribution. Whether our t-value falls within the region of rejection is dependent on whether the obtained t (t_{obt}) falls beyond t_{cv}. We determine the critical value by referring to table B.3.

In table B.3, we look for the t_{cv} that corresponds to a two-tailed alternative hypothesis where $\alpha = .05$ and $df = N - 1 = 9 - 1 = 8$. Using this information, we find that $t_{cv} = 2.306$. Therefore, t_{obt} is not within the region of rejection. We do not reject H_0 and, thus, have no evidence to support H_1; that is, we have no evidence that the population of psychology majors differ significantly on ACT scores from the rest of the student body at this university.

The t-test, like the z-test, is a parametric procedure; as such, its validity is dependent on certain assumptions:

- that the data are measured on an interval or ratio scale;
- that the sample has been randomly selected, so as to be representative of the population;

- that the observations are independent; in other words, that the observation of one participant had no effect on the performance or observation of another; and
- that the population distribution of the scores is normal.

Violating these assumptions makes the t-test less powerful, so that it is more difficult to detect differences between the sample and the population.

The single-sample t-test is used to compare a sample mean to a population mean when a z-test is not possible. Primarily, this would be when the population mean is known, but the population standard deviation is not known. When neither a z-test nor a t-test is appropriate, the researcher may wish to consider a nonparametric test; such tests are described in most introductory-level statistics texts.

The Independent-Samples *t*-Test

The **independent-samples t-test** is used to compare the means of two separate, independent groups (samples) of data. For example, let's assume that a graduate student is interested in determining if noise is a help or a hindrance when studying. This researcher decides to operationally define "noise" as radio static, and expects to find that individuals who are required to study a list of words in the static condition will recall fewer words than those who study in a quiet condition. Thus, the null and alternative hypotheses are as follows:

$$H_0 : \mu_{\text{quiet condition}} = \mu_{\text{static condition}} \text{ or } H_0 = \mu_q = \mu_s$$

$$H_1 : \mu_{\text{quiet condition}} > \mu_{\text{static condition}} \text{ or } H_1 = \mu_q > \mu_s$$

The researcher solicits the assistance of 20 volunteers, who are randomly assigned to either the control (quiet) condition or the experimental (static) condition. Each participant is tested individually. He or she sits at a desk in a quiet room and is fitted with a set of headphones. The headphones serve to block out all other extraneous noise for those in the control group or to present radio static from an attached receiver for those in the experimental group. Each participant is presented with a list of 50 words randomly chosen from a dictionary. The participants study this list for 10 minutes and then complete a free recall task in which they try to write down as many of the words as they can recall. Hypothetical results for the participants are presented in table A.6.

**Table A.6   Number of Words Recalled by Participants in
Two Separate Noise Conditions**

Quiet (X_1)	Static (X_2)
20	12
15	17
22	18
19	12
17	11
21	13
18	15
21	16
18	11
19	14

The researcher now needs to determine whether the mean for the silence condition is significantly greater than the mean for the static condition. In the single-sample t-test discussed earlier, a single sample mean was compared to a population mean. To compare two sample means, we will also use a t-test—the independent-samples t-test. The general formula for the independent-samples t-test is as follows:

$$t = \frac{(\bar{X}_1 - \bar{X}_2) - (\mu_1 - \mu_2)}{s_{\bar{X}_1 - \bar{X}_2}}$$

In essence, this looks like a double version of the single-sample t-test formula. Instead of comparing a single sample with a single population, however, the difference between two sample means is compared here with the difference between two population means. In most research involving the independent-samples t-test, the null hypothesis is that there is no difference between μ_1 and μ_2; the difference is zero. Thus, we can simplify this formula somewhat by dropping the difference between the populations:

$$t = \frac{\bar{X}_1 - \bar{X}_2}{s_{\bar{X}_1 - \bar{X}_2}}$$

The standard error used in the independent-samples t-test is officially called the **standard error of differences between means**. It is the standard deviation for the sampling distribution composed of differences between sample means (rather than a sampling distribution of sample means).

In the independent-samples t-test, we are determining how far from the difference between the population means lies the difference between our sample means. If the difference between our sample means is relatively large, it will fall in one of the tails of the distribution, far from the difference between the population means, which is zero according to our null hypothesis. To determine the distance from the difference of the population means, we need to convert our mean differences to standard errors. As you may recall, the formula for the standard error for a single sample is as follows:

$$s_{\bar{X}} = \frac{s}{\sqrt{N}}$$

Algebraically, this may be written in the equivalent form:

$$s_{\bar{X}} = \sqrt{\frac{s^2}{N}}$$

Correspondingly, the formula for the standard error for the independent-samples t-test is as follows:

$$s_{\bar{X}_1 - \bar{X}_2} = \sqrt{\frac{s_1^2}{n_1} + \frac{s_2^2}{n_2}}$$

Thus, by analogy with the single-samples t-test, the formula for determining t is as follows:

$$t = \frac{\bar{X}_1 - \bar{X}_2}{\sqrt{\frac{s_1^2}{n_1} + \frac{s_2^2}{n_2}}}$$

In these formulas, n refers to the number of scores in each group, whereas N, as used previously, refers to the total number of scores in the entire study.

Let's use this formula to determine if there is a significant difference between the noise and static conditions, on the basis of the data in table A.7. First, we calculate the mean scores:

Table A.7   Squares and Sums of Scores for Free Recall Task

Silence (X_1)	X_1^2	Static (X_2)	X_2^2
20	400	12	144
15	225	17	289
22	484	18	324
19	361	12	144
17	289	11	121
21	441	13	169
18	324	15	225
21	441	16	256
18	324	11	121
19	361	14	196
Sums: 190	3650	139	1989

$$\overline{X}_1 = \frac{\Sigma X_1}{n_1} = \frac{190}{10} = 19$$

$$\overline{X}_2 = \frac{\Sigma X_2}{n_2} = \frac{139}{10} = 13.9$$

Next we calculate the squares of the sample standard deviations:

$$s_1^2 = \frac{\Sigma X_1^2 - \dfrac{\left(\Sigma X_1\right)^2}{n_1}}{n_1 - 1}$$

$$= \frac{3650 - \dfrac{190^2}{10}}{9}$$

$$= \frac{3650 - 3610}{9}$$

$$= \frac{40}{9} = 4.4444$$

$$s_2^2 = \frac{\Sigma X_2^2 - \dfrac{\left(\Sigma X_2\right)^2}{n_2}}{n_2 - 1}$$

$$= \frac{1989 - \dfrac{139^2}{10}}{9}$$

$$= \frac{1989 - 1932.1}{9}$$

$$= \frac{56.9}{9} = 6.3222$$

We can now determine t:

$$t = \frac{\overline{X}_1 - \overline{X}_2}{\sqrt{\dfrac{s_1^2}{n_1} + \dfrac{s_2^2}{n_2}}}$$

$$= \frac{19 - 13.9}{\sqrt{\dfrac{4.4444}{10} + \dfrac{6.3222}{10}}}$$

$$= \frac{5.1}{\sqrt{1.0767}}$$

$$= \frac{5.1}{1.0376} = 4.915$$

Our t_{obt} = 4.915. We now consult table B.3 in appendix B to find t_{cv}. Our alternative hypothesis was one-tailed, and α = .05. Two estimates of the standard deviation are being made, one with $n_1 - 1$ degrees of freedom and one with $n_2 - 1$ degrees of freedom. Hence, the degrees of freedom for the independent-samples t-test are $(n_1 - 1) + (n_2 - 1)$ or $n_1 + n_2 - 2$. In this case, the degrees of freedom are 18. The t_{cv} for a one-tailed test with 18 degrees of freedom is 1.734. Our t_{obt} falls beyond the critical value and thus is in the region of rejection. Accordingly, we reject the null hypothesis and support the alternative hypothesis that more words can be recalled after studying in the quiet condition than in the static condition. These statistical results would be written in an article as: $t(18) = 14.55, p <$ .05. This tells the reader the t value obtained and the degrees of freedom and states that t_{obt} is significant with α at .05. The statement $p < .05$ means that the probability of making a Type I error was less than .05.

The formula for the independent-samples t-test provided here is appropriate for use when n is the same for both samples; however, it needs to be modified for those situations where there are more participants in one group than in the other. In the case of unequal n, the variances of the two samples are averaged together; each variance is weighted by its degrees of freedom. This new measure is called the **pooled variance**. The formula for the pooled variance is as follows:

$$s_p^2 = \frac{(n_1 - 1)s_1^2 + (n_2 - 1)s_2^2}{n_1 + n_2 - 2}$$

The formula for t now looks like this:

$$t = \frac{\overline{X}_1 - \overline{X}_2}{\sqrt{\dfrac{s_p^2}{n_1} + \dfrac{s_p^2}{n_2}}} = \frac{\overline{X}_1 - \overline{X}_2}{\sqrt{s_p^2\left(\dfrac{1}{n_1} + \dfrac{1}{n_2}\right)}}$$

This formula may be used even when the samples are of equal size, without affecting the value of the standard error. When the samples are of unequal size, however, it must be used.

The assumptions of the independent-samples t-test are the same as those for the single-sample t—that is, that the data are measured on an interval or ratio scale; that the underlying distribution is normal; and that the observations are independent. An additional assumption of the t-test for independent samples is that the variances of the two populations are homogeneous; that is, they should be the same. Statisticians have demonstrated that, if the sample sizes are equal, heterogeneity of variance is not a problem. However, it is a concern if the sample sizes are not equal; in that case, a correction needs to be made. The actual correction is beyond the scope of this text but can be found in statistics textbooks by Hinkle, Wiersma, and Jurs (2003) or Howell (2002).

The Correlated-Samples *t*-Test

The **correlated-samples *t*-test**—also called the dependent or dependent-samples *t*-test, the matched-pairs *t*-test, the paired-samples *t*-test, or the repeated measures *t*-test—is used to compare the means of two conditions within one study. Typically, a set of subjects will be tested twice on some measure, such as a depression score before and after treatment or a weight measurement before and after a diet program. This analysis might also be used when two types of stimuli are being compared—for instance, when study participants recall concrete and abstract words or when their reading speeds for sentences with or without figurative phrases are compared. Finally, a correlated-samples *t*-test is also appropriately used in a matched-pairs or yoked design, where the study includes two different groups of participants, but participants are paired across groups in some manner, such as husbands and wives compared on marital satisfaction scores.

Consider an experiment in which participants rolled up a ball of string. Each participant was tested twice, once while standing alone and once while standing next to another person who was also rolling up a ball of string. (How would you control for practice or fatigue effects?) The researcher expected to find that, with no instructions to compete, the mere presence of another person performing the same task would induce the subjects to perform the string-rolling task more quickly. The amount of time needed to complete the task in each condition was measured; the data are provided in table A.8.

Table A.8   Amount of Time, in Seconds, Each Person Took to Roll a Ball of String, in Two Conditions

Participant	Alone	With other
1	10.6	8.7
2	15.8	10.2
3	12.5	9.4
4	11.3	11.2
5	10.9	11.1
6	13.6	9.3
7	15.7	13.6
8	14.9	12.8

Because each participant provided each pair of scores, a correlated-samples *t*-test would be an appropriate way to compare the means of each condition. Our null hypothesis for this test is that the means will not differ:

$$H_0 : \mu_{1(\text{alone})} - \mu_{2(\text{with other})} = 0$$

The alternative hypothesis is that the condition where the ball roller is alone will have a larger mean than the condition where another person is present:

$$H_1 : \mu_1 - \mu_2 > 0$$

Therefore, we have a one-tailed test of the null hypothesis.

If the null hypothesis is true, the difference between the two sample means will tend to be zero. If the presence of another ball roller does decrease rolling time, we would expect a mean difference larger than zero. To test our null hypothesis, as with the independent-samples t-test, we will consider the likelihood that our obtained difference between the means could have been randomly chosen. As before, we set α at .05. If the probability of randomly selecting our obtained difference from the sampling distribution that represents the null hypothesis is less than .05, we reject the null hypothesis and support the alternative.

Although we have two sets of scores, our calculations of the correlated-samples t-test involve transforming those two sets into one set by creating a set of **difference scores**, the difference between X_1 and X_2 for each pair of scores. This computation is shown in table A.9.

Table A.9   Difference Scores for Each Pair of String-Rolling Scores

Participant	Alone	With other	d (difference scores)
1	10.6	8.7	1.9
2	15.8	10.2	5.6
3	12.5	9.4	3.1
4	11.3	11.2	0.1
5	10.9	11.1	−0.2
6	13.6	9.3	4.3
7	15.7	13.6	2.1
8	14.9	12.8	2.1
			19.0

We now have one set of scores, the difference scores. We compare the mean of these difference scores with zero, which is the difference between μ_1 and μ_2 according to the null hypothesis. The calculations from this point on are analogous to those in the single-sample t-test. The formula for the single-sample t-test is as follows:

$$t = \frac{\overline{X} - \mu}{s_{\overline{X}}}$$

The formula for the correlated-samples t-test takes the following form:

$$t = \frac{\bar{d} - 0}{s_{\bar{d}}}$$

where $\bar{d}$ is the mean of the difference scores; $s_{\bar{d}}$ is the standard error of the difference scores.

There is considerable similarity between these two formulas. The zero in the correlated-samples formula is directly analogous to the μ in the single-sample formula. In the single-sample formula, the μ is the mean of the sampling distribution of scores. In the correlated-samples formula, the zero is the mean of the sampling distribution of difference scores. Difference scores serve as the scores in a correlated-samples t-test, and the standard error of those difference scores simply has a new symbol. As we know, the standard error is calculated from the following formula:

$$s_{\bar{X}} = \frac{s}{\sqrt{n}}$$

Likewise, the standard error of the difference scores is calculated as follows:

$$s_{\bar{d}} = \frac{s_d}{\sqrt{n}}$$

where s_d is the standard deviation of the difference scores, which is calculated in the same manner as the standard deviation for any scores:

$$s_d = \sqrt{\frac{\sum d^2 - \frac{(\sum d)^2}{n}}{n-1}}$$

Finally, the degrees of freedom for both the single-sample and the correlated-samples t-tests are both $n - 1$. For the correlated-samples t-test, n is the number of difference scores. On the basis of the data in table A.10, we calculate the values needed for the correlated-samples t-test:

Table A.10 The Ball-Rolling Data, Including the Squares of the Difference Scores

Participant	Alone	With other	d	d^2
1	10.6	8.7	1.9	3.61
2	15.8	10.2	5.6	31.36
3	12.5	9.4	3.1	9.61
4	11.3	11.2	0.1	0.01
5	10.9	11.1	−0.2	0.04
6	13.6	9.3	4.3	18.49
7	15.7	13.6	2.1	4.41
8	14.9	12.8	2.1	4.41
		Sums:	19.0	71.94

$$s_d = \sqrt{\frac{71.94 - \frac{19^2}{8}}{8-1}} = \sqrt{\frac{71.94 - 45.125}{7}} = \sqrt{\frac{26.815}{7}}$$

$$= \sqrt{3.8307} = 1.957$$

$$s_{\bar{d}} = \frac{1.957}{\sqrt{n}} = 0.6920$$

$$\bar{d} = \frac{\Sigma d}{n} = \frac{19}{8} = 2.375$$

We can now determine t:

$$t = \frac{\bar{d} - 0}{s_{\bar{d}}} = \frac{2.375}{0.6920} = 3.4321$$

Thus, our obtained t value is 3.4321. The degrees of freedom is: $df = n - 1 = 8 - 1 = 7$. To determine the t_{cv}, we again consult table B.3 in appendix B. Our alternative hypothesis was one-tailed, and α was set at .05. Hence, $t_{cv} = 1.895$. Therefore, the obtained t falls within the region of rejection. This suggests there is a significant difference between the two conditions. In other words, a person will roll a ball of string more rapidly when another person nearby is performing the same task than when no one else is present.

The correlated-samples t-test is used to compare means between two sets of paired scores. It is an inferential statistical procedure so it can only be used when the data are measured on an interval or ratio scale and meet a number of other assumptions: that the population of difference scores are normally distributed; that the variances of the two sets of scores are homogeneous; and that the sample of participants is a random sample from the population it is meant to represent, or that the participants were randomly assigned to conditions.

χ^2 GOODNESS-OF-FIT TEST AND χ^2 TEST OF INDEPENDENCE

A **nonparametric test** is a statistical test that does not test a hypothesis about a parameter of the sampled population; that is, no population parameters need to be known or estimated. Nonparametric tests tend to be based on fewer assumptions about the data set or the population from which the data were sampled and, hence, are sometimes called assumption-free tests (or assumption-freer tests, because they are not totally free of assumptions). Nonparametric tests are often easier to calculate than parametric tests. Spearman's rho, which was introduced earlier, is a nonparametric alternative to Pearson's r.

Another nonparametric test is the χ^2 (spelled *chi* and pronounced with a hard *c*) **Goodness-of-Fit test**, which is useful for comparing categorical information to what might be expected by chance (or expected on the basis of some other information). It is a nondirectional test. In other words, the alternative hypothesis is neither one-tailed nor two-tailed; it is simply that the obtained data do not fit the expected frequencies. Let's consider an example where the χ^2 Goodness-of-Fit test would be appropriate.

Stories are often told of animals that find their way back home across many miles. Some researchers have wondered if people also have a homing instinct, an internal compass that may help them maintain their orientation in unknown places. In one study, after being shown which way north was, each participant was blindfolded, spun around several times, and then asked to point in an arbitrarily chosen direction (north, south, east, or west). Subjects were allowed 45 degrees of error on either side of the direction. Each participant's response was recorded as either correct or incorrect. In this study, 19 individuals were tested; nine were correct and ten were incorrect.

According to chance, each participant had a 25% chance of being correct and a 75% chance of being incorrect. Another way to think of this is that 25% of the participants in a group would be expected to be correct and 75% to be incorrect. For 19 participants, we would expect 4.75 participants to be correct and 14.25 participants to be incorrect. The expected frequencies are calculated by multiplying the number of observations (N) by the probability of membership in each category.

To conduct a χ^2 Goodness-of-Fit, we need to compare our obtained frequencies of correct and incorrect responses to our expected frequencies of these responses. The obtained and expected frequencies are as follows:

	Frequency of correct responses	Frequency of incorrect responses
Frequency obtained	9	10
Frequency expected	4.75	14.25

How can we tell if our obtained frequencies fit the expected frequencies, or if our obtained frequencies differ significantly from those expected? We must calculate χ^2 by means of the following formula:

$$\chi^2 = \Sigma \frac{(O-E)^2}{E}$$

where O is the obtained frequency; E is the expected frequency.

The null hypothesis is rejected if the χ^2_{obt} is greater than χ^2_{cv}. The χ^2_{cv} is obtained from table B.5 in appendix B. The degrees of freedom for the χ^2 Goodness-of-Fit test are calculated as the number of categories minus 1. In this example, there are two categories (correct and incorrect), therefore $df = 2 - 1 = 1$. In table B.5, we find that, for $\alpha = .05$ and one degree of freedom, $\chi^2_{cv} = 3.841$. We will be able to reject the null hypothesis if our χ^2_{obt} is greater than 3.841. The χ^2_{obt} is calculated as follows:

$$\chi^2 = \Sigma \frac{(O-E)^2}{E}$$
$$= \frac{(9-4.75)^2}{4.75} + \frac{(10-14.25)^2}{14.25}$$
$$= \frac{4.25^2}{4.75} + \frac{(-4.25)^2}{14.25}$$
$$= \frac{18.0625}{4.75} + \frac{18.0625}{14.25}$$
$$= 3.8026 + 1.2675 = 5.0701$$

The χ^2_{obt} is greater than 3.841. Thus, we can reject the null hypothesis and state that the frequencies of correct and incorrect responses obtained are significantly greater than would be expected by chance. By comparing the obtained frequencies with the expected frequencies for each category, we can see that the participants were correct more frequently than would be expected.

Conditions of Appropriate Use of the χ^2 Goodness-of-Fit Test

The χ^2 Goodness-of-Fit test is a nonparametric test. What that means, from a practical standpoint, is that it is less restrictive than a parametric test; however, it is still based on certain assumptions.

To be able to generalize to the population, the sample must be randomly selected. Perhaps more importantly, the observations must be independent. This means that each observation must be generated by a different participant, and the score of one participant has no effect on the scores of the other subjects. Thus, in the example of blindly pointing toward a direction, the observations would not be independent if each participant took more than one turn in pointing towards a direction.

Another important issue in the χ^2 test is that the expected frequencies should not be very small. A small expected frequency has a greater impact on the total χ^2 value than does a large expected frequency; this is especially problematic when the expected frequency is smaller than five. The χ^2 Goodness-of-Fit should probably not be conducted if even one expected frequency is less than five. If this problem does arise, more data should be collected to increase the expected frequencies.

Assuming that these requirements have been met, the χ^2 Goodness-of-Fit can be conducted and will provide useful information. This test is appropriate when the data are frequencies measured on a nominal scale. This means that the data are categorical. Data that have been originally measured on a higher-level scale (ordinal, interval, or ratio) can typically be transformed to categorical data. For example, test scores in percentage of questions answered correctly can be transformed to letter grades, and the frequencies of students with As, Bs, Cs, Ds, and Fs can be assessed and compared to some expected frequencies.

χ^2 Test of Homogeneity of Proportions and Test of Independence

The χ^2 test of homogeneity of proportions and the closely allied χ^2 test of independence are extensions of the χ^2 Goodness-of-Fit test. In fact, the formula is the same:

$$\chi^2 = \Sigma \frac{(O-E)^2}{E}$$

It is used when frequency data for two or more samples (or one sample divided into two or more groups) have been collected on a categorical variable; that is, when there are no quantitative scores for the individuals in each group, but only a frequency count for each subcategory.

The χ^2 test of homogeneity of proportions and the χ^2 test of independence use the same formula and critical values, but differ on how subjects are chosen. When two (or more) random samples are chosen and each participant's response is classified as belonging to one of two or more categories, the test is called the χ^2 **test of homogeneity of proportions**. When one random sample is chosen and each participant is classified as belonging to one of two (or more) groups, the test is called the χ^2 **test of independence**; in this case, the participants' responses are also classified as belonging to one of two or more categories.

An example may clarify this difference. Imagine that we select a single sample of drivers and ask the drivers whether their car was produced by an American company or a foreign company and whether they are satisfied or dissatisfied with the car's performance. Because one sample of subjects is grouped according to their responses (American or foreign car and satisfied or dissatisfied with performance), the appropriate test is the χ^2 test of independence.

Now assume a sample of owners of foreign cars and a sample of owners of American cars are asked to indicate if they were satisfied or dissatisfied with their cars' performance. Because two separate samples were chosen, the appropriate χ^2 test is the test of homogeneity of proportions.

Suppose I am interested in the career goals of psychology majors planning to go to graduate school. Specifically, I want to know if the plans of sophomore majors differ from those of seniors; that is, do the sophomores change their minds? I randomly select 50 sophomore majors and 50 senior majors, all of whom have indicated a desire to go to graduate school. I ask each individual whether he or she plans to enter a clinical psychology program, an experimental psychology program, or some other type of psychology program. I then organize my data in a contingency table, as follows:

| | | Type of psychology graduate program | | | |
		Clinical	Experimental	Other	Row totals
Class	Seniors	30	8	12	50
standing	Sophomores	36	5	9	50
	Column totals	66	13	21	100

To calculate the expected frequencies, we need to take into account that plans for attending a clinical program are more prevalent than plans to attend other types of programs. This means that the probability of choosing the clinical program is greater than the probabilities for the other two options. We need to take these probabilities into consideration when calculating our expected values. We do so on the basis of the column and row totals. The formula for calculating the expected frequency for each cell is as follows:

$$E = \frac{(RT)(CT)}{N}$$

where RT is the row total; CT is the column total; and N is the total number of observations.

Thus, for seniors, the expected frequency would be computed as follows:

$$E = \frac{50(66)}{100} = \frac{3300}{100} = 33$$

The contingency table with the expected frequencies (in parentheses) is as follows:

| | | Type of psychology graduate program | | | |
		Clinical	Experimental	Other	Row totals
	Seniors	30 (33)	8 (6.5)	12 (10.5)	50
Class standing	Sophomores	36 (33)	5 (6.5)	9 (10.5)	50
	Column totals	66	13	21	100

Now χ^2 is calculated in the same manner as for the χ^2 Goodness-of-Fit:

$$\chi^2 = \Sigma \frac{(O-E)^2}{E}$$

$$= 0.2727 + 0.3462 + 0.2143 + 0.2727 + 0.3462 + 0.2143$$

$$= 1.6664$$

For the contingency table $df = (r-1)(c-1)$, where r is the number of rows and c is the number of columns. Thus, in this example, $df = (2-1)(3-1) = 2$. We now use table B.5 in appendix B to identify the χ^2_{cv} for $df = 2$ and $\alpha = .05$. The $\chi^2_{cv} = 5.991$; our obtained value of 1.6664 does not exceed the critical value. We fail to reject the null hypothesis, which is that the proportion of students who plan to attend a certain type of graduate program is *independent* of the students' sophomore or senior standing. If reported in an article, this result might be presented as: $\chi^2 (2, N = 100) = 1.67, p > .05$ (or N.S., which stands for *not significant*).

The null hypothesis for the test of homogeneity of proportions is that the proportion of participants from each sample choosing each category of response is equivalent. In other words, the null hypothesis for our example is that the proportion of seniors indicating a preference for a clinical program is roughly the same as the proportion of sophomores indicating a preference for a clinical program, and that this is also true for the proportions of students preferring an experimental program or some other program. The alternative hypothesis is that these proportions are not equivalent across the samples and therefore, class standing is *associated* with preference for a type of graduate program.

The null hypothesis for the test of independence is somewhat different. Suppose that we choose a large random sample of students and ask them to indicate whether they are science majors or not, and whether the last book they read for pleasure was fiction or nonfiction. The χ^2 test of independence would be appropriate for analyzing this data. The null hypothesis, informally stated, is that these factors are not associated—that they are independent factors. More formally, the null hypothesis is that the probability of a respondent having read one type of book is independent of the probability that the respondent holds a particular major. The alternative hypothesis is much like that for the test of homogeneity of proportions—that major and type of book read are associated with one another.

Assumptions of the χ^2 Test

The assumptions underlying the χ^2 test of independence are the same as those for the χ^2 Goodness-of-Fit: the sample must be random, and the observations must be independent of each other. In addition, an issue related to sample size arises for the test of independence and the test of homogeneity of proportions. If any of the expected frequencies are less than 10 and you have a 2 × 2 contingency table, *Yates' correction for continuity* should probably be used.

Yates' correction for continuity simply involves subtracting 0.5 from the difference between each observed and expected frequency when calculating the χ^2 statistic. The χ^2 formula including Yates' correction is as follows:

$$\chi^2 = \Sigma \frac{(|O - E| - 0.5)^2}{E}$$

Actually, there is something of a controversy about using the Yates' correction. Camilli and Hopkins (1978) argue against its use, because they feel it reduces the Power of the χ^2 test too greatly. Kirk (1990), on the other hand, recommends it whenever any expected frequency is not much greater than 10. To avoid the problem, whenever possible, collect enough data that expected frequencies are greater than 10.

Finally, note that in the case of a response variable that has two options—such as yes or no, agree or disagree—it is important to include both responses in the contingency table. Do not be tempted to create a table that includes only the positive responses (or only the negative responses); this would distort the data and invalidate the test.

As an example, suppose a researcher asked a sample of citizens the following: If there was an election tomorrow, would you vote for the current president? Do you consider yourself to be a Democrat, Republican, or other? If the researcher looked only at the data of those who would vote for the current president, the data might look like this:

	Democrat	Republican	Other
Would vote for president	50	50	35

The researcher might then conduct a χ^2 Goodness-of-Fit test and find a χ^2 of 3.968. The researcher would fail to reject the null hypothesis and conclude that there is no evidence that support for the president differs among Democrats, Republicans, and others. However, if the data of those who would not vote for the president are also included, the data might look like this:

	Democrat	Republican	Other
Would vote for president	50	50	35
Would not vote for president	150	25	20

Now the researcher appropriately conducts the χ^2 test of independence and calculates a χ^2 of 53.276. This time the null hypothesis is rejected; support for the president is associated with the respondent's political party. The moral of this story is to include all of the data, and not just the positive or negative responses.

EFFECT SIZE

Knowing that there is a significant difference between two groups tells part of the story, but it doesn't indicate how large or small the effect is, or the magnitude of the effect. The magnitude of the effect is indicated by the **effect size**. With just two groups being compared, the effect size is expressed as a z-score, an indication of the size of the difference between the means as measured in standard deviations. The formula is:

$$d = \frac{\overline{X}_1 - \overline{X}_2}{s}$$

where s = the standard deviation using the pooled-variance, that is the square root of the pooled-variance.

Cohen (1965) suggested that an effect size of roughly .25 should be considered small, medium would be about .50, and a large effect size would be 1.00 or greater; however, these are only guidelines that will not fit every situation. One researcher's small effect size might be considered medium by another.

Different research designs will require different formulas for calculating effect size. These can be found in many statistical textbooks.

SUMMARY

This appendix offers only the very briefest of introductions to statistical techniques. There is much more to know; those intending to conduct their own research are encouraged to consult statistical textbooks for a greater selection of appropriate statistical techniques.

IMPORTANT TERMS AND CONCEPTS

average deviation (A.D.)

bimodal

chi-squared (χ^2)
  Goodness-of-Fit test

chi-squared (χ^2) test of
  homogeneity of proportions

chi-squared (χ^2) test
  of independence

correlated-samples t-test

degrees of freedom

difference scores

effect size

independent-samples t-test

mean

median

mode

multimodal

nonparametric test

Pearson's product-moment
  correlation coefficient
  (or Pearson's r)

pooled variance

range

single-sample t-test

Spearman's rho

standard deviation

standard error of differences
  between means

t-distributions (or Student's
  t-distributions)

variance

z-score

Statistical Tables

Table B.1   Random Numbers

Row
number

00000	10097	32533	76520	13586	34673	54876	80959	09117	39292	74945
00001	37542	04805	64894	74296	24805	24037	20636	10402	00822	91665
00002	08422	68953	19645	09303	23209	02560	15953	34764	35080	33606
00003	99019	02529	09376	70715	38311	31165	88676	74397	04436	27659
00004	12807	99970	80157	36147	64032	36653	98951	16877	12171	76833
00005	66065	74717	34072	76850	36697	36170	65813	39885	11199	29170
00006	31060	10805	45571	82406	35303	42614	86799	07439	23403	09732
00007	85269	77602	02051	65692	68665	74818	73053	85247	18623	88579
00008	63573	32135	05325	47048	90553	57548	28468	28709	83491	25624
00009	73769	45753	03529	64778	35808	34282	60935	20344	35273	88435
00010	98520	17767	14905	68607	22109	40558	60970	93433	50500	73998
00011	11805	05431	39808	27732	50725	68248	29405	24201	52775	67851
00012	83452	99634	06288	98033	13746	70078	18475	40610	68711	77817
00013	88685	40200	86507	58401	36766	67951	90364	76493	29609	11062
00014	99594	67348	87517	64969	91826	08928	93785	61368	23478	34113
00015	65481	17674	17468	50950	58047	76974	73039	57186	40218	16544
00016	80124	35635	17727	08015	45318	22374	21115	78253	14385	53763
00017	74350	99817	77402	77214	43236	00210	45521	64237	96286	02655
00018	69916	26803	66252	29148	36936	87203	76621	13990	94400	56418
00019	09893	20505	14225	68514	46427	56788	96297	78822	54382	14598
00020	91499	14523	68479	27686	46162	83554	94750	89923	37089	20048
00021	80336	94598	26940	36858	70297	34135	53140	33340	42050	82341
00022	44104	81949	85157	47954	32979	26575	57600	40881	22222	06413
00023	12550	73742	11100	02040	12860	74697	96644	89439	28707	25815
00024	63606	49329	16505	34484	40219	52563	43651	77082	07207	31790
00025	61196	90446	26457	47774	51924	33729	65394	59593	42582	60527
00026	15474	45266	95270	79953	59367	83848	82396	10118	33211	59466
00027	94557	28573	67897	54387	54622	44431	91190	42592	92927	45973
00028	42481	16213	97344	08721	16868	48767	03071	12059	25701	46670
00029	23523	78317	73208	89837	68935	91416	26252	29663	05522	82562

Row
number

00030	04493	52494	75246	33824	45862	51025	61962	79335	65337	12472
00031	00549	97654	64051	88159	96119	63896	54692	82391	23287	29529
00032	35963	15307	26898	09354	33351	35462	77974	50024	90103	39333
00033	59808	08391	45427	26842	83609	49700	13021	24892	78565	20106
00034	46058	85236	01390	92286	77281	44077	93910	83647	70617	42941
00035	32179	00597	87379	25241	05567	07007	86743	17157	85394	11838
00036	69234	61406	20117	45204	15956	60000	18743	92423	97118	96338
00037	19565	41430	01758	75379	40419	21585	66674	36806	84962	85207
00038	45155	14938	19476	07246	43667	94543	59047	90033	20826	69541
00039	94864	31994	36168	10851	34888	81553	01540	35456	05014	51176
00040	98086	24826	45240	28404	44999	08896	39094	73407	35441	31880
00041	33185	16232	41941	50949	89435	48581	88695	41994	37548	73043
00042	80951	00406	96382	70774	20151	23387	25016	25298	94624	61171
00043	79752	49140	71961	28296	69861	02591	74852	20539	00387	59579
00044	18633	32537	98145	06571	31010	24674	05455	61427	77938	91936
00045	74029	43902	77557	32270	97790	17119	52527	58021	80814	51748
00046	54178	45611	80993	37143	05335	12969	56127	19255	36040	90324
00047	11664	49883	52079	84827	59381	71539	09973	33440	88461	23356
00048	48324	77928	31249	64710	02295	36870	32307	57546	15020	09994
00049	69074	94138	87637	91976	35584	04401	10518	21615	01848	76938
00050	09188	20097	32825	39527	04220	86304	83389	87374	64278	58044
00051	90045	85497	51981	50654	94938	81997	91870	76150	68476	64659
00052	73189	50207	47677	26269	62290	64464	27124	67018	41361	82760
00053	75768	76490	20971	87749	90429	12272	95375	05871	93823	43178
00054	54016	44056	66281	31003	00682	27398	20714	53295	07706	17813
00055	08358	69910	78542	42785	13661	58873	04618	97553	31223	08420
00056	28306	03264	81333	10591	40510	07893	32604	60475	94119	01840
00057	53840	86233	81594	13628	51215	90290	28466	68795	77762	20791
00058	91757	53741	61613	62669	50263	90212	55781	76514	83483	47055
00059	89415	92694	00397	58391	12607	17646	48949	72306	94541	37408
00060	77513	03820	86864	29901	68414	82774	51908	13980	72893	55507
00061	19502	37174	69979	20288	55210	29773	74287	75251	65344	67415
00062	21818	59313	93278	81757	05686	73156	07082	85046	31853	38452
00063	51474	66499	68107	23621	94049	91345	42836	09191	08007	45449
00064	99559	68331	62535	24170	69777	12830	74819	78142	43860	72834
00065	33713	48007	93584	72869	51926	64721	58303	29822	93174	93972
00066	85274	86893	11303	22970	28834	34137	73515	90400	71148	43643
00067	84133	89640	44035	52166	73852	70091	61222	60561	62327	18423
00068	56732	16234	17395	96131	10123	91622	85496	57560	81604	18880
00069	65138	56806	87648	85261	34313	65861	45875	21069	85644	47277
00070	38001	02176	81719	11711	71602	92937	74219	64049	65584	49698
00071	37402	96397	01304	77586	56271	10086	47324	62605	40030	37438
00072	97125	40348	87083	31417	21815	39250	75237	62047	15501	29578
00073	21826	41134	47143	34072	64638	85902	49139	06441	03856	54552
00074	73135	42742	95719	09035	85794	74296	08789	88156	64691	19202
00075	07638	77929	03061	18072	96207	44156	23821	99538	04713	66994
00076	60528	83441	07954	19814	59175	20695	05533	52139	61212	06455

(continued)

Table B.1 *(continued)*

Row
number

00077	83596	35655	06958	92983	05128	09719	77433	53783	92301	50498
00078	10850	62746	99599	10507	13499	06319	53075	71839	06410	19362
00079	39820	98952	43622	63147	64421	80814	43800	09351	31024	73167
00080	59580	06478	75569	78800	88835	54486	23768	06156	04111	08408
00081	38508	07341	23793	48763	90822	97022	17719	04207	95954	49953
00082	30692	70668	94688	16127	56196	80091	82067	63400	05462	69200
00083	65443	95659	18238	27437	49632	24041	08337	65676	96299	90836
00084	27267	50264	13192	72294	07477	44606	17985	48911	97341	30358
00085	91307	06991	19072	24210	36699	53728	28825	35793	28976	66252
00086	68434	94688	84473	13622	62126	98408	12843	82590	09815	93146
00087	48908	15877	54745	24591	35700	04754	83824	52692	54130	55160
00088	06913	45197	42672	78601	11883	09528	63011	98901	14974	40344
00089	10455	16019	14210	33712	91342	37821	88325	80851	43667	70883
00090	12883	97343	65027	61184	04285	01392	17974	15077	90712	26769
00091	21778	30976	38807	36961	31649	42096	63281	02023	08816	47449
00092	19523	59515	65122	59659	86283	68258	69572	13798	16435	91529
00093	67245	52670	35583	16563	79246	86686	76463	34222	26655	90802
00094	60584	47377	07500	37992	45134	26529	26760	83637	41326	44344
00095	53853	41377	36066	94850	58838	73859	49364	73331	96240	43642
00096	24637	38736	74384	89342	52623	07992	12369	18601	03742	83873
00097	83080	12451	38992	22815	07759	51777	97377	27585	51972	37867
00098	16444	24334	36151	99073	27493	70939	85130	32552	54846	54759
00099	60790	18157	57178	65762	11161	78576	45819	52979	65130	04860
00100	03991	10461	93716	16894	66083	24653	84609	58232	88618	19161
00101	38555	95554	32886	59780	08355	60860	29735	47762	71299	23853
00102	17546	73704	92052	46215	55121	29281	59076	07936	27954	58909
00103	32643	52861	95819	06831	00911	98936	76355	93779	80863	00514
00104	69572	68777	39510	35905	14060	40619	29549	69616	33564	60780
00105	24122	66591	27699	06494	14845	46672	61958	77100	90899	75754
00106	61196	30231	92962	61773	41839	55382	17267	70943	78038	70267
00107	30532	21704	10274	12202	39685	23309	10061	68829	55986	66485
00108	03788	97599	75867	20717	74416	53166	35208	33374	87539	08823
00109	48228	63379	85783	47619	53152	67433	35663	52972	16818	60311
00110	60365	94653	35075	33949	42614	29297	01918	28316	98953	73231
00111	83799	42402	56623	34442	34994	41374	70071	14736	09958	18065
00112	32960	07405	36409	83232	99385	41600	11133	07586	15917	06253
00113	19322	53845	57620	52606	66497	68646	78138	66559	19640	99413
00114	11220	94747	07399	37408	48509	23929	27482	45476	85244	35159
00115	31751	57260	68980	05339	15470	48355	88651	22596	03152	19121
00116	88492	99382	14454	04504	20094	98977	74843	93413	22109	78508
00117	30934	47744	07481	83828	73788	06533	28597	20405	94205	20380
00118	22888	48893	27499	98748	60530	45128	74022	84617	82037	10268
00119	78212	16993	35902	91386	44372	15486	65741	14014	87481	37220
00120	41849	84547	46850	52326	34677	58300	74910	64345	19325	81549

Row number

00121	46352	33049	69248	93460	45305	07521	61318	31855	14413	70951
00122	11087	96294	14013	31792	59747	67277	76503	34513	39663	77544
00123	52701	08337	56303	87315	16520	69676	11654	99893	02181	68161
00124	57275	36898	81304	48585	68652	27376	92852	55866	88448	03584
00125	20857	73156	70284	24326	79375	95220	01159	63267	10622	48391
00126	15633	84924	90415	93614	33521	26665	55823	47641	86225	31704
00127	92694	48297	39904	02115	59589	49067	66821	41575	49767	04037
00128	77613	19019	88152	00080	20554	91409	96277	48257	50816	97616
00129	38688	32486	45134	63545	59404	72059	43947	51680	43852	59693
00130	25163	01889	70014	15021	41290	67312	71857	15957	68971	11403
00131	65251	07629	37239	33295	05870	01119	92784	26340	18477	65622
00132	36815	43625	18637	37509	82444	99005	04921	73701	14707	93997
00133	64397	11692	05327	82162	20247	81759	45197	25332	83745	22567
00134	04515	25624	95096	67946	48460	85558	15191	18782	16930	33361
00135	83761	60873	43253	84145	60833	25983	01291	41349	20368	07126
00136	14387	06345	80854	09279	43529	06318	38384	74761	41196	37480
00137	51321	92246	80088	77074	88722	56736	66164	49431	66919	31678
00138	72472	00008	80890	18002	94813	31900	54155	83436	35352	54131
00139	05466	55306	93128	18464	74457	90561	72848	11834	79982	68416
00140	39528	72484	82474	25593	48545	35247	18619	13674	18611	19241
00141	P1616	18711	53342	44276	75122	11724	74627	73707	58319	15997
00142	07586	16120	82641	22820	92904	13141	32392	19763	61199	67940
00143	90767	04235	13574	17200	69902	63742	78464	22501	18627	90872
00144	40188	28193	29593	88627	94972	11598	62095	36787	00441	58997
00145	34414	82157	86887	55087	19152	00023	12302	80783	32624	68691
00146	63439	75363	44989	16822	36024	00867	76378	41605	65961	73488
00147	67049	09070	93399	45547	94458	74284	05041	49807	20288	34060
00148	79495	04146	52162	90286	54158	34243	46978	35482	59362	95938
00149	91704	30552	04737	21031	75051	93029	47665	64382	99782	93478
00150	94015	46874	32444	48277	59820	96163	64654	25843	41145	42820
00151	74108	88222	88570	74015	25704	91035	01755	14750	48968	38603
00152	62880	87873	95160	59221	22304	90314	72877	17334	39283	04149
00153	11748	12102	80580	41867	17710	59621	06554	07850	73950	79552
00154	17944	05600	60478	03343	25852	58905	57216	39618	49856	99326
00155	66067	42792	95043	52680	46780	56487	09971	59481	37006	22186
00156	54244	91030	45547	70818	59849	96169	61459	21647	87417	17198
00157	30945	57589	31732	57260	47670	07654	46376	25366	94746	49580
00158	69170	37403	86995	90307	94304	71803	26825	05511	12459	91314
00159	08345	88975	35841	85771	08105	59987	87112	21476	14713	71181
00160	27767	43584	85301	88977	29490	69714	73035	41207	74699	09310
00161	13025	14338	54066	15243	47724	66733	47431	43905	31048	56699
00162	80217	36292	98525	24335	24432	24896	43277	58874	11466	16082
00163	10875	62004	90391	61105	57411	06368	53856	30743	08670	84741
00164	54127	57326	26629	19087	24472	88779	30540	27886	61732	75454
00165	60311	42824	37301	42678	45990	43242	17374	52003	70707	70214
00166	49739	71484	92003	98086	76668	73209	59202	11973	02902	33250
00167	78626	51594	16453	94614	39014	97066	83012	09832	25571	77628

(continued)

Table B.1 (continued)

**Row
number**

00168	66692	13986	99837	00582	81232	44987	09504	96412	90193	79568
00169	44071	28091	07362	97703	76447	42537	98524	97831	65704	09514
00170	41468	85149	49554	17994	14924	39650	95294	00556	70481	06905
00171	94559	37559	49678	53119	70312	05682	66986	34099	74474	20740
00172	41615	70360	64114	58660	90850	64618	80620	51790	11436	38072
00173	50273	93113	41794	86861	24781	89683	55411	85667	77535	99892
00174	41396	80504	90670	08289	40902	05069	95083	06783	28102	57816
00175	25807	24260	71520	78920	72682	07385	90726	57166	98884	08583
00176	06170	97965	88302	98041	21443	41808	68984	83620	89747	98882
00177	60808	54444	74412	81105	01176	28838	36421	16489	18059	51061
00178	80940	44893	10408	36222	80582	71944	92638	40333	67054	16067
00179	19516	90120	46759	71643	13177	55292	21036	82808	77501	97427
00180	49386	54480	23604	23554	21785	41101	91178	10174	29420	90438
00181	06312	88940	15995	69321	47458	64809	98189	81851	29651	84215
00182	60942	00307	11897	92674	40405	68032	96717	54244	10701	41393
00183	92329	98932	78284	46347	71209	92061	39448	93136	25722	08564
00184	77936	63574	31384	51924	85561	29671	58137	17820	22751	36518
00185	38101	77756	11657	13897	95889	57067	47648	13885	70669	93406
00186	39641	69457	91339	22502	92613	89719	11947	56203	19324	20504
00187	84054	40455	99396	63680	67667	60631	69181	96845	38525	11600
00188	47468	03577	57649	63266	24700	71594	14004	23153	69249	05747
00189	43321	31370	28977	23896	76479	68562	62342	07589	08899	05985
00190	64281	61826	18555	64937	13173	33365	78851	16499	87064	13075
00191	66847	70495	32350	02985	86716	38746	26313	77463	55387	72681
00192	72461	33230	21529	53424	92581	02262	78438	66276	18396	73538
00193	21032	91050	13058	16218	12470	56500	15292	76139	59526	52113
00194	95362	67011	06651	16136	01016	00857	55018	56374	35824	71708
00195	49712	97380	10404	55452	34030	60726	75211	10271	36633	68424
00196	58275	61764	97586	54716	50259	46345	87195	46092	26787	60939
00197	89514	11788	68224	23417	73959	76145	30342	40277	11049	72049
00198	15472	50669	48139	36732	46874	37088	63465	09819	58869	35220
00199	12120	86124	51247	44302	60883	52109	21437	36786	49226	77837

Table B.2   Areas under the Normal Curve

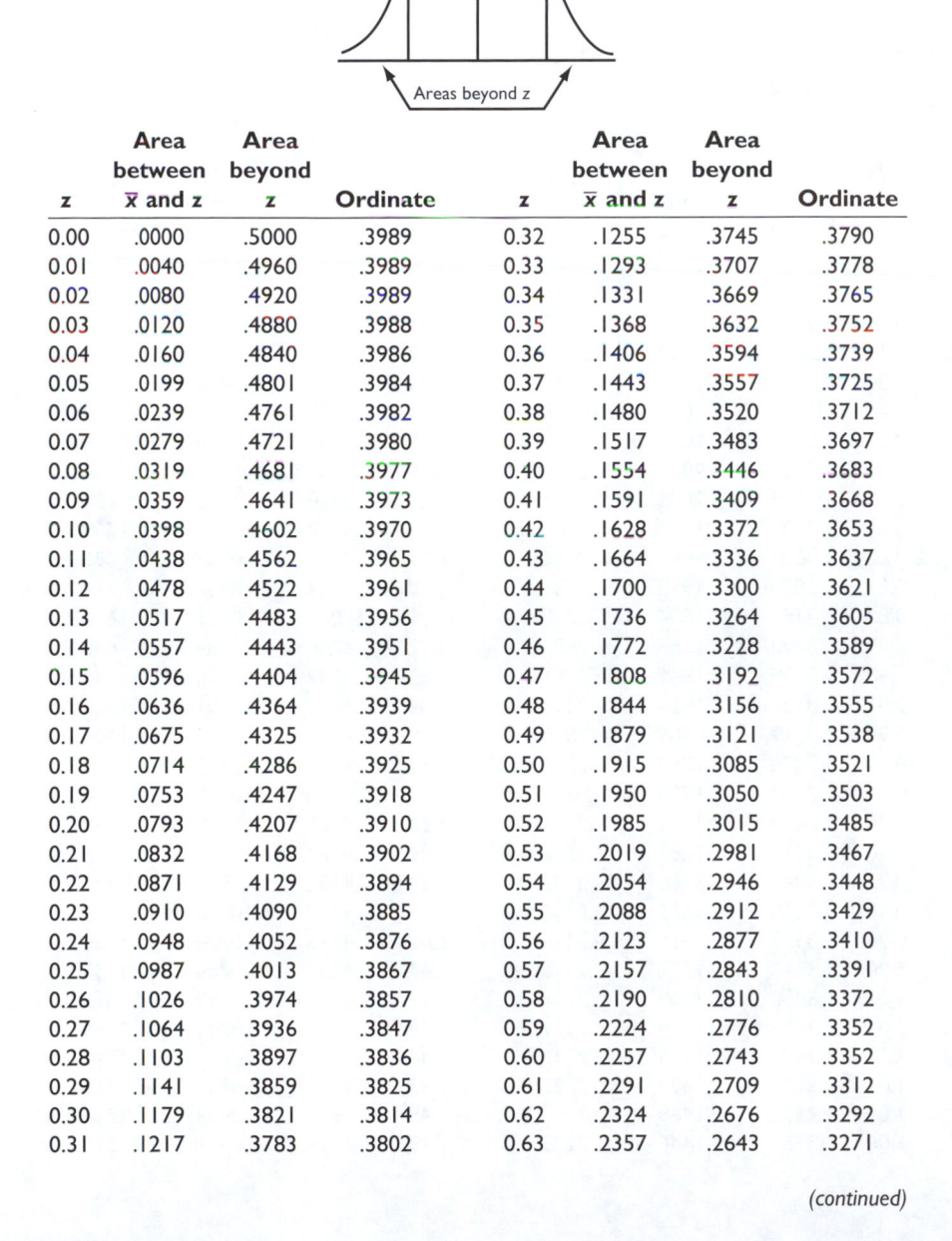

z	Area between $\bar{x}$ and z	Area beyond z	Ordinate	z	Area between $\bar{x}$ and z	Area beyond z	Ordinate
0.00	.0000	.5000	.3989	0.32	.1255	.3745	.3790
0.01	.0040	.4960	.3989	0.33	.1293	.3707	.3778
0.02	.0080	.4920	.3989	0.34	.1331	.3669	.3765
0.03	.0120	.4880	.3988	0.35	.1368	.3632	.3752
0.04	.0160	.4840	.3986	0.36	.1406	.3594	.3739
0.05	.0199	.4801	.3984	0.37	.1443	.3557	.3725
0.06	.0239	.4761	.3982	0.38	.1480	.3520	.3712
0.07	.0279	.4721	.3980	0.39	.1517	.3483	.3697
0.08	.0319	.4681	.3977	0.40	.1554	.3446	.3683
0.09	.0359	.4641	.3973	0.41	.1591	.3409	.3668
0.10	.0398	.4602	.3970	0.42	.1628	.3372	.3653
0.11	.0438	.4562	.3965	0.43	.1664	.3336	.3637
0.12	.0478	.4522	.3961	0.44	.1700	.3300	.3621
0.13	.0517	.4483	.3956	0.45	.1736	.3264	.3605
0.14	.0557	.4443	.3951	0.46	.1772	.3228	.3589
0.15	.0596	.4404	.3945	0.47	.1808	.3192	.3572
0.16	.0636	.4364	.3939	0.48	.1844	.3156	.3555
0.17	.0675	.4325	.3932	0.49	.1879	.3121	.3538
0.18	.0714	.4286	.3925	0.50	.1915	.3085	.3521
0.19	.0753	.4247	.3918	0.51	.1950	.3050	.3503
0.20	.0793	.4207	.3910	0.52	.1985	.3015	.3485
0.21	.0832	.4168	.3902	0.53	.2019	.2981	.3467
0.22	.0871	.4129	.3894	0.54	.2054	.2946	.3448
0.23	.0910	.4090	.3885	0.55	.2088	.2912	.3429
0.24	.0948	.4052	.3876	0.56	.2123	.2877	.3410
0.25	.0987	.4013	.3867	0.57	.2157	.2843	.3391
0.26	.1026	.3974	.3857	0.58	.2190	.2810	.3372
0.27	.1064	.3936	.3847	0.59	.2224	.2776	.3352
0.28	.1103	.3897	.3836	0.60	.2257	.2743	.3352
0.29	.1141	.3859	.3825	0.61	.2291	.2709	.3312
0.30	.1179	.3821	.3814	0.62	.2324	.2676	.3292
0.31	.1217	.3783	.3802	0.63	.2357	.2643	.3271

(continued)

Table B.2 *(continued)*

z	Area between $\bar{x}$ and z	Area beyond z	Ordinate	z	Area between $\bar{x}$ and z	Area beyond z	Ordinate
0.64	.2389	.2611	.3251	1.07	.3577	.1423	.2251
0.65	.2422	.2578	.3230	1.08	.3599	.1401	.2227
0.66	.2454	.2546	.3209	1.09	.3621	.1379	.2203
0.67	.2486	.2514	.3187	1.10	.3643	.1357	.2179
0.68	.2517	.2483	.3166	1.11	.3665	.1335	.2155
0.69	.2549	.2451	.3144	1.12	.3686	.1314	.2131
0.70	.2580	.2420	.3123	1.13	.3708	.1292	.2107
0.71	.2611	.2389	.3101	1.14	.3729	.1271	.2083
0.72	.2642	.2358	.3079	1.15	.3749	.1251	.2059
0.73	.2673	.2327	.3056	1.16	.3770	.1230	.2036
0.74	.2704	.2296	.3034	1.17	.3790	.1210	.2012
0.75	.2734	.2266	.3011	1.18	.3810	.1190	.1989
0.76	.2764	.2236	.2989	1.19	.3830	.1170	.1965
0.77	.2794	.2206	.2966	1.20	.3849	.1151	.1942
0.78	.2823	.2177	.2943	1.21	.3869	.1131	.1919
0.79	.2852	.2148	.2920	1.22	.3888	.1112	.1895
0.80	.2881	.2119	.2897	1.23	.3907	.1093	.1872
0.81	.2910	.2090	.2874	1.24	.3925	.1075	.1849
0.82	.2939	.2061	.2850	1.25	.3944	.1056	.1826
0.83	.2967	.2033	.2827	1.26	.3962	.1038	.1804
0.84	.2995	.2005	.2803	1.27	.3980	.1020	.1781
0.85	.3023	.1977	.2780	1.28	.3997	.1003	.1758
0.86	.3051	.1949	.2756	1.29	.4015	.0985	.1736
0.87	.3078	.1922	.2732	1.30	.4032	.0968	.1714
0.88	.3106	.1894	.2709	1.31	.4049	.0951	.1691
0.89	.3133	.1867	.2685	1.32	.4066	.0934	.1669
0.90	.3159	.1841	.2661	1.33	.4082	.0918	.1647
0.91	.3186	.1814	.2637	1.34	.4099	.0901	.1626
0.92	.3212	.1788	.2613	1.35	.4115	.0885	.1604
0.93	.3238	.1762	.2589	1.36	.4131	.0869	.1582
0.94	.3264	.1736	.2565	1.37	.4147	.0853	.1561
0.95	.3289	.1711	.2541	1.38	.4162	.0838	.1539
0.96	.3315	.1685	.2516	1.39	.4177	.0823	.1518
0.97	.3340	.1660	.2492	1.40	.4192	.0808	.1497
0.98	.3365	.1635	.2468	1.41	.4207	.0793	.1476
0.99	.3389	.1611	.2444	1.42	.4222	.0778	.1456
1.00	.3413	.1587	.2420	1.43	.4236	.0764	.1435
1.01	.3438	.1562	.2396	1.44	.4251	.0749	.1415
1.02	.3461	.1539	.2371	1.45	.4265	.0735	.1394
1.03	.3485	.1515	.2347	1.46	.4279	.0721	.1374
1.04	.3508	.1492	.2323	1.47	.4292	.0708	.1354
1.05	.3531	.1469	.2299	1.48	.4306	.0694	.1334
1.06	.3554	.1446	.2275	1.49	.4319	.0681	.1315

z	Area between $\bar{x}$ and z	Area beyond z	Ordinate	z	Area between $\bar{x}$ and z	Area beyond z	Ordinate
1.50	.4332	.0668	.1295	1.96	.4750	.0250	.0584
1.51	.4345	.0655	.1276	1.97	.4756	.0244	.0573
1.52	.4357	.0643	.1257	1.98	.4761	.0239	.0562
1.53	.4370	.0630	.1238	1.99	.4767	.0233	.0551
1.54	.4382	.0618	.1219	2.00	.4772	.0228	.0540
1.55	.4394	.0606	.1200	2.01	.4778	.0222	.0529
1.56	.4406	.0594	.1182	2.02	.4783	.0217	.0519
1.57	.4418	.0582	.1163	2.03	.4788	.0212	.0508
1.58	.4429	.0571	.1145	2.04	.4793	.0207	.0498
1.59	.4441	.0559	.1127	2.05	.4798	.0202	.0488
1.60	.4452	.0548	.1109	2.06	.4803	.0197	.0478
1.61	.4463	.0537	.1092	2.07	.4808	.0192	.0468
1.62	.4474	.0526	.1074	2.08	.4812	.0188	.0459
1.63	.4484	.0516	.1057	2.09	.4817	.0183	.0449
1.64	.4495	.0505	.1040	2.10	.4821	.0179	.0440
1.65	.4505	.0495	.1023	2.11	.4826	.0174	.0431
1.66	.4515	.0485	.1006	2.12	.4830	.0170	.0422
1.67	.4525	.0475	.0989	2.13	.4834	.0166	.0413
1.68	.4535	.0465	.0973	2.14	.4838	.0162	.0404
1.69	.4545	.0455	.0957	2.15	.4842	.0158	.0395
1.70	.4554	.0446	.0940	2.16	.4846	.0154	.0387
1.71	.4564	.0436	.0925	2.17	.4850	.0150	.0379
1.72	.4573	.0427	.0909	2.18	.4854	.0146	.0371
1.73	.4582	.0418	.0893	2.19	.4857	.0143	.0363
1.74	.4591	.0409	.0878	2.20	.4861	.0139	.0355
1.75	.4599	.0401	.0863	2.21	.4864	.0136	.0347
1.76	.4608	.0392	.0848	2.22	.4868	.0132	.0339
1.77	.4616	.0384	.0833	2.23	.4871	.0129	.0332
1.78	.4625	.0375	.0818	2.24	.4875	.0125	.0325
1.79	.4633	.0367	.0804	2.25	.4878	.0122	.0317
1.80	.4641	.0359	.0790	2.26	.4881	.0119	.0310
1.81	.4649	.0351	.0775	2.27	.4884	.0116	.0303
1.82	.4656	.0344	.0761	2.28	.4887	.0113	.0297
1.83	.4664	.0336	.0748	2.29	.4890	.0110	.0290
1.84	.4671	.0329	.0734	2.30	.4893	.0107	.0283
1.85	.4678	.0322	.0721	2.31	.4896	.0104	.0277
1.86	.4686	.0314	.0707	2.32	.4898	.0102	.0270
1.87	.4693	.0307	.0694	2.33	.4901	.0099	.0264
1.88	.4699	.0301	.0681	2.34	.4904	.0096	.0258
1.89	.4706	.0294	.0669	2.35	.4906	.0094	.0252
1.90	.4713	.0287	.0656	2.36	.4909	.0091	.0246
1.91	.4719	.0281	.0644	2.37	.4911	.0089	.0241
1.92	.4726	.0274	.0632	2.38	.4913	.0087	.0235
1.93	.4732	.0268	.0620	2.39	.4916	.0084	.0229
1.94	.4738	.0262	.0608	2.40	.4918	.0082	.0224
1.95	.4744	.0256	.0596	2.41	.4920	.0080	.0219

(continued)

Table B.2 *(continued)*

z	Area between $\bar{x}$ and z	Area beyond z	Ordinate	z	Area between $\bar{x}$ and z	Area beyond z	Ordinate
2.42	.4922	.0078	.0213	2.85	.4978	.0022	.0069
2.43	.4925	.0075	.0208	2.86	.4979	.0021	.0067
2.44	.4927	.0073	.0203	2.87	.4979	.0021	.0065
2.45	.4929	.0071	.0198	2.88	.4980	.0020	.0063
2.46	.4931	.0069	.0194	2.89	.4981	.0019	.0061
2.47	.4932	.0068	.0189	2.90	.4981	.0019	.0060
2.48	.4934	.0066	.0184	2.91	.4982	.0018	.0058
2.49	.4936	.0064	.0180	2.92	.4982	.0018	.0056
2.50	.4938	.0062	.0175	2.93	.4983	.0017	.0055
2.51	.4940	.0060	.0171	2.94	.4984	.0016	.0053
2.52	.4941	.0059	.0167	2.95	.4984	.0016	.0051
2.53	.4943	.0057	.0163	2.96	.4985	.0015	.0050
2.54	.4945	.0055	.0158	2.97	.4985	.0015	.0048
2.55	.4946	.0054	.0154	2.98	.4986	.0014	.0047
2.56	.4948	.0052	.0151	2.99	.4986	.0014	.0046
2.57	.4949	.0051	.0147	3.00	.4987	.0013	.0044
2.58	.4951	.0049	.0143	3.01	.4987	.0013	.0033
2.59	.4952	.0048	.0139	3.02	.4987	.0013	.0024
2.60	.4953	.0047	.0136	3.03	.4988	.0012	.0017
2.61	.4955	.0045	.0132	3.04	.4988	.0012	.0012
2.62	.4856	.0044	.0129	3.05	.4989	.0011	.0009
2.63	.4957	.0043	.0126	3.06	.4989	.0011	.0006
2.64	.4959	.0041	.0122	3.07	.4989	.0011	.0004
2.65	.4960	.0040	.0119	3.08	.4990	.0010	.0003
2.66	.4961	.0039	.0116	3.09	.4990	.0010	.0002*
2.67	.4962	.0038	.0113	3.10	.4990	.0010	
2.68	.4963	.0037	.0110	3.11	.4991	.0009	
2.69	.4964	.0036	.0107	3.12	.4991	.0009	
2.70	.4965	.0035	.0104	3.13	.4991	.0009	
2.71	.4966	.0034	.0101	3.14	.4992	.0008	
2.72	.4967	.0033	.0099	3.15	.4992	.0008	
2.73	.4968	.0032	.0096	3.16	.4992	.0008	
2.74	.4969	.0031	.0093	3.17	.4992	.0008	
2.75	.4970	.0030	.0091	3.18	.4993	.0007	
2.76	.4971	.0029	.0088	3.19	.4993	.0007	
2.77	.4972	.0028	.0086	3.20	.4993	.0007	
2.78	.4973	.0027	.0084	3.21	.4993	.0007	
2.79	.4974	.0026	.0081	3.22	.4994	.0006	
2.80	.4974	.0026	.0079	3.23	.4994	.0006	
2.81	.4975	.0025	.0077	3.24	.4994	.0006	
2.82	.4976	.0024	.0075	3.25	.4994	.0006	
2.83	.4977	.0023	.0073	3.30	.4995	.0005	
2.84	.4977	.0023	.0071	3.35	.4996	.0004	

z	Area between $\bar{x}$ and z	Area beyond z	Ordinate	z	Area between $\bar{x}$ and z	Area beyond z	Ordinate
3.40	.4997	.0003		3.70	.4999	.0001	
3.45	.4997	.0003		3.80	.4999	.0001	
3.50	.4998	.0002		3.90	.49995	.00005	
3.60	.4998	.0002		4.00	.49997	.00003	

* For values of z greater than 3.09, the height of the curve is negligible, and the value of the ordinate is close to zero.

Source: From R. A. Fisher and F. Yates, *Statistical Tables for Biological, Agricultural, and Medical Research, Sixth Edition.* Published by Longman Group, Ltd. London, 1974. Reprinted with permission of Pearson Education.

Table B.3 Critical Values for the t-Distribution

	Level of significance for one-tailed test					
	.10	.05	.025	.01	.005	.0005
	Level of significance for two-tailed test					
df	.20	.10	.05	.02	.01	.001
1	3.078	6.314	12.706	31.821	63.657	636.619
2	1.886	2.920	4.303	6.965	9.925	31.598
3	1.638	2.353	3.182	4.541	5.841	12.941
4	1.533	2.132	2.776	3.747	4.604	8.610
5	1.476	2.015	2.571	3.365	4.032	6.859
6	1.440	1.943	2.447	3.143	3.707	5.959
7	1.415	1.895	2.365	2.998	3.499	5.405
8	1.397	1.860	2.306	2.896	3.355	5.041
9	1.383	1.833	2.262	2.821	3.250	4.781
10	1.372	1.812	2.228	2.764	3.169	4.587
11	1.363	1.796	2.201	2.718	3.106	4.437
12	1.356	1.782	2.179	2.681	3.055	4.318
13	1.350	1.771	2.160	2.650	3.012	4.221
14	1.345	1.761	2.145	2.624	2.977	4.140
15	1.341	1.753	2.131	2.602	2.947	4.073
16	1.337	1.746	2.120	2.583	2.921	4.015
17	1.333	1.740	2.110	2.567	2.898	3.965
18	1.330	1.734	2.101	2.552	2.878	3.922
19	1.328	1.729	2.093	2.539	2.861	3.883
20	1.325	1.725	2.086	2.528	2.845	3.850
21	1.323	1.721	2.080	2.518	2.831	3.819
22	1.321	1.717	2.074	2.508	2.819	3.792
23	1.319	1.714	2.069	2.500	2.807	3.767
24	1.318	1.711	2.064	2.492	2.797	3.745
25	1.316	1.708	2.060	2.485	2.787	3.725
26	1.315	1.706	2.056	2.479	2.779	3.707
27	1.314	1.703	2.052	2.473	2.771	3.690
28	1.313	1.701	2.048	2.467	2.763	3.674
29	1.311	1.699	2.045	2.462	2.756	3.659
30	1.310	1.697	2.042	2.457	2.750	3.646
40	1.303	1.684	2.021	2.423	2.704	3.551
60	1.296	1.671	2.000	2.390	2.660	3.460
120	1.289	1.658	1.980	2.358	2.617	3.373
∞	1.282	1.645	1.960	2.326	2.576	3.291

Source: From R. A. Fisher and F. Yates, *Statistical Tables for Biological, Agricultural, and Medical Research, Sixth Edition.* Published by Longman Group, Ltd. London, 1974. Reprinted with permission of Pearson Education.

Table B.4   Critical Values of the Correlation Coefficients

	Level of significance for one-tailed test			
	.05	.025	.01	.005
	Level of significance for two-tailed test			
df	.10	.05	.02	.01
1	.988	.997	.9995	.9999
2	.900	.950	.980	.990
3	.805	.878	.934	.959
4	.729	.811	.882	.917
5	.669	.754	.833	.874
6	.622	.707	.789	.834
7	.582	.666	.750	.798
8	.549	.632	.716	.765
9	.521	.602	.685	.735
10	.497	.576	.658	.708
11	.476	.553	.634	.684
12	.458	.532	.612	.661
13	.441	.514	.592	.641
14	.426	.497	.574	.623
15	.412	.482	.558	.606
16	.400	.468	.542	.590
17	.389	.456	.528	.575
18	.378	.444	.516	.561
19	.369	.433	.503	.549
20	.360	.423	.492	.537
21	.352	.413	.482	.526
22	.344	.404	.472	.515
23	.337	.396	.462	.505
24	.330	.388	.453	.496
25	.323	.381	.445	.487
26	.317	.374	.437	.479
27	.311	.367	.430	.471
28	.306	.361	.423	.463
29	.301	.355	.416	.456
30	.296	.349	.409	.449
35	.275	.325	.381	.418
40	.257	.304	.358	.393
45	.243	.288	.338	.372
50	.231	.273	.322	.354
60	.211	.250	.295	.325
70	.195	.232	.274	.303
80	.183	.217	.256	.283
90	.173	.205	.242	.267
100	.164	.195	.230	.254

Source: From R. A. Fisher and F. Yates, *Statistical Tables for Biological, Agricultural, and Medical Research, Sixth Edition.* Published by Longman Group, Ltd. London, 1974. Reprinted with permission of Pearson Education.

Table B.5 Critical Values of χ^2

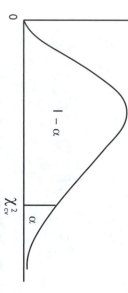

df	.99	.98	.95	.90	.80	.70	.50	.30	.20	.10	.05	.02	.01	.001
1	.03157	.03628	.00393	.0158	.0642	.148	.455	1.074	1.642	2.706	3.841	5.412	6.635	10.827
2	.0201	.0404	.103	.211	.446	.713	1.386	2.408	3.219	4.605	5.991	7.824	9.210	13.815
3	.115	.185	.352	.584	1.005	1.424	2.366	3.665	4.642	6.251	7.815	9.837	11.345	16.266
4	.297	.429	.711	1.064	1.649	2.195	3.357	4.878	5.989	7.779	9.488	11.668	13.277	18.467
5	.554	.752	1.145	1.610	2.343	3.000	4.351	6.064	7.289	9.236	11.070	13.388	15.086	20.515
6	.872	1.134	1.635	2.204	3.070	3.828	5.348	7.231	8.558	10.645	12.592	15.033	16.812	22.457
7	1.239	1.564	2.167	2.833	3.822	4.671	6.346	8.383	9.803	12.017	14.067	16.622	18.475	24.322
8	1.646	2.032	2.733	3.490	4.594	5.527	7.344	9.524	11.030	13.362	15.507	18.168	20.090	26.125
9	2.088	2.532	3.325	4.168	5.380	6.393	8.343	10.656	12.242	14.684	16.919	19.679	21.666	27.877
10	2.558	3.059	3.940	4.865	6.179	7.267	9.342	11.781	13.442	15.987	18.307	21.161	23.209	29.588
11	3.053	3.609	4.575	5.578	6.989	8.148	10.341	12.899	14.631	17.275	19.675	22.618	24.725	31.264
12	3.571	4.178	5.226	6.304	7.807	9.034	11.340	14.011	15.812	18.549	21.026	24.054	26.217	32.909
13	4.107	4.765	5.892	7.042	8.634	9.926	12.340	15.119	16.985	19.812	22.362	25.472	27.688	34.528
14	4.660	5.368	6.571	7.790	9.467	10.821	13.339	16.222	18.151	21.064	23.685	26.873	29.141	36.123

Level of significance (α)

df													
15	5.229	5.985	7.261	8.547	10.307	11.721	14.339	17.322	19.311	22.307	24.996	28.259	30.578	37.697
16	5.812	6.614	7.962	9.312	11.152	12.624	15.338	18.418	20.465	23.542	26.296	29.633	32.000	39.252
17	6.408	7.255	8.672	10.085	12.002	13.531	16.338	19.511	21.615	24.769	27.587	30.995	33.409	40.790
18	7.015	7.906	9.390	10.865	12.857	14.440	17.338	20.601	22.760	25.989	28.869	32.346	34.805	42.312
19	7.633	8.567	10.117	11.651	13.716	15.352	18.338	21.689	23.900	27.204	30.144	33.687	36.191	43.820
20	8.260	9.237	10.851	12.443	14.578	16.266	19.337	22.775	25.038	28.412	31.410	35.020	37.566	45.315
21	8.897	9.915	11.591	13.240	15.445	17.182	20.337	23.858	26.171	29.615	32.671	36.343	38.932	46.797
22	9.542	10.600	12.338	14.041	16.314	18.101	21.337	24.939	27.301	30.813	33.924	37.659	40.289	48.268
23	10.196	11.293	13.091	14.848	17.187	19.021	22.337	26.018	28.429	32.007	35.172	38.968	41.638	49.728
24	10.856	11.992	13.848	15.659	18.062	19.943	23.337	27.096	29.553	33.196	36.415	40.270	42.980	51.179
25	11.524	12.697	14.611	16.473	18.940	20.867	24.337	28.172	30.675	34.382	37.652	41.566	44.314	52.620
26	12.198	13.409	15.379	17.292	19.820	21.792	25.336	29.246	31.795	35.563	38.885	42.856	45.642	54.052
27	12.879	14.125	16.151	18.114	20.703	22.719	26.336	30.319	32.912	36.741	40.113	44.140	46.963	55.476
28	13.565	14.847	16.928	18.939	21.588	23.647	27.336	31.391	34.027	37.916	41.337	45.419	48.278	56.893
29	14.256	15.574	17.708	19.768	22.475	24.577	28.336	32.461	35.139	39.087	42.557	46.693	49.588	58.302
30*	14.953	16.306	18.493	20.599	23.364	25.508	29.336	33.530	36.250	40.256	43.773	47.962	50.892	59.703

* For $df > 30$, the expression $\sqrt{2\chi^2} - \sqrt{2df - 1}$ may be used as a normal deviation with unit variance.

Source: From R. A. Fisher and F. Yates, *Statistical Tables for Biological, Agricultural, and Medical Research, Sixth Edition*. Published by Longman Group, Ltd. London, 1974. Reprinted with permission of Pearson Education.

Empirical Research Reports in Psychology
What They Are, What They Say, Where to Find Them, How to Write Them

RESEARCH REPORTS: WHAT THEY ARE

The standard—and perhaps most prestigious—method of presenting the results of psychological research to other members of the discipline is by publishing a research report in one of the many scholarly journals. This appendix discusses the review process used to choose articles for publication in psychological journals, the types of articles published in journals, and how you can go about finding articles on particular topics. The last section of this appendix will focus on writing your own research report.

Journals in print are thin paperback books that contain numerous short articles; they are published monthly, bimonthly, or quarterly. Libraries will usually bind an entire year (or more frequently) of a journal into a single volume to prevent individual issues from getting lost and to protect the material. Increasingly, scholarly journals are appearing on the Internet. The Miami University Libraries Web site has a listing of 80 electronic journals in psychology.

Many scholarly journals do not sell advertising space and earn most of their money through annual subscriptions. These subscription rates are not trivial; individual rates might be $25, $75, or more per year, while institutional rates—the rates that libraries are charged—are typically in the hundreds of dollars. For this reason, many smaller libraries may not have much more than the most standard journals in a discipline in print form; they simply cannot afford the annual institutional subscription rate for very many print journals. Increasingly, an Internet user can find an article via an electronic search, but then be asked to purchase that article, a practice that can add up quickly for some topics. For subscribers and article purchasers to get their money's worth from a journal, it is important that the journal present the highest-quality material available. To do so, journals select articles for publication carefully, using a thorough review process.

THE REVIEW PROCESS

Each manuscript received by a journal is assessed by the editor for appropriateness to that journal. Obviously, a manuscript on adult memory processes sent to *Child Development* would be returned to the author with the suggestion that it be submitted to a different journal. If the editor believes the topic is appropriate, the manuscript is then sent to reviewers.

The review process used by many scholarly journals is called **blind review.** In a blind review, reviewers read and critique a manuscript without any knowledge of its author or authors. In this manner, manuscripts written by major researchers in a discipline and those written by first-time authors are given equal attention. The reviewers, who are experts in the topic addressed by the manuscript, evaluate the quality of the research procedure, the logic of the hypotheses, the appropriateness of the statistical analyses, and the thoroughness of the discussion. The reviewers might suggest topics or findings that need to be addressed, other statistical tests that need to be performed, or improvements to the research method itself.

Reviewers make one of three recommendations to the editor: that the manuscript be accepted for publication as is; that certain revisions be made and that the author(s) then resubmit the manuscript for reconsideration; or that the article be rejected and not published in the journal. The editor then takes the reviewers' comments into consideration and makes the final decision about the manuscript.

The entire process—from initial submission of the manuscript for review to publication in the journal—can take as little as three months or more than a year. Of course, this does not include the time it takes to research an area, design a study, collect the data, perform the statistical analyses, and write the report. The articles that you encounter in a psychology journal are the result of a great deal of effort and time on the parts of authors, editors, and reviewers. Ideally, this effort results in a high-quality publication.

EMPIRICAL RESEARCH REPORTS: WHAT THEY SAY

Research reports are the most common type of article published in psychology journals. Publication as a journal article is the preferred manner of disseminating research results in psychology. The research reports published in psychology journals, as well as those published in journals for many other disciplines, are written and organized according to the organizational, referencing, and writing style described in the *Publication Manual of the American Psychological Association* (the APA manual). The particular format described in the APA manual (APA, 2001) is referred to as **APA style.** Research reports written in APA style have six important parts:

1. An abstract (a very brief description of the study and its results) appears before the body of the article and is reproduced in reference texts and computerized literature search systems.

2. An introduction.

3. A methods section, which describes the procedures used in the investigation.

4. A description of the statistical results.

5. A discussion of those results.

6. A list of all of the references cited in the paper.

A sample manuscript at the end of this appendix goes into more detail about each subsection and demonstrates how the paper should be typed.

LITERATURE REVIEW FOR PSYCHOLOGICAL RESEARCH: WHERE TO FIND RESEARCH REPORTS

Conducting a search for literature that is relevant to a particular topic can be a challenging endeavor, especially when you consider that hundreds of journals and thousands of articles are published every year. Luckily, there are reference sources and computer programs to aid you in your literature search.

A very important printed reference source for psychological research articles is *Psychological Abstracts*, which is a listing of the abstracts of articles printed in a multitude of psychological journals. A new edition of *Psychological Abstracts* is published every month. And every year, a subject index and an author index are published. These indexes (which are also published for each monthly issue) list the abstracts by an abstract number under the appropriate author or authors and under the relevant subject headings or key terms.

Another printed source of references is the *Social Science Index (SSI)*. This is a quarterly subject and author index of publications in the social sciences. The subject headings in the *SSI* can be useful for suggesting other headings you may not have thought of, because they make use of "see also" and "see reference" commands. The "see also" command leads the user to related or more specific subject headings. The "see reference" command supplies a more appropriate subject heading than the one used. In the front of each issue is a list of the periodicals that are indexed.

In addition to printed reference sources, computer systems can be used for literature searches. Two of the computer systems relevant to psychology are PsycArticles and PsycINFO. PsycArticles provides links to the full text of articles from 50 journals from the APA. There are numerous other databases that are also relevant to psychology, but might lean toward the health sciences (such as Medline) or education (such as ERIC [Education Resources Information Center] or WilsonSelectPlus).

In general, to use these systems the user conducts a search by author, by title of the reference (if it's known), or by using keywords or subject headings. Because these computer systems can sometimes generate a lengthy list of references, it is easy to forget that they have their limitations. Not all journals will be listed (nor in the published indexes, for that matter), and computer systems are not able to span the full-length of time that research has been conducted in most areas. Very early references, and sometimes very new references, could be missing.

To begin a literature search, you need to consider your topic and how to find information on that topic. Most of your literature searches, whether in print sources or on a computer system, will be conducted by searching under appropriate subject headings using keywords. In *Psychological Abstracts* and the *SSI*, the abstract numbers or information about the abstract will be listed in the subject index under keywords. In a computer search, the computer will search for all of the articles in which those keywords were identified as important by the author. Spend some time thinking about the appropriate keywords to use in your search. If it is available to you, you might skim through the *Thesaurus of Psychological Index Terms* for ideas and appropriate subject headings. *Psychological Abstracts* uses subject headings from this source. The online database you use may also include a thesaurus of keywords to help you better focus your literature search.

What sources you use for a literature search will have an impact on the amount and usefulness of the references that are cited. As an example, I used several different online systems to search three different databases using the keywords *happiness* and *language*. The different services provided me with as little as one citation (a full-text online article) and as many as 119. I was provided with four different systems I could use to search the ERIC database and each search provided me with a different number of citations ranging from 52 to 62. Only by looking through the results of these various searches would I be able to determine if I was getting various subsets of the 119 references that PsycINFO provided me, or if I actually had more than that at my disposal. The lesson here is don't depend on only one system for searching one database if you are trying to do a comprehensive literature search.

Limiting yourself to online sources or even a combination of online and print sources might be limiting your literature search. Books, edited books of research projects, and textbooks can all be excellent sources for some of the mainstay references for a topic. How else can you find relevant references? Consult the list of holdings for your library, and seek advice from a reference librarian. Reference librarians have graduate degrees in library science; they hold an incredible wealth of information about accessing the works you need in the library.

The best source of all when conducting a literature search in psychology may be the reference lists of other relevant articles. Once you have found a few related articles, a quick perusal of their reference lists will tell you what the important papers are in the area (the ones that show up on every reference list) and will supply you with the reference citation. Psychology journals also publish review articles that summarize research in a particular area. If you are lucky enough to find a relevant review article, its reference list can be an invaluable source for your literature search.

Unless you have access to a large university library, your library probably won't house all of the journals that you need. Do not be shy about using interlibrary loan. Interlibrary loan is a nationwide cooperative system that allows borrowers to receive books and articles from libraries other than their own. Photocopies of articles can be sent to you via your library, often for no charge, and books will be lent for a predetermined period of time. The catch with interlibrary loan is the need to plan ahead. It can take several days to several weeks (and unfortunately, when books are not on the shelf, several months) for the information you requested to get to you. Be kind, be patient, and be early.

Finally, for a complete and up-to-date literature review, you will want to read the most recently published work, and that work may not yet be listed in any of the indexing systems. To find these works, you will need to browse through the most important journals in the field that you are researching.

Finally, it is very important to actually find and read the primary sources—that is, the relevant original articles. Do not depend on secondary sources, which are someone else's interpretation of the original article. It's amazing how many errors are passed on from article to article because researchers fail to check the primary source. This is damaging to the reputation of the articles' authors and bad for the pool of information in psychology.

Literature searches are time-consuming, and occasionally frustrating, but rewarding in the long run. Using one strategy—such as a reference list of books or a computer search system—will not provide you with a complete listing of all the relevant articles on a topic. A complete literature search requires the use of multiple strategies to yield the maximum number of the most relevant sources.

RESEARCH PROPOSALS AND REPORTS: HOW TO WRITE THEM

As you proceed in psychology, you will sooner or later have to write a research proposal or an article-like report of a research project. In this section, I will discuss the type of writing and the format appropriate to research descriptions and proposals.

If you have read articles from psychology journals, you've probably noticed that some are relatively straightforward and easily understood, while others are much more difficult to decipher. I used to think that if I had a hard time with an article, I wasn't smart enough to understand it. Later, I came to realize that if I couldn't understand an article, it wasn't because of me, but because of the article. The writing style was usually too complicated; the author had used unnecessarily big words and confusing sentence structures to say things that could have been expressed much more simply. Good writing—in English, psychology, biology, or business—follows the same principle: Clear thoughts and precise word choice yield quality writing.

Clear thinking is probably the more difficult aspect of writing. The writer needs to know at the outset exactly what she or he wants to say. This is where an outline can be useful. I know many people balk at the use of an outline and, to be honest, I don't use outlines in the way my English teachers taught me. Usually, I begin writing, then inspiration strikes and I suddenly understand what I want to say. At that point, I jot down an outline of sorts—often just a list of topics in an order that I think might be appropriate—which is subject to change. I then start writing all over again, because usually what I've already written just doesn't stack up now that I have the clarity of thought to write well.

Outlines are not mandatory; what is important is to write an organized paper. Organization helps the writer to think clearly about the topic, and helps the reader to understand the finished article. Organized material is always easier to understand than disorganized material. Lack of organization at any level—the paper as a whole, the subsections of the paper, the paragraphs, the sentences—will make the work less comprehensible.

We have already discussed the basic organization of a research report in psychology. It has an abstract, introduction, methods section, results section, discussion section, and references. The organization of a research proposal is quite similar. A proposal is the description of a study that could be conducted. It will contain an introduction, methods section, expected results section, and references. Whereas the methods section in a research article is written in the past tense, the methods section in a research proposal is written in the future tense. Also, the expected results section of the proposal replaces the results and discussion sections of the article; in the expected results section, the author describes what results he or she would expect to find if the study were conducted, and why these results would be expected.

Each subsection also has its own organization. These subsections will be described more thoroughly within the sample paper later in this appendix.

Paragraphs and sentences also need to be organized. A paragraph typically has a topic sentence, a body that builds on or expands on the topic sentence, and a conclusion. The conclusion can serve as a summary or as a transition to the next topic.

Whatever the next topic is, there must be a transition between paragraphs; otherwise, the paper reads like an arbitrarily chosen list of topics. You want the reader to progress through your paper without struggling to see how the paragraphs are related. In your paper and in your paragraphs, the statements you begin with and the statements you end with are of special import. The reader remembers what was said there and uses that information to better understand the paper.

The beginnings and endings of sentences are also important. These too receive more emphasis and are better remembered than the words in the middle of a sentence. Consider these sentences:

1. However, the difference between the two groups was relatively small.

2. The difference between the groups, however, was relatively small.

In the first sentence, the word "however" emphasizes the contrast between this statement and some previous statement. In the second sentence, the emphasis is on the difference between the groups, which, secondarily, is contrasted with some previous statement. The author would use the first sentence if the contrast is important and the second sentence if the difference between the groups is most important. Carefully choose the words you place at these points of emphasis.

Selecting the words for your sentences is an important task and should not be taken lightly. If you do not own a dictionary and a thesaurus, they are well worth the investment. Every word has a specific meaning; even similar words provide different nuances and emphases. Choosing the best words to describe your thoughts has two benefits. First, it is easier for the reader to understand you; second, you need fewer words.

Scientific writing should be clear, concise, and to the point. In addition, the standard organization of the paper aids the reader in understanding its content because the different types of information are presented in predictable locations. The literature review is at the beginning; the description of the methods is in the middle; and the discussion of the results is at the end. In the next section, we'll examine a standard research summary format. The section is presented in accordance with APA style and illustrates the correct spacing, proper use of headings, appropriate width of margins, and so on.[1]

---

[1] In the following sample paper, several sample references have been provided as illustrations. Only the APA (2001) citations refer to an actual source.

Running head: A SHORT VERSION OF THE TITLE ALL IN CAPITALS

The Title

Is Centered about Here

The Author(s) Name(s)

The Author(s) Institutional Affiliation

Abstract

An abstract is a brief summary of the contents of the article. This is the section of the article that will appear in *Psychological Abstracts*, in the PsycLit database, and in other indexes and computer search systems. The abstract should tell the reader, in no more than 120 words, what problem was studied, the specific characteristics of subjects (such as gender, age, number, etc.), what the experimental method entailed (briefly), the statistical results (including significance levels), what the conclusions were, and what the results implied (APA, 2001). Writing a good, clear, short abstract requires practice and editing. It should not be indented and all numbers should be typed as Arabic numerals, not as words, unless they begin a sentence.

The Title

This next section is the introduction. In this section, the author should introduce the problem. Do not leave the reader wondering about the topic of your research project.

To provide the reader with enough knowledge to understand the importance and relevance of your research, some background on the topic will need to be provided. This is where you review the most relevant previous research. Typically, a research article will not contain a comprehensive review of the literature (APA, 2001). A research proposal for a dissertation or thesis, however, might very well require a thorough description of previous research.

When reviewing the literature, be sure to organize your review so that the discussion of the previous research flows logically. For example, the review might be organized around important concepts or similar methodologies. Try to begin each paragraph with a clear and relevant transition from the previous paragraph. Make the introduction more than a list of project descriptions.

When describing the previous research it is essential that your sources be cited properly. When describing a study, even when using only your own words, you *must* cite the author(s) of that research. Similarly, if you paraphrase someone's ideas about a theory or concept, you must give the original thinker the credit that is due and cite that person in the text and reference list. Failure to cite sources appropriately (and that often means at least one citation per paragraph in an introduction) is plagiarism. Accusations of plagiarism can stop a career before it starts.

In APA style, references are cited by the last name(s) of the author(s) and the date of publication. For instance, if this sentence were a restatement of something said or suggested by Smith and Jones in 1993, one way to cite them would be to put the citation information in parentheses at the end of the sentence (Smith & Jones, 1993). Or, I could be more direct and state: Smith and Jones, in their 1993 discussion of plagiarism, argued that failure to cite sources should be penalized by death. If the entire paragraph is a description of a particular study, a person, or a person's ideas, then the author(s) and date can be presented in parentheses at the end of the paragraph (Smith & Jones, 1993).

Sometimes there will be more than two authors for a given study. If there are three to five authors, then the first time the reference is cited all of the authors are listed (Smith, Jones, Young, & Green, 1998). The next time this reference is used in the paper only the first author is listed, the rest are referred to by et al., which means "and others" (Smith et al., 1998). If there are six or more authors, then the very first time you refer to this source list only the first author's surname, followed by et al., and the date of publication. In the reference list, however, all of the authors' surnames and first initials are to be listed.

Sometimes, you might want to quote someone directly. If the quote is under 40 words, "put the quote within quotation marks, and follow the quote with the source and page number" (Meyer, 1987, p. 123). Or similarly, the author might be mentioned earlier in the sentence, such as: As Meyer (1987) noted in her earlier work on quotations, "Quotations should be used sparingly, and only when they add to the content of the paper" (p. 123). [Notice, by the way, that when the author was mentioned in the previous sentence, the date of the publication appears in parentheses immediately after the author's name.]

Quotes longer than 40 words require that the wording appear in a block quotation such as this:

> For a block quotation, the left margin is set in five spaces or a ½ inch (1.3 cm), and the first word of each additional paragraph within the quote is set in an additional five spaces. Note, however, that the right margin remains at the same place and that the quote is typed double-spaced, just as the rest of the paper is. When the quote is complete, if the appropriate citation information did not appear immediately prior to the quotation it is provided in parentheses at the end. This includes the author(s), the publication date, and the page number. Note the placement of the concluding period for block and text quotations. (Sullivan & Sullivan, 1991, p. 78)

Finally, after the relevant literature has been reviewed, you are ready to tell your readers about the present study. In the final paragraphs of the introduction you should briefly describe your project in general terms (you will be supplying the nitty-gritty details in the methods section). This is also where your hypotheses should be introduced and the rationale for your expectations are made clear.

Method

Participants

The first subsection of the method section is typically the participants section. In this section, you would describe the participants of your study. How many participated? How were they selected and how were they compensated? Or were they volunteers? How were they assigned to the experimental conditions and how many were in each condition? Were the participants selected based on some criterion? Describe the sample on relevant demographics, such as gender, ethnicity, health status, language preference, or other factors that might be important to your study (APA, 2004).

Materials (or *Apparatus*, if more appropriate)

In this next subsection the materials and equipment used in the study are described. If equipment is used, such as a tachistoscope, calipers, computers, or scales, then this subsection is typically referred to as the *Apparatus* subsection. If the research involves the use of paper-and-pencil tests or specially designed computer software, then the subsection is usually referred to as the *Materials* subsection.

Standard equipment, such as tables, chairs, pens, pencils, and paper need not be described in detail. But custom-made equipment should be described thoroughly, perhaps including a drawing or picture of the item (APA, 2001). The make and model number of manufactured equipment is also provided. Psychological tests that are used in a project should also be described in this section, and included with the description should be information about the tests' validity and reliability.

Design and Procedure (or often just *Procedure)*

In the procedure section, the author(s) explain, clearly and completely, all of the steps that were taken to conduct the research. The authors should describe how people were assigned to groups, or how it was determined whether they met the criterion for admittance to the study. Any counterbalancing or other measures used to control or balance the effects of extraneous variables should be described here. The instructions to the subjects should be paraphrased or summarized, such as: The subjects were asked to study the list of 20 words for 5 minutes. However, if the instructions included the experimental manipulation, that is, the different instructions are being compared, then the instructions should be presented verbatim (APA, 2001).

The Method section is something like a recipe for the research. The research should be described in sufficient detail regarding what was done, how it was done, and with what materials or equipment so that a reader could replicate the study.

Results

In this section, the type of data collected and the statistical techniques used to analyze them are described. The results of the analyses are also presented and general conclusions are made. For example, an author might say: The results of the independent-samples *t*-test was significant, t (12) = 7.62, $p < .05$; the subjects in the mnemonic condition recalled significantly more words ($M = 15.73$, $SD = 3.25$) than those in the control condition ($M = 9.36$, $SD = 2.96$). The M and SD stand for mean and standard deviation, respectively, and are standard usage in APA manuscripts.

You should not expound on why these particular results occurred. The implications of the results are to be presented in the discussion section.

When presenting the results of statistical analyses, you should assume that the reader has a basic understanding of statistics. You do not need to explain the concept of rejecting the null hypothesis or what a *t*-test is used for. You should supply the reader with information about the value of the test statistics, the degrees of freedom, the probability level, as well as information about the means, correlations, and standard deviations so that the reader can thoroughly understand the magnitude of the results (even if the results are not significant) (APA, 2001).

Sometimes, a table or a figure (a graph, picture, or drawing) is a more efficient and more easily understood way of presenting data than to try to list means and standard deviations in the text. Figures and tables, however, cost the publishers money to produce, so you should use as few as possible. Any tables or figures that are included should be referred to in the text, and the reader should be told what to look for in that table, such as the means for the groups or the correlations among the variables.

When typing a table, the table is typed double-spaced, as is the rest of the manuscript. The organization of the table must be done carefully so as to make the data easily comprehensible. The APA publication manual (APA, 2001) provides several examples of appropriate table formats. When preparing the manuscript, the table is typed or printed on a separate piece of paper and is put at the back of the manuscript. An example is presented at the end of this sample paper (see table 1).

Discussion

In the introduction the background for the study was provided and hypotheses were described. The methods section described how the study was carried out, and the results section described the data that had been collected. In the discussion section, you can now interpret those data, relating them back to the previous research. For many researchers, this is the most interesting part of the paper to write because it allows them to express what they see as the most important implications and contributions of the research, even when the research does not come out as expected.

Typically, the discussion begins with a general statement of support or nonsupport for the author's hypotheses. From this point, the author might wish to discuss why some results did not come out as expected, what the implications of the present results are in relation to previous work, or the underlying theory of the project. What has this project contributed? What questions has it answered? What possible alternative explanations are there for the results? What are paths that future researchers might follow? Answering these questions should provide a basis for the discussion of your project.

Conducting research in psychology is a rewarding process, and an important part of that process is communicating the results to other colleagues. The organization presented here is standard in psychology. It allows researchers to quickly read a report and understand what was done, why it was done, and what it means. The information is presented succinctly, but with enough detail so that a reader can evaluate the quality of the project or attempt to replicate the results. I hope that this information will not only aid you in writing your own research reports, but also in reading and evaluating the reports of others. Research is how we gain knowledge in psychology and reading the report of the original researcher is to be handed knowledge directly from the discoverer.

References

American Psychological Association. (2001). *Publication manual of the American Psychological Association*. Washington, DC: Author.

[Note: this is called a hanging format, the first line is flush with the margin and subsequent lines of the citation are indented ½ inch (1.3 cm or 5 spaces).]

Meyer, R. C. (1987). The title of an article is typed like this. *The Journal is Italicized, 23*, 34–37.

[Note: the number 23 is the volume number and it is italicized. The numbers 34–37 are page numbers, they are not italicized.]

Smith, J. K., & Jones, R. L. (1993). The title. *The Journal, 12*, 44–78.

Smith, J. K., Jones, R. L., Young, T. W., & Green, G. G. (1978). The article title. *The Journal, 17*, 56–68.

Sullivan, J. D., & Sullivan, W. S. (1991). *The title of a book*. Long Grove, IL: Waveland Press.

Table 1

Mean Body-Dissatisfaction Scores for Males and Females Who Had and Had Not Eaten

	Eating condition			
	Had eaten		Had not eaten	
Gender	M	SD	M	SD
Males	6.67	2.45	4.74	2.21
Females	9.13	3.49	6.49	1.96

$n = 12$ per condition.

IMPORTANT TERMS AND CONCEPTS

APA style   blind review

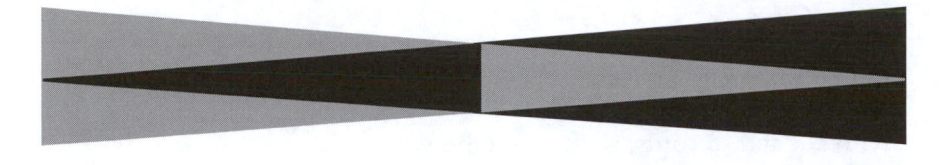

Glossary

ABAB design a single-subject research design in which baseline (A) is followed by the intervention (B), then by withdrawal (A), and then by the introduction of the intervention again (B).

ABBA counterbalancing a technique in which each participant experiences condition A followed by B and condition B followed by A.

accidental sample see convenience sample.

accretion measures traces or products that accumulate as a result of some behavior.

accuracy one of the criteria by which the value of a scientific theory is judged. An accurate theory fits the known facts.

action checklist a checklist used to record the presence or absence of specific behaviors and characteristics.

alpha (α) the probability of making a Type I error.

alternating-treatments design (or **between-series design**) a single-subject design in which two (or more) treatments are introduced to the subject randomly or systematically, so that the effectiveness of each treatment may be compared.

alternative (or **research**) **hypothesis (H_1 or sometimes H_A)** the prediction that the researcher is making about the results of the research; the researcher predicts that there will be a difference between the groups being compared.

American Psychological Association (APA) a national organization of psychologists and people in related fields.

analysis of variance (ANOVA) an inferential statistical test for comparing the means of three or more groups.

anonymous of unknown identity.

APA ethical principles in the conduct of research guidelines generated by the APA for conducting research in which people are the participants.

APA principles for the care and use of animals guidelines for the use of animals in research.

APA style the editorial style and organizational format for manuscripts suggested by the American Psychological Association and published in the *Publication Manual of the American Psychological Association* (2001).

applied research   research whose results are immediately relevant in a practical setting or situation.

archival data   records, written or otherwise.

archival data studies   the assessment of written and other records to make inferences about behaviors, beliefs, attitudes, and so on.

attribute variable   see subject variable.

authority   a method of knowing that entails accepting the word of a respected source.

average deviation (A.D.)   the mean distance of each datum in a distribution from the mean of that distribution. The corresponding formula is as follows:

$$A.D. = \frac{\Sigma |X - \mu|}{N}$$

baseline   a measurement of the dependent variable that is taken before the manipulation of the independent variable; used extensively in single-subject designs.

basic research   research whose results may be of no immediate practical use.

behavior sampling   observing subsets of a participant's behavior by observing behavior at different times and/or in different situations.

beliefs   statements that are based on personal feelings and subjective knowledge about things that cannot be tested scientifically.

beta (β)   the probability of making a Type II error.

between-groups research design   a research design in which the performance of participants in two or more groups is compared.

between-groups variance   an estimate of the effect of the independent variable plus error variance.

between-series design   see alternating-treatments design.

biased sample   a subset of a population that overrepresents or underrepresents population subgroups.

bimodal   having two mode scores.

blind review   review of a manuscript for a scholarly journal by reviewers who do not know the name of the manuscript's author or authors.

block randomization   a complete within-subjects design that involves the random presentation of blocks of conditions; each block is composed of single presentations of each experimental condition.

carryover effect   in a within-subjects design, the result obtained when one experimental condition affects performance in another condition.

case studies   descriptions of an individual and his or her experiences that typically do not involve the systematic observation of the person's behavior.

ceiling effect   the situation in which the dependent variable yields scores at or near the top limit of the measurement tool for one or all of the conditions.

changing-criterion design   a single-subject design used to assess an intervention when the criterion for that intervention is routinely changed.

checklist   a tool used for data collection during observational studies. See also action checklist and static checklist.

chi-squared (χ^2) Goodness-of-Fit test   a nonparametric test that compares the categorical observations obtained to the values expected on the basis of previous knowledge, hypotheses, or chance.

chi-squared (χ^2) test of homogeneity of proportions   a nonparametric test used when two random samples are chosen and each participant's response is classified as belonging to one of two or more categories. This test determines whether the proportions of responses in each category are equivalent for both samples.

chi-squared (χ^2) test of independence   a nonparametric test used when frequency data for two or more samples (or one sample divided into two or more groups) have been collected on a categorical variable. This test determines whether the two independent variables are associated or independent.

closed questions   survey, interview, or test questions that ask the respondent to choose from alternative potential answers.

cluster sampling   a technique in which clusters of elements that represent the population are identified and then all of the elements in those clusters are included in the sample.

comparable treatment of groups   a necessary condition for conducting research using a between-groups design.

complete within-subjects design   a research design in which each participant experiences each experimental condition several times, until he or she has received all possible orders of the conditions.

confederate   a person with knowledge of the experiment posing as a participant.

confidentiality   secrecy about the identity of research participants.

confound   an uncontrolled, extraneous variable—or other flaw in the research design—that yields alternative explanations for the results and thus limits the study's internal validity.

confounded results   results of an investigation that can be explained in various ways because of the presence of one or more extraneous variables.

content analysis   a coding system that is used to record data regarding the content of records.

continuous (or **running**) **records**   archival records that are maintained and added to on a routine basis.

control   a goal of research in psychology, to control some behaviors by understanding their causes.

control group or control condition   the group or condition within an investigation that does not receive the treatment being tested. The control group is used to demonstrate that any difference between the performance of the control group and the performance of the experimental group was a result of the independent variable and not of some other aspect of the experiment.

controlled trace measures   a trace or product that cannot occur without the involvement of the researcher.

convenience (or **accidental** or **haphazard**) **sample**   a sample composed of individuals who happened to be in the right place at the right time; not to be confused with a random sample.

correlated-samples *t*-test   a parametric test used to compare the means of two related samples or the means provided by one set of subjects tested twice. The formula for the correlated-samples *t*-test is as follows:

$$t = \frac{\bar{d} - 0}{s_{\bar{d}}}$$

where $\bar{d}$ is the mean of the difference scores; $s_{\bar{d}}$ is the standard error of the difference scores. This test is also called the dependent or dependent-samples *t*-test, the matched-pairs *t*-test, the paired-samples *t*-test, or the repeated-measures *t*-test.

correlation   a measure of the degree of relationship between two variables. The strength of the relationship is represented by the absolute value of the correlation coefficient. The direction of the relationship is represented by the sign of the correlation coefficient.

correlational study   an investigation in which relationships between or among variables can be identified, but causal inferences cannot be made because of the possible effects of uncontrolled variables.

counterbalancing   a procedure for distributing the effect of an extraneous variable across the experimental conditions within a within-subjects design.

cross-sectional design   a design typically used to look at differences between different age-groups.

data   recorded observations.

data reduction   the coding of notes and tapes to reduce the amount of information obtained to a more manageable level.

debriefing   fully explaining the purpose of the experiment to the participants, usually after the experiment is over.

deception   lying to, or misleading, research participants.

degrees of freedom   the number of observations that may freely vary; it is equal to the number of observations minus the number of restrictions placed on those observations.

demand characteristics   cues inadvertently provided by the researcher, the research materials, or the research setting that supply the research participant with information about the purpose of the investigation.

demographic questions   survey questions about the characteristics of a sample, such as average age, racial composition, and socioeconomic status.

dependent variable   what the experimenter measures in both the experimental and control groups.

description   a goal of scientific research, to describe when behavior is likely to occur.

descriptive statistics   procedures that organize, summarize, and describe a set of data.

desensitization   a technique in which the observer slowly moves closer to the participants until he or she can sit near or even among them without disturbing them.

difference scores   the result of subtracting one score from another.

discontinuous records   archival records that are produced less continuously than running records, or perhaps only once.

disguised participant studies   studies in which the researcher is an active participant in the research situation but the other participants do not know that the researcher is observing their behavior.

documents   written or filmed material that (a) is not a record and (b) wasn't created in response to some task or request by the investigator.

double-barreled questions   a survey, interview, or test question worded in such a manner as to ask more than one question at the same time.

double-blind procedure   a research procedure in which neither the experimenter nor the participants know to which condition the participants have been assigned.

ecological validity   the extent to which study results can be readily generalized to real life.

effect size   an indicator of the magnitude of a statistical difference.

elements   members of the sample.

erosion measures   traces or products that result from the wearing away of material.

error variance   the variation among scores that is not caused by the independent variable but instead is caused by random factors or by extraneous variables.

event sampling   the random or systematic selection of events that include the behavior of interest.

experimental group or experimental condition   the group or condition in an investigation that receives a treatment.

experimenter bias   the effect of the experimenter's expectations on the outcome of a study.

experimenter effect   the confound arising when behavior differences in a study are caused by the participation of different experimenters.

experiments   investigations in which two (or more) equivalent groups of subjects are treated in exactly the same way, except that the independent variable is different. Differences in measurements of the dependent variable can then be attributed to the difference in the independent variable. In experiments, causal inferences are possible.

explanation   a goal of research, to explain phenomena.

external validity   the extent to which the results of an investigation can be generalized beyond the original study.

extraneous variables   variables—other than the independent variable— that can affect the dependent variable.

factor   an independent variable.

factorial design   a research design in which the effect of two or more independent variables on a dependent variable is assessed.

fatigue effect   the confound arising when participants' performance on a task declines because they have repeated the task.

field experiments   highly controlled observational studies in a natural setting, where the researcher manipulates an independent variable to assess its effect on a dependent variable.

filter question   a survey or interview question that instructs the respondent or interviewer as to what the next question should be for different answers by the respondent.

floor effect   the situation in which the dependent variable yields scores at or near the lower limit of the measurement tool for one or all conditions.

free consent   consent given without coercion or pressure to comply.

funnel questions   a set of survey or interview questions ordered from the most general question to the most specific question.

graphs of the cell means   an important technique for presenting the results of a factorial design so that they can be more easily interpreted.

habituation   a technique in which the observer appears in the research setting numerous times until his or her presence no longer appears to affect the participants' behavior.

haphazard sample   see convenience sample.

Hawthorne effect   the effect of observers on the behavior of subjects in the social sciences.

higher-order designs   factorial designs that involve more than one independent variable.

history effect   a change in participants' performance on the dependent measure due to an event that occurs during the course of the investigation.

hypothesis   a possible answer to a research question. Scientific investigations are often designed to test a hypothesis.

idiographic   related to the study of individuals. Idiographic research attempts to identify patterns of behavior within the individual.

incomplete within-subjects design   a research design in which each participant receives a unique order of the conditions and may receive each condition more than once, but does not receive all possible orderings of the conditions.

independent variable   the variable in an investigation that the researcher changes or manipulates. The grouping variable in an investigation.

independent-samples *t*-test   a parametric test for comparing sample means of two independent groups of scores. The general formula for the independent *t*-test is as follows:

$$t = \frac{\left(\bar{X}_1 - \bar{X}_2\right) - \left(\mu_1 - \mu_2\right)}{s_{\bar{X}_1 - \bar{X}_2}}$$

informed consent form   a form given in advance to each participant in a research project; it describes the purpose of the study and what the participant will be asked to do and includes any known risks or benefits of the study.

institutional review boards (IRBs)   committees of individuals with diverse backgrounds who review proposals for research with human participants.

instrumentation effect   the confound arising when a measuring device fails to measure in the same manner across observations.

interaction effect   in a factorial design, the effect of a dependent measure on an independent variable within each level of each independent variable.

interaction of selection with other threats to internal validity   the confound arising when comparison groups are not equivalent and an extraneous variable affects one group but not the other.

internal validity   the extent to which a study actually answers the research questions that it was designed to answer. A study with good internal validity has no confounds and only one explanation for the results.

interobserver reliability   the degree to which a measurement procedure yields consistent results when used by different observers. One general formula for interobserver reliability is as follows:

$$\frac{\text{Number of agreements}}{\text{Number of opportunities for agreement}} \times 100$$

interval scale   a measurement scale characterized by equal units of measurement throughout the scale. Thus, measurements made with an interval scale provide information about both the order and the relative quantity of the characteristic being measured. Interval scales of measurement, however, do not have a true zero value; thus, negative values are meaningful.

interviewer bias   the confound that arises when an interviewer's behaviors, questions, or recording procedures result in data that are consistent with the interviewer's personal beliefs and constitute an inaccurate record of the respondent's true opinions or behavior.

intuition   a way of knowing based on the individual's own gut reaction.

Latin square   a technique for an incomplete within-subjects design in which each condition is presented in each ordinal position and is presented before and after each other condition. The number of sequences necessary is equal to the number of conditions in the study; thus, writing one sequence on each line, we obtain a square. A Latin square for four conditions is as follows:

ABCD
BDAC
CADB
DCBA

laws   specific statements that are generally expressed in the form of a mathematical equation with only a few variables. Laws have so much empirical support that their accuracy is beyond reasonable doubt.

leading questions   survey, interview, or test questions in which information is presented in such a manner that the respondent is more likely to give the answer that the researcher wants.

levels (or **conditions**) **of the independent variable**   the groups or categories within the independent variable; for example, depression and elation may be levels of an independent variable called mood.

loaded questions   survey, interview, or test questions that include non-neutral or emotionally laden terms.

longitudinal design   a repeated-measures design meant to look for changes that occur over time.

mail surveys   written, self-administered questionnaires.

main effect   the effect of an independent variable on a dependent measure within a factorial design.

marginal means   the average of scores for each level of an independent variable, disregarding other independent variables. Marginal means are used in factorial designs to interpret main effects.

matching   identifying pairs (or triplets, quadruplets, and so on) of participants who measure similarly on a characteristic that is related to the dependent variable and then randomly assigning each of these participants to separate experimental conditions.

maturation effect   a change in the participants' performance on the dependent variable due simply to the passage of time.

mean   the arithmetic average of the scores in a distribution of scores. The mean is calculated by adding the scores in the distribution and dividing by the number of scores. The formula for the mean is as follows:

$$\mu = \frac{\Sigma X}{N} \quad \text{or} \quad \bar{X} = \frac{\Sigma X}{N}$$

measurement   systematically assigning numbers to objects, events, or characteristics according to a set of rules.

measures of central tendency   statistical characteristics describing the approximate center of a distribution of scores; they include the mean, the median, and sometimes the mode.

measures of dispersion   statistical characteristics that describe how spread out the scores are in a distribution; they include the range, average deviation, standard deviation, and the variance.

median   the middle score, or 50th percentile, in a set of scores.

minimal risk a situation in which the risk to the participants of a research project is no greater than that encountered in daily life.

mixed (or **split-plot**) **design** a factorial design involving at least one between-groups and one within-subjects variable.

mode the score in a set of discrete data that occurs most frequently.

multimodal containing more than two mode scores.

multiple time-series design a quasi-experimental design that combines the time-series design and the pretest-posttest design with nonequivalent groups by making multiple observations of an experimental group and its nonequivalent control group.

multiple-baselines design a single-subject design in which the effectiveness of a treatment is assessed on two or more behaviors or across two or more situations.

narrative record a running record of behavior occurring in a given situation. Narrative records can be created by audiotaping or videotaping a situation, or by means of handwritten notes.

natural trace measures traces or products that occur without researcher intervention.

naturalistic observation unobtrusively observing behaviors in the natural setting. The investigator does nothing to interfere with the participants' behavior.

negative correlation a relationship between two variables such that, as one variable increases, the other variable decreases.

nominal scale a scale of measurement that categorizes objects or individuals. The order of the categories is arbitrary and unimportant.

nomothetic related to the study of groups in an attempt to identify general laws and principles of behavior.

nonequivalent-control-group design a type of quasi-experimental design in which the experimental group is compared with a comparable, but not equivalent, control group.

nonparametric test a statistical test that does not require as many assumptions about the population represented by the sample as does a parametric test. Also called assumption-free tests or assumption-freer tests.

nonprobability sampling techniques the sample is formed without considering the probability of each member of the population.

nonreactive not affected by the act of acquiring the measures.

nonsystematic subject mortality the loss of data when participants withdraw from a study or their data cannot be used for reasons unrelated to the experiment itself.

null hypothesis (H_0) the prediction that there is no difference between the groups being compared. The null hypothesis is true if the population that the sample is from is the same as the population with which it is being compared.

objective devoid of influences from attitudes and beliefs.

observer bias   bias introduced into data collection by the beliefs and attitudes of the observer.

one-tailed hypothesis   a type of alternative hypothesis in which the researcher predicts the direction of the difference between the groups being compared.

open-ended questions   survey, interview, or test questions that do not provide specific options for answers but instead provide room or time for the respondent to formulate his or her own response.

operational definition   a definition of the exact procedures used to produce a phenomenon or to measure some variable.

ordinal scale   a measurement scale in which objects or individuals are categorized and the order of the categories is important. The order of the categories reflects an increase in the amount of the characteristic being measured. The categories need not be of equal size.

outliers   scores in a distribution that are inordinately large or small relative to the other scores.

parameter   a characteristic of a population.

parametric tests   statistical tests in which the sample statistics are assumed to be estimates of population parameters.

parsimony   the assumption that, of two equally accurate explanations, the one based on simpler assumptions is preferable.

participant observation   studies in which the researcher is an active participant in the situation along with the participants who are being observed.

Pearson's product-moment correlation coefficient (or **Pearson's r**)   a statistic used to determine the correlation between two variables measured on either a ratio or an interval scale. The raw score formula is as follows:

$$r_{xy} = \frac{N\Sigma XY - \Sigma X\Sigma Y}{\sqrt{\left[N\Sigma X^2 - (\Sigma X)^2\right]\left[N\Sigma Y^2 - (\Sigma Y)^2\right]}}$$

personal interviews   a type of survey that involves a person-to-person meeting between the interviewer and respondent.

physical trace measure   data generated from physical evidence in the absence of the individuals whose behavior was responsible for the evidence.

physical trace studies   investigations involving the study of physical evidence left by individuals' behavior.

pilot study   a smaller, preliminary study conducted to answer questions about procedures for the full scale version of the investigation.

placebo   an inert substance or treatment that has no physical effect on the participants.

placebo effect   the confound arising when a behavior change is apparent after the introduction of an intervention, even though the intervention is known to be ineffectual.

pooled variance   the average variance of two samples weighted by the degrees of freedom for each sample.

population   all of the individuals to whom a research project is meant to generalize.

positive correlation   a relationship between two variables such that, as one variable increases, the other variable also increases.

Power   the probability of detecting a difference between the groups in the study when the null hypothesis is false. Power is calculated as $1 - \beta$.

practice effect   the confound arising when participants' performance on a task improves because they have repeated the task.

precision   a criterion by which theories are evaluated on how precisely they are stated. A more precisely stated theory is considered better than one containing vague statements.

predictions   an objective of research, to predict when behaviors or phenomena will occur.

preexperimental design   a simple type of research design in an applied setting that yields results for which there are several alternative explanations.

pretest and posttest measures   measurements made in a nonequivalent-control-group design before and after the introduction of a treatment to the experimental group.

pretest-posttest design   a research design in which one or more groups of subjects are tested before and after some treatment is administered to the experimental group.

pretest-posttest design with nonequivalent groups   a type of quasi-experimental design in which the experimental group is compared with a comparable, but not equivalent, control group.

pretesting   a measurement made before the introduction of an independent variable.

principles   statements that predict a phenomenon with a certain level of probability.

privacy   an invisible physical or psychological buffer zone or boundary around a person.

products   physical evidence created by individuals.

quasi-experimental design   a type of research design in which non-equivalent groups are compared, a single group is observed a number of times, or both of these techniques are combined.

quota sampling   a sampling technique in which differing numbers of participants are chosen for each sample from various subgroups of a population by identifying convenient sources of subgroup members and soliciting participants from these sources.

random assignment   assigning participants to experimental conditions within an investigation in a manner such that each participant is equally likely to be assigned to each condition.

random order with rotation   a technique for presenting conditions to participants in an incomplete within-subjects design. In this approach, the experimental conditions are ordered randomly and the first subject receives this order. Another order of the conditions is obtained by moving the first condition to the last place and shifting all of the other conditions up one; the next subject receives this order. Then the conditions are moved one place forward again, and the previously first condition is shifted to last place; the next subject receives this order. This rotation continues until each condition has occupied each position in the sequence.

random sample   a sample in which the elements were selected randomly from a sampling frame.

random selection   a manner of sample selection in which all members of the population are equally likely to be chosen as part of the sample. This should not be confused with haphazardly or arbitrarily choosing elements for a sample.

range   the number of possible values for scores in a discrete data set; for a data set taken from a continuous distribution, the interval of scores covered by the data.

ratio scale   a measurement scale that provides information about order; all units are of equal size throughout the scale, and there is a true zero value. The true zero allows ratios of values to be formed.

rational-inductive argument   a way of knowing based on reasoning.

reactive measure   a measurement of behavior that is susceptible to reactivity.

reactivity   the tendency for behavior to change when participants know that they are being observed.

records   written statements presented to provide an account or attest to an event. Records are produced for the consumption of another. Do not confuse with documents.

region of rejection   the area of a sampling distribution beyond the critical value of the test statistic. If a score falls within the region of rejection, H_0 is rejected.

regression toward the mean   the phenomenon that extreme scores tend to be less extreme upon retesting; they move toward the mean.

reliability   the consistency with which the same results are obtained from the same test, instrument, or procedure.

repeated-measures design   a research design in which one group of subjects is tested two or more times by means of the same measurement tool.

research hypothesis   see alternative hypothesis.

response rate   the extent to which people who receive a survey or are approached to complete an interview complete the survey or interview. A formula for the response rate is as follows:

$$\frac{\text{Number of responses}}{\text{Number in sample} - (\text{Ineligible and undeliverable resquests})} \times 100$$

reversal design   a single-subject design in which the effectiveness of an intervention is determined by withdrawing the intervention and introducing a new and opposite intervention.

risk   the potential for physical or psychological harm to a research participant.

running records   see continuous records.

sample   a subset of a population.

sampling bias   the extent to which a sample does not represent the underlying population.

sampling distribution   a frequency distribution of sample means.

sampling frame   a list of all of the members of a population; the sampling frame serves as the operational definition of the population.

scattergram   a graphical representation of a correlation between two variables.

scientific method   a set of procedures used to gain information in the sciences; it involves systematic observations obtained in an objective manner that avoids biases by the observer or by the participants in the study.

scientific misconduct   acts in which a researcher modifies or lies about data so that the results of the research will be more impressive.

selection bias   the confound arising when there are differences between the comparison groups within a study.

selective deposit   the circumstance that all traces are not equally representative of past behavior.

selective survival   the confound arising when some subset of trace or product evidence does not endure over time.

sensitivity of the dependent variable   the ability of the dependent variable to demonstrate subtle differences between the experimental conditions.

significant difference   a difference between two descriptive statistics—such as means—that is of such a magnitude as to be unlikely to have occurred by chance alone.

single-blind procedure   a research procedure in which either the participants or the experimenter does not know to which condition the participants have been assigned.

single-sample *t*-test   a parametric test used to compare the mean of a single sample to a population mean.

single-subject designs   research designs in which only one subject need be observed. The goal in single-subject designs is to eliminate as many alternative hypotheses for the results as possible.

situation sampling   making observations in different settings and circumstances in order to obtain a representative sample of behavior.

snowball sampling   a sampling technique in which research participants are asked to identify other potential participants.

socially desirable responses   responses that reflect what is deemed appropriate by society but do not necessarily reflect the respondent's true beliefs, attitudes, or behaviors.

Spearman's rho a statistic used to determine the correlation between two variables that have been ranked. The formula is as follows:

$$\rho = 1 - \frac{6\Sigma d^2}{N(N^2 - 1)}$$

split-plot design see mixed design.

standard deviation the square root of the variance:

$$\sigma = \sqrt{\sigma^2} \quad \text{or} \quad s = \sqrt{s^2}$$

standard error of differences between means the standard deviation for the sampling distribution composed of differences between sample means.

static checklist a checklist used to record characteristics that will not change during the course of the observations.

statistical analysis the summarization and analysis of data.

stratified random sampling stratified sampling in which members of the sample are chosen randomly.

stratified sampling a sampling technique intended to guarantee that the sample will be representative of specific subgroups of the population, called strata. The sampling frame is divided into such strata, and then the elements of the sample are chosen from the strata.

Student's *t*-distributions a family of distributions that, like the normal distribution, are symmetric and bell-shaped; in contrast to the normal distribution, however, there is a different distribution for each sample size.

subject attrition see subject mortality.

subject bias all of the biases and expectations that a participant brings to a study.

subject mortality (or **subject attrition**) the loss of data when participants withdraw from a study or their data cannot be used.

subject (or **attribute**) **variable** a measurable characteristic of the participant, such as height, weight, or gender, that cannot be manipulated by a researcher. When used as an independent variable, subject variables provide correlational information but not causal information.

subjective influenced by biases and irrational beliefs.

superstition a method of knowing based on irrational beliefs.

systematic subject mortality the loss of data occurring when more participants from one experimental condition withdraw from a study than another.

***t*-distributions** see Student's *t*-distributions.

***t*-test** an inferential statistical test for comparing two means.

telephone surveys surveys conducted over the telephone.

testability a criterion by which theories are evaluated. A testable theory is one that can, in principle, be proven wrong.

testing effect the phenomenon in which repeated testing leads to better scores.

theory   a set of related statements that explain and predict phenomena. The statements used in a theory can be laws, principles, or beliefs.

time sampling   a technique where the times at which observations will be made are determined in an effort to obtain a representative sample of behaviors. Time sampling may be done randomly or systematically.

time-series design   a type of quasi-experimental design in which multiple observations are made of a single group.

traces   evidence left as a by-product of behavior.

two-tailed hypothesis   a type of alternative hypothesis in which the researcher simply predicts that the two groups being compared will differ, but does not predict the direction of that difference.

Type I error   rejecting the null hypothesis when it is true.

Type II error   failing to reject the null hypothesis when it is false.

undisguised participant studies   studies in which the researcher is an active participant in the research situation and the other participants are aware that the researcher is observing their behavior.

validity   the extent to which the dependent variable is measuring what it purports to measure.

variance   a measure of dispersion in which the average squared deviation from the mean is determined for a distribution of scores. The formula is as follows:

$$\sigma^2 = \frac{\Sigma(X-\mu)^2}{N} \quad \text{or} \quad s^2 = \frac{\Sigma(X-\mu)^2}{N-1}$$

The raw score formula is as follows:

$$\sigma^2 = \frac{\Sigma X^2 - \frac{(\Sigma X)^2}{N}}{N} \quad \text{or} \quad s^2 = \frac{\Sigma X^2 - \frac{(\Sigma X)^2}{N}}{N-1}$$

withdrawal design   a single-subject design in which an intervention is introduced after baseline and then withdrawn to determine whether the intervention affects performance.

within-group variance   an estimate of the population error variance.

within-subjects design   a research design in which each participant receives each level of the independent variable at least once.

z-score   standard score that indicates how many standard deviations a raw score is above or below the mean. The formula for the z-score is as follows:

$$z = \frac{X-\bar{X}}{s}$$

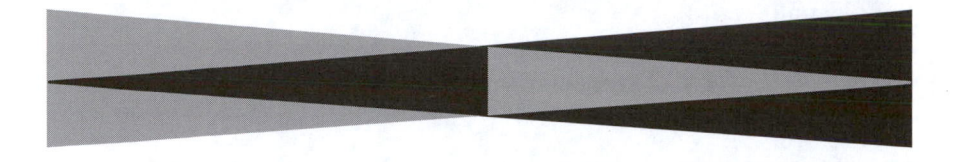

Bibliography

American Psychological Association (APA). (1981). Ethical principles of psychologists. *American Psychologist, 36*, 638.

American Psychological Association (APA). (1982). *Ethical principles in the conduct of research with human participants.* Washington, DC: Author.

American Psychological Association (APA). (1996). Guidelines for the ethical conduct in the care and use of animals [Brochure]. Washington, DC: Author.

American Psychological Association (APA). (2001). *Publication manual of the American Psychological Association* (5th ed.). Washington, DC: Author.

American Psychological Association (APA). (2002). *Ethical principles of psychologists and code of conduct.* Washington, DC: Author.

Baldwin, E. (1993). The case for animal research. *Journal of Social Issues, 49*, 121–131.

Bales, J. (1988, November). Bruening pleads guilty in scientific fraud case. *APA Monitor*, p. 12.

Barber, T. X., & Silver, M. J. (1968). Fact, fiction, and the experimenter bias effect. *Psychological Bulletin Monograph Supplement, 70*(6, Pt. 2), 1–29.

Barlow, D. H., & Hersen, M. (1984). *Single case experimental designs.* New York: Pergamon Press.

Black student posted racist notes. (1993, February 24). *The Chronicle of Higher Education*, p. 5.

Bowd, A. D., & Shapiro, K. J. (1993). The case against laboratory animal research in psychology. *Journal of Social Issues, 49*, 133–142.

Brigham, C. C. (1923). *A study of American intelligence.* Princeton, NJ: Princeton University Press.

Brink, N., Dulal, N., Paulhus, P., Wolf, S., Chong, C., Barry, S., Andreutti, L., & Saini, S. (1995). *Canadian Journal of Psychology*: A review of subject, language, funding, experimental vs. clinical, and place of origin of research articles published from 1974 to 1992. *Psybernetika* (Winter). Retrieved December 20, 2005, from http://www.sfu.ca/~wwwpsyb/index.htm

Camilli, G., & Hopkins, K. D. (1978). Applicability of chi-square to 2 × 2 contingency tables with small expected frequencies. *Psychological Bulletin, 85*, 163–167.

Campbell, D. T., & Stanley, J. C. (1963). *Experimental and quasi-experimental designs for research.* Chicago: Rand McNally.

Chermak, S. M. (1993). Interested bystanders: An examination of crime victims in the news media and how their involvement in the news production process affects the final news product. *Dissertation Abstracts International, 54* (04), 1550A.

Cicchetti, D. U. (1972). Extension of multiple-range tests to interaction tables in analysis of variance: A rapid approximate solution. *Psychological Bulletin, 77,* 405–408.

Cohen, J. (1965). Some statistical issues in psychological research. In B. B. Woman (Ed.), *Handbook of clinical psychology* (pp. 95–121). New York: McGraw-Hill.

Cook, T. D., & Campbell, D. T. (1979). *Quasi-experimentation: Design and analysis issues for field settings.* Boston: Houghton Mifflin.

Dillman, D. A. (1978). *Mail and telephone surveys: The total design method.* New York: Wiley.

Ebbinghaus, H. (1913). *Memory* (H. A. Ruger & C. E. Bussenius, Trans.). New York: Teachers College Press, Columbia University.

Erdos, P. L. (1983). *Professional mail surveys.* Malabar, FL: Robert E. Krieger.

Erikson, D. (1990, June). Blood feud: Researchers begin fighting back against animal-rights activists. *Scientific American,* pp. 17–18.

Etaugh, C. (1980). Effects of nonmaternal care on children: Research evidence and popular views. *American Psychologist, 35,* 309–319.

Etaugh, C., Carlson, P., & Williams, B. (July, 1992). *Changing attitudes toward day care and maternal employment as portrayed in women's magazines: 1977–1990.* Paper presented at the meeting of the Twenty-Fifth International Congress of Psychology, Brussels, Belgium.

Eysenck, H. J. (1977). Sir Cyril Burt. *American Psychologist, 32,* 674–676.

Finley, C., & Corty, E. (1993). Rape on the campus: The prevalence of sexual assault while enrolled in college. *Journal of College Student Development, 34,* 113–117.

Gage, N. L. (Ed.). (1963). *Handbook of research on teaching.* Chicago: Rand McNally.

Gershman, J. (2004, June 18). *Columbia committee probes a possibly fraudulent study.* Retrieved on May 23, 2005, from http://www.web.lexis-nexis.com

Gravetter, F. J., & Wallnau, L. B. (1985). *Statistics for the behavioral sciences: A first course for students of psychology and education.* St. Paul, MN: West.

Grisso, T., Baldwin, E., Blanck, P. D., Rotheram-Borus, M. J., Schooler, N. R., & Thompson, T. (1991, July). Standards in research: APN's mechanism for monitoring the challenges. *American Psychologist, 46,* 758–766.

Groves, R. M., & Kahn, R. L. (1979). *Surveys by telephone: A national comparison with personal interviews.* New York: Academic.

Hersen, M., & Barlow, D. H. (1976). *Single-case experimental designs: Strategies for studying behavior change.* New York: Pergamon.

Hinkle, D. E., Wiersma, W., & Jurs, S. G. (1982). *Basic behavioral statistics.* Boston: Houghton Mifflin.

Hinkle, D. E., Wiersma, W., & Jurs, S. G. (2003). *Applied statistics for the behavioral sciences* (5th ed.). Boston: Houghton Mifflin.

Hochstim, J. R. (1967). A critical comparison of three strategies of collecting data from households. *Journal of American Statistical Association, 62,* 154–159.

Howell, D. C. (2002). *Statistical methods for psychology* (5th ed.). Belmont, CA: Wadsworth.

Hurd, M. W. (1989). *Short-term memory before and during treatment of sleep apnea.* Unpublished masters thesis, Bradley University, Peoria, Illinois.

Jensen, A. R. (1983). Sir Cyril Burt: A personal recollection. *Association of Educational Psychologists Journal, 6,* 13–20.

Jones, S. R. G. (1992). Was there a Hawthorne effect? *American Journal of Sociology, 98,* 451–468.

Kalat, J. W. (1990). *Introduction to psychology* (2nd ed.). Belmont, CA: Wadsworth.

Kantowitz, B. H., Roediger, H. L., III, & Elmes, D. G. (1991). *Experimental psychology: Understanding psychological research.* St. Paul, MN: West.

Kirk, R. E. (1990). *Statistics: An introduction* (3rd ed.). Fort Worth, TX: Holt, Rinehart, & Winston.

Kirkham, G. L. (1975). Doc cop. *Human Behavior, 4,* 16–23.

Koocher, G. P. (1977). Bathroom behavior and human dignity. *Journal of Personality and Social Psychology, 35,* 120–121.

Kratochwill, T. R. (Ed.). (1978). *Single subject research: Strategies for evaluating change.* New York: Academic.

Leavitt, F. (1991). *Research methods for behavioral scientists.* Dubuque, IA: W. C. Brown.

McAskie, M. (1979). On "Sir Cyril Burt in perspective." *American Psychologist, 34,* 92–93.

Merriam-Webster. (2003). *Merriam-Webster's collegiate dictionary* (11th ed.). Springfield, MA: Author.

Middlemist, R. D., Knowles, E. S., & Matter, C. F. (1976). Personal space invasions in the lavatory: Suggestive evidence for arousal. *Journal of Personality and Social Psychology, 33,* 541–546.

Middlemist, R. D., Knowles, E. S., & Matter, C. F. (1977). What to do and what to report: A reply to Koocher. *Journal of Personality and Social Psychology, 35,* 122–124.

Milgram, S. (1963). Behavioral study of obedience. *Journal of Abnormal and Social Psychology, 67,* 371–378.

Milgram, S. (1977). Ethical issues in the study of obedience. In S. Milgram (Ed.), *The individual in a social world* (pp. 188–199). Reading, MA: Addison-Wesley.

Miller, N. E. (1985). The value of behavioral research on animals. *American Psychologist, 40,* 423–440.

Munro, M. (2004, February 28). *Rogue scientist tarnished U of A research team: Technician falsified experiments, altered work by colleagues.* Retrieved on May 23, 2005, from http://www.web.lexis-nexis.com

National Institute of Environmental Health Sciences. (2000). *Respect for life: Using fewer animals—some landmarks* (NIH Publication No. 90-3170). Retrieved December 23, 2005, from http://www.niehs.nih.gov/oc/factsheets/wrl/iccvam.htm

National Institutes of Health. (1996). *Guide for the care and use of laboratory animals* (NIH Publication No. 85-23). Washington, DC: U.S. Government Printing Office.

Pavlov, I. P. (1928). *Lectures on conditioned reflexes.* New York: International Publishers.

Pihl, R. D., Zacchia, C., & Zeichner, A. (1981). Follow-up analysis of the use of deception and aversive contingencies in psychological experiments. *Psychological Reports, 48,* 927–930.

Pope, K. S., & Vetter, V. A. (1992). Ethical dilemmas encountered by members of the American Psychological Association: A national survey. *American Psychologist, 47,* 397–411.

Popper, K. R. (1959). *The logic of scientific discovery.* New York: Basic Books.

Public Welfare, 45 C.F.R. §§ 46.101–02 (June 23, 2005).

Raymond, C. (1991, May). Study of patient histories suggests Freud suppressed or distorted facts that contradicted his theories. *Chronicle of Higher Education, 37*(37), 4–6.

Ring, K., Wallston, X., & Corey, M. (1970). Mode of debriefing as a factor affecting reaction to a Milgram-type obedience experiment: An ethical inquiry. *Representative Research in Social Psychology, 1,* 67–88.

Roman, M. (1988, April). When good scientists turn bad. *Discover,* pp. 50–58.

Rosenhan, D. L. (1973, January). On being sane in insane places. *Science, 179,* 250–258.

Rosenthal, R. (1978). How often are our numbers wrong? *American Psychologist, 33,* 1005–1007.

Schabner, D. (2002, February 26). *New front on ecoterror? Some want to target high-profile activists in battle on ecoterror.* Retrieved December 23, 3005, from http:// www.rickross.com/reference/animal/animal24.html

Shaughnessy, J. J., & Zechmeister, E. G. (1990). *Research methods in psychology* (2nd ed.). New York: McGraw-Hill.

Sidman, M. (1960). *Tactics of scientific research: Evaluating experimental data in psychology.* New York: Basic Books.

Sieber, J. E., & Stanley, B. (1988). Ethical and professional dimensions of socially sensitive research. *American Psychologist, 43,* 49–55.

Smith, S. S., & Richardson, D. (1983). Amelioration of deception and harm in psychological research: The important role of debriefing. *Journal of Personality and Social Psychology, 44,* 1075–1082.

Snyderman, M., & Herrnstein, R. J. (1983). Intelligence tests and the Immigration Act of 1924. *American Psychologist, 38,* 986–995.

Stein, R. (2005, March 18). *Researcher fabricated data in studies on women: Scientist to enter plea and pay fine in federal case.* Retrieved on May 23, 2005, from http:// web.lexis-nexis.com

Stevens, S. S. (1951). Mathematics, measurement, and psychophysics. In S. S. Stevens (Ed.), *Handbook of experimental psychology.* New York: Wiley.

Sudman, S., & Bradburn, N. B. (1982). *Asking questions: A practical guide to questionnaire design.* San Francisco: Jossey-Bass.

Svenson, S., & White, K. (1995). A content analysis of horoscopes. *Genetics, Social, and General Psychology Monographs, 121,* 5–38.

Taylor, C. R., Lee, J. Y., & Stern, B. B. (1995). Portrayals of African, Hispanic, and Asian Americans in magazine advertising. *American Behavioral Scientist, 38,* 608–621.

Tryon, W. W. (1982). A simplified time series analysis for evaluating treatment interventions. *Journal of Applied Behavior Analysis, 15,* 423–429.

UPI. (2005, January 10). *CBS News fires 4 for flawed Bush reporting.* Retrieved May 23, 2005, from http://www.web.lexis-nexis.com

Van Lawick-Goodall, J. (1971). *In the shadow of man.* Boston: Houghton Mifflin.

Wahl, O. F., Borostovik, L., & Rieppi, R. (1995). Schizophrenia in popular periodicals. *Community Mental Health Journal, 31,* 239–248.

Webb, E. J., Campbell, D. T., Schwartz, R. D., Sechrest, L., & Grove, J. B. (1981). *Nonreactive measures in the social sciences.* Boston: Houghton Mifflin.

Zurawik, D. (2005, May 5). *Rather's career put in harsh light as anchorman retires, colleagues, peers criticize his flawed Bush report.* Retrieved May 23, 2005, from http://www.web.lexis-nexis.com

Index